3/99

Required Reading

REQUIRED READING

SOCIOLOGY'S MOST INFLUENTIAL BOOKS

Edited by Dan Clawson

UNIVERSITY OF MASSACHUSETTS PRESS   *Amherst*

Copyright © 1998 by
The University of Massachusetts Press
All rights reserved
Printed in the United States of America
LC 98-11944
ISBN 1-55849-152-X (cloth); 153-8 (pbk.)
Designed by Milenda Nan Ok Lee
Set in Sabon and Stone Sans Semibold
Printed and bound by Braun-Brumfield, Inc.
Library of Congress Cataloging-in-Publication Data
Required reading : sociology's most influential books / edited by Dan
    Clawson.
        p.   cm.
    Includes bibliographical references.
    ISBN 1-55849-152-X (alk. paper). —
ISBN 1-55849-153-8 (pbk. : alk. paper)
    1. Sociology — Book reviews.   2. Sociology literature.   3. Best
books.   I. Clawson, Dan.
HM73.R45   1998
301 — dc21   98-11944
                                                           CIP
British Library Cataloguing in Publication data are available.

CONTENTS

1 VARIETIES OF INFLUENCE

Canon and Anti-Canon for a Fragmented Discipline
DAN CLAWSON AND ROBERT ZUSSMAN   3

Best-Sellers by American Sociologists:
An Exploratory Study
HERBERT J. GANS   19

2 STATE PROCESSES

On Theda Skocpol, *States and Social Revolutions*

How to Become a Dominant American Social Scientist:
The Case of Theda Skocpol
JEFF GOODWIN   31

On Charles Tilly, *From Mobilization to Revolution*

Historicization of Protest as a Route to General Theory:
Stepping Back to Move Forward
ROGER V. GOULD   39

On Michel Foucault, *Discipline and Punish*

Discipline and Punish:
The Birth of a Postmodern Middle-Range
JONATHAN SIMON   47

On Charles Murray, *Losing Ground*

Charles Murray: Losing Ground, Gaining Power
THEODORE J. LOWI AND GWENDOLYN MINK   55

3 TOOLS AND FRAMEWORKS

On Norman H. Nie, Dale H. Bent, and C. Hadlai Hull, *SPSS*
Doing It Ourselves
BARRY WELLMAN   71

On Clifford Geertz, *The Interpretation of Culture*
Geertz's Ambiguous Legacy
ANN SWIDLER   79

On Pierre Bourdieu, *Outline of a Theory of Practice*
Sociology's Other Poststructuralism
CRAIG CALHOUN   85

4 APPROACHES TO THE ECONOMY AND ECONOMIC PROCESSES

On Gary Becker, *A Treatise on the Family*
Gary Becker on the Family:
His Genius, Impact, and Blind Spots
PAULA ENGLAND AND MICHELLE J. BUDIG   95

On Arlie Hochschild, *The Managed Heart*
Emotion Management as Emotional Labor
LYNN SMITH-LOVIN   113

On David Featherman and Robert Hauser,
Opportunity and Change
Models of Influence
DAVID B. GRUSKY AND KIM A. WEEDEN   121

On Harry Braverman, *Labor and Monopoly Capital*
A Classic of Its Time
MICHAEL BURAWOY   135

On Rosabeth Moss Kanter,
Men and Women of the Corporation
What's Gender Got to Do with It?
CHRISTINE L. WILLIAMS   141

On Immanuel Wallerstein, *The Modern World System*
Promethean Sociology
HARRIET FRIEDMANN   149

5   RACE AND GENDER FORMATION

On William J. Wilson, *The Declining Significance of Race*

What's Race Got to Do with It?
ALDON MORRIS   157

On Edward Said, *Orientalism*

Empire and Knowledge:
More Troubles, New Opportunities for Sociology
STEVEN SEIDMAN   167

On Nancy Chodorow, *The Reproduction of Mothering*

The Gendering of Social Theory:
Sociology and Its Discontents
BARBARA LASLETT   173

On Boston's Women's Health Book Collective,
Our Bodies, Ourselves

Feminist Subversions
LINDA GORDON AND BARRIE THORNE   181

6   THE MEANING OF THIS LIST

Sociological Politics and *Contemporary Sociology's*
Ten Most Influential Books
GERALD MARWELL   189

Taking the List as It Stands:
What Does It Say about Sociology Today?
RACHEL A. ROSENFELD   197

Who's In? Who's Out?
CHARLES LEMERT   207

Contributors' Notes   215

Required Reading

1 VARIETIES OF INFLUENCE

CANON AND ANTI-CANON FOR A FRAGMENTED DISCIPLINE

DAN CLAWSON AND ROBERT ZUSSMAN

How do we dare—how does anyone dare, especially now—to claim that there is such a thing as "Required Reading" in sociology? The notion of required reading implies agreement. But agreement is hard to come by. The synthesis wrought by the early University of Chicago sociologists is long gone. The Parsonian synthesis has come and gone. Only Alvin Gouldner's "Crisis" has come and stayed: But the very point of Gouldner's crisis was that the old syntheses have disappeared without replacement. To be sure, there is no lack of candidates— theoretical, metatheoretical, methodological—for unifying principles in sociology. Yet, whatever the intellectual virtues of these candidates, it is clear that none has succeeded in unifying the field in practice. Indeed, in a touch of mildly postmodern irony, we might note that the only grounds for consensus in sociology is an acknowledgment of dissensus. How do we dare to claim that the books discussed in this volume are required reading?

INFLUENTIAL BOOKS

This book (now much expanded) began as a (May 1996) special issue of *Contemporary Sociology,* marking that journal's twenty-fifth anniversary. The project was initiated by Clawson, then beginning his second year as the journal's editor. After discussing the project with his local board—a group of sociologists and sociological fellow travelers clustered around Amherst, Massachusetts—Clawson asked the full twenty-eight-member board of editors to nominate books they considered among the most influential of the previous twenty-five years. Books that received significant support then entered a second round of voting. Many board members insisted that a number of books were essential to the list. Others found it agony to choose any books at all. In the end, however, there was a surprising agreement about the selections. Still, it is unlikely that any member of the board would have chosen exactly the same ten selections that appeared in the journal, and several board members strongly objected to one or another of the included books. In one case (*Our Bodies, Ourselves*), the decision to include a book was made almost entirely by Clawson on his own, at the urging of some but to the dismay of others.

Required Reading adds seven new books to the original list of ten that first appeared in *Contemporary Sociology:* Gary Becker, *A Treatise on the Family* (reviewed by Paula England and Michelle J. Budig); David Featherman and Robert Hauser, *Opportunity and Change* (David B. Grusky and Kim A. Weeden); Arlie Hochschild, *The Managed Heart* (Lynn Smith-Lovin); Rosabeth Moss Kanter, *Men and Women of the Corporation* (Christine L. Williams); Charles Murray, *Losing Ground* (Theodore J. Lowi and Gwendolyn Mink); Norman H. Nie et al., *SPSS* (Barry Wellman); and Charles Tilly, *From Mobilization to Revolution* (Roger Gould). The initial list generated a great deal of discussion and commentary — in offices and hallways, on electronic listservs, and in letters to both *Contemporary Sociology* and *Footnotes* (the newsletter of the American Sociological Association) — and the expanded list represents an effort to incorporate these comments. Except for the *SPSS* manual, all of the additional books were actively considered for the original list. In the case of the *SPSS* manual, Barry Wellman made so powerful a case for its inclusion, and raised such interesting issues in doing so, that Clawson added it to the list even though no one else had proposed it.[1] In addition to the seven additional reviews, the present volume also adds Herbert Gans's list and analysis of the best-selling books in sociology and Gerald Marwell's proposal for alternative criteria of influence, as well as concluding essays by Charles Lemert and Rachel Rosenfeld on the implications of the list itself.

Throughout the process of selecting books, only two criteria were explicit. First, in keeping with the origins of the list as a commemoration of *Contemporary Sociology*'s twenty-fifth anniversary, all of the books had to have been published since 1972. Although this criterion turned out to be somewhat less clear-cut than it might at first appear —

---

1. In addition, Clawson attempted to find a reviewer for Christopher Jencks's *Inequality,* but four different people declined the invitation, and the book was eventually dropped from the list. In sharp contrast, a total of only three potential authors declined the opportunity to discuss the seventeen books included here.

is, for example, the date for Geertz's *Interpretation of Cultures* the publication date of the book itself or the dates for the individual essays included in it? — it presented no great difficulties. The second criterion, about which much more later, did: The seventeen books included on the list are emphatically not the editor's choices, or the *Contemporary Sociology* board's collective choices, as the "best" books in sociology. Rather, they constitute a list of the most influential books. In this sense, the list represents a second-order judgment: It is not a compilation based on the editor's or board's judgments of the books themselves so much as their judgment of the judgment of other sociologists. Although we certainly think highly of most of the books included on the list, the list itself should be understood less as a claim about the quality of the included books and more as a claim about the state of the discipline.

CANONIZATION

Any list of the sort proposed here implies at least a hint of canon making. Indeed, this may be why the list generated a great deal of controversy. This controversy, however, was not all of a piece. On the one hand, there were objections to the creation of any canon. On the other hand, there were objections to the particular canon represented here. We discuss these two types of objections in turn.

The strongest argument against any effort at canonization was made by Jerry Watts, a sociologist and political scientist, a scholar of African American intellectuals, and a member of the *Contemporary Sociology* board. Watts opposes not only the notion of required reading but even the milder formulation of a list of most influential books. He would have been happier if the list had been characterized, with a ruthless sense of limits, as "some books that some people think have had some influence."

His argument is as follows: A canon is a mechanism of inclusion but also, by virtue of its inclusions, a mechanism of exclusion. In the particular case of this list, it is a codification of arbitrary tastes. The judgments to include one book rather than another are highly subjective, but placing a book on a list of most influential books gives it an appearance of objectivity that will virtually inevitably validate the text on grounds independent of the ideas it contains. For example, we might want to encourage someone to read Bourdieu for a specific purpose, for the insights and ideas he provides in making sense of an important sociological problem. Placing Bourdieu on a decontextualized list, however, means that Bourdieu or, perhaps more precisely, *Outline of a Theory of Practice* will become an object of veneration, read and cited less for its contributions to an understanding of the social world than as an object of ritualistic veneration. This process will fetishize the texts.

As Jeff Goodwin points out in his essay on Skocpol's *States and Social Revolutions,* references to a canonical text do not mean that it has been read. Goodwin suggests that this comes close to serving as a defining characteristic of a canonical text — one that is used as a source of authority and legitimation (or as an object of attack), rather than as a source of insight and ideas. The canon then becomes a burden, suffocating new ideas. References to Bourdieu — or Foucault or Geertz — become a substitute for analysis and rigorous argument.

Moreover, when a canon is created, the status of each text is intensified by the other texts in the canon. Thus, for example, if someone questions the importance of Wallerstein's *Modern World System* or Chodorow's *Reproduction of Mothering,* those books will gain authority not on the basis of their own merit, but simply by their association with the works of Foucault, Geertz, or Bourdieu on the canonical list.

All these points are well taken. But there is also more to say. First, if this is an exercise in canon formation — as it surely is, at least to some degree — it differs markedly from most such ventures. The original Christian canon was determined on the basis of doctrinal purity (Guillory 1995), and the most common argument for including a work in a canon is that it is the best, an exemplar of the sort of work that should be done. The works included here, however, were selected on the basis of their influence and not on anything approaching doctrinal purity. They represent an attempt to assess where we are, not where we should be.

Second, if the canon is a mechanism of exclusion — which it is — it may also be, simultaneously and dialectically, a means of opening up the field, a way of providing validation and authority for works that have been enormously influential, but which have not been accepted by "mainstream" sociology. A list that includes Foucault and Said, and perhaps even Wallerstein, Geertz, and Chodorow, supports those who find these authors stimulating and insightful and encourages them to insist that this too is sociology, that these works cannot be dismissed or ignored. Although there are surely biases that inform the selections, no one could mistake a list that includes both Foucault and Featherman, both Said and the *SPSS* manual, for a narrow or exclusionary version of sociology. Quite the reverse: We think of the list as one that celebrates sociology's methodological, substantive, and conceptual diversity.

It is, however, precisely the diversity of the list that has disturbed others. For example, Gerald Marwell, a former editor of the *American Sociological Review*, argues, in the essay included in this book, that the diversity of the list is a consequence of a failure to specify what is meant by "influence." In particular, we might want to distinguish among a variety of different audiences for sociology and specify influence on: sociologists publishing in core sociology journals, all other U.S. sociologists (including both those who publish books and those who publish little if at all), sociologists outside the United States, all other social scientists or natural scientists or scholars in the humanities, students or on an elusive general public, policymakers, or the actual formation of policy.

If the concept of influence were specified more precisely, it would lend itself to measurement in a way that an imprecise concept does not. We would ourselves be very much interested to see efforts to measure the influence of different books on social policy or on the required curricula of graduate programs. In different ways this is what Herbert Gans and Gerald Marwell do in the essays included in this book. Gans's painstaking compilation of sociological best-sellers provides a rough indicator of influence on a general reading public. Marwell's use of the *Social Science Citation Index* is, by contrast, an attempt to measure influence on a "sociological core."

Citation counts from the *Social Science Citation Index* are almost certainly the most common form of efforts to quantify influence. Widely used and often yielding fascinating results, such counts are nonetheless highly problematic for the problem at hand.[2] The *Social*

2. For example, in a rigorous analysis, Cronin et al. (1993) use quantitative criteria to determine the ten sociology journals with the highest impact on citations. They then examine citations in those journals and report that, for the period 1981–1990, the fifteen individuals most frequently cited in these journals are Otis Dudley Duncan (526), James S. Coleman (364), Robert M. Hauser (292), Erik Olin Wright (210), Michael T. Hannan (181), John W. Meyer (168), Arthur L. Stinchcombe (162), Charles Tilly (153), Clifford C. Clogg (148),

Science Citation Index is far more appropriate as a measure of article than of book influence; although it includes references to both books and articles, it is limited to citations from journals, omitting citations from books. If sociology were organized differently, this might not be a serious consideration. But, as is well documented, sociology is characterized by a strong distinction between a book culture and an article culture. As a result, *Social Science Citation Index* counts will produce lists of the books and articles that most influence article sociologists rather than those that most influence book sociologists. Of the twenty-eight sociologists most frequently cited in high-impact sociology journals, as reported by Cronin et al., none appeared on the original *Contemporary Sociology* list and only two (Hauser and Tilly) appear on the expanded list. (None at all appears on Gans's list of sociological best-sellers.) Moreover, in the last twenty-five years, the authors of the books on the original *Contemporary Sociology* list have published a total of only four articles in the *American Sociological Review* or the *American Journal of Sociology,* although several have written book reviews for the latter. We do not, however, take this as evidence that the *Contemporary Sociology* list is wrong. Rather, we take it as evidence of the enormity of the distance between sociology's book culture and its article culture.

Measures of one or another form of influence are valuable, but we would argue for judgment rather than measurement and for a general notion of influence in preference to a specified and limited one. Even if we could surmount technical problems in the measurement of well-specified concepts of influence, we would be left having to decide which of those concepts to use. If Clawson had specified one concept rather than another or, in a foolishly heroic effort at precision, had even attempted to specify different weights for different aspects of influence (30 percent for influence on policy, 20 percent for influence on core sociology journals, 10 percent for influence on all countries other than the United States, and so on), this decision would surely have provoked even more strident (and justified) objections than the list itself. Thus, assessing influence in general is unavoidably a matter of judgment. Moreover, as valuable as more specified conceptions of influence may be, a general, unspecified concept of influence retains a common-language

---

Christopher S. Jencks (127), Aage B. Sorensen (116), Mark S. Granovetter (112), James N. Baron (104), Harrison White (100), and Joan Huber (99).

meaning of considerable power. We note, in this respect, that the National Research Council faced a similar issue in its massive study of the quality of graduate programs. Although the NRC included twenty quantitative indicators of the quality of departments in its report, their primary summary measure — and the measure most often cited by administrators and in public discussions — relied on a question that asked respondents to evaluate the "scholarly quality" of departmental faculty, with no further specification of what might be meant by quality.

Judgment, then, is fundamental to a discipline. Judgments — not measurements — decide what should be taught, what should be read, what should be published, and (for that matter) what should be cited. It is these judgments that give the discipline boundaries and shape. And these judgments cannot — and probably should not — be avoided. We might ask that the criteria for these judgments be made as explicit as possible. We might ask that the social process that goes into making these judgments also be made explicit (as we have tried to do here). And we might ask that these judgments be collective rather than individual. As Calhoun and Land (1989) noted in their review of Smelser's *Handbook of Sociology,* a handbook is "a powerful statement of the disciplinary canon and, as such, too important and difficult a task for a single editor." They recommend instead that such decisions be made by editorial boards "composed of members from diverse specialties of the discipline, schools of thought, and geographical regions." It is for parallel reasons that Clawson, reserving some room for editorial discretion, turned the selection process over to the editorial board of *Contemporary Sociology.*

The original charge to the board of *Contemporary Sociology* was to select influential books, without any further specification. It was an admittedly diffuse concept and its ambiguities are altogether apparent in the list itself. Thus, *Our Bodies, Ourselves* is neither the work of sociologists nor does it appear at all in the *Social Science Citation Index*[3] but it has sold three times as many copies as the book Gans identifies as the sociological best-seller, Riesman's *Lonely Crowd.* Clearly the implicit criterion by which *Our Bodies* is included is not influence on core sociology but some idea of its influence on American culture in an area of concern to many sociologists. Thus, William

---

3. Given the ambiguity of the "author" of *Our Bodies,* and the variety of ways the book might be cited, it is possible that we missed citations to it in *SSCI.*

Julius Wilson's *Declining Significance of Race* fares less well in terms of both citations and sales than his own later *Truly Disadvantaged*. Here the implicit criterion involves not large numbers of sociologists or general readers so much as influence on key audiences, both academic and in social policy. The eclecticism of the list does make it hard to interpret. But eclecticism is also one of the list's strengths.

Sociology is itself eclectic. The notion of required reading assumes a core. But sociology does not have a single core. It is a discipline that addresses itself simultaneously to other sociologists, scholars in other disciplines, students, general readers, and those who make policy. Any attempt to establish a single criterion of influence would, of necessity, exclude many of these audiences. Perhaps it would be better to let each of the congeries of sociologists concerned with a particular audience go its own way. But sociologists also have to live together — in their associations, in their departments, and in their joint membership within the cultural category of sociologist as it is understood by others (even if sociologists themselves are prepared to disavow its meaningfulness). Sociology may not have a single common language. But sociologists can, to take the metaphor seriously, be multilingual. If, to understand their colleagues, all sociologists need to speak the language of multiple regressions, so, too, they need at least a reading knowledge of Foucault and Bourdieu, of world system and managed hearts. How do we dare to claim that these seventeen books are required reading? They are required in the specific sense that they are necessary to understand the concepts and preoccupations of a significant proportion of the discipline's practitioners.

INFLUENTIAL BOOKS

In the course of making the case for including the *SPSS* manual among the most influential books in sociology, Barry Wellman asks whether it is the findings themselves or the tools that enable us to make those findings that are more important. Wellman answers his own question with a "vote for the toolmakers because they give us the eyes to see things." Wellman's argument is compelling: We would also extend it. Tools do not consist solely of methods narrowly understood but also of concepts and modes of analysis more generally. Indeed, one distinguishing characteristic of many of the books included on the most influential list is precisely that they have provided sociologists with just such tools. It is not, for example, the particular content of Foucault's observations about nineteenth-century prisons or Geertz's observations about Balinese cockfights or even Kanter's observations about men and women in contemporary corporations that engages us. Rather, it is what Foucault shows us about how to analyze discourse, what Geertz shows us about how to analyze local cultures, and what Kanter shows us about how to analyze structures that provide the basis for their enduring influence.

None of the books included on the list is a grand theoretical statement in the tradition of Talcott Parsons. To be sure, a few books on the list — Tilly's, by Gould's reading, and perhaps Chodorow's and Bourdieu's — are explicitly and self-consciously theoretical. But even these are not grand theories. Similarly, a few books on the list deal with phenomena of enormous scope: What, indeed, could be of greater scope than Skocpol's analysis of revolutions in the making of the modern world or than Wallerstein's analysis of nothing less than a world system? But neither Skocpol nor Wallerstein imagines her- or himself engaged in acts of abstract or formal theory. Geertz's theoretical significance is, as Ann Swidler points out, largely dependent on his antitheoretical stance. And, as Jonathan Simon points out in his essay in this volume, something of the same sort might be said for Foucault. On the one hand, Foucault is arguably the single figure of the past several decades who has most influenced the way theorists talk about theory; and a great number of social scientists (along with an even greater number of scholars in the humanities) identify themselves either as Foucauldians or, in muted tribute, as post-Foucauldians. On the other hand, Foucault's theoretical stance is rarely explicit, developed primarily in a series of exemplary empirical studies, each limited to a particular discourse. In Simon's fine phrase, Foucault's work represents the "birth of a postmodern middle-range."

It is altogether to the point that the large majority (fourteen of seventeen) of the books discussed in this volume were first published in the 1970s. It is, of course, possible that it simply takes time before a book's influence is felt and recognized. And it is equally possible that the overrepresentation of books from the 1970s represents the *Contemporary Sociology* board's generational bias.[4] Although the board is geograph-

---

4. The *Contemporary Sociology* board was designed to include a broad representation of specialty areas, but is unbalanced geographically (half the members are concentrated within

ically heterogeneous, aside from the concentration around Amherst, and includes an intentionally wide range of specialty areas, it is generationally more homogenous: twenty-two of twenty-eight board members received their degrees in the 1970s or 1980s. It may be that the choice of books represents intellectual preoccupations formed in graduate school and the early stages of careers. But there is another possibility as well. With the ending of the intellectual dominance of structural-functionalism, there was ample room for new perspectives and orientations. With the entrance of far larger numbers of women and people of color than had previously characterized sociology and with the coming of age of a generation whose formative intellectual influences were (negatively or positively) the radical movements of the 1960s, there was a much enlarged audience for these new orientations. For these reasons, it is altogether possible that the 1970s were a moment of unusual innovation in sociology and that, for better or worse, it is the intellectual legacy of that decade with which we now live.

Some of the books on the *Contemporary Sociology* list seem to have been thrust into prominence by social forces and social movements that may have been crystallized by, but nonetheless preceded, the book's publication. The success of Charles Murray's *Losing Ground,* let alone *The Bell Curve,* seems to have depended less on the book's merits than on the support for the position it articulated among powerful political forces. (In Murray's case, in particular, this support was not simply abstract or part of a *weltenschaung:* His book was actively promoted by the Manhattan Institute and was made available to academic and media supporters long before it could be read by neutral critics [Escoffier 1988; Smith 1991].) This point, of course, applies not only to works of the right: As Aldon Morris argues in his essay, there

---

fifty miles of Amherst, Massachusetts), focuses on book (not article) sociology, and over-represents left and feminist perspectives. Of the twenty-eight board members, twenty-one are white and seven are members of minority groups; sixteen are women and twelve are men; four were based outside the United States. Four members of the board received their doctoral degrees in the 1960s, eight in the 1970s, fourteen in the 1980s, and two in the 1990s. The members of the board who participated in the selection of the most influential books were Douglas Anderton, Maxine Baca Zinn, John Braithwaite, Michael Burawoy, Margaret Cerullo, Mary Ann Clawson, N. J. Demerath III, Rick Fantasia, Naomi Gerstel, Linda Gordon, David Grusky, John Hewitt, Nazli Kibria, Deborah King, Michèle Lamont, Arnlaug Leira, John Lie, Patricia Yancey Martin, Ruth Milkman, Valentine Moghadam, Aldon Morris, Constance Nathanson, Deirdre Royster, Janet Salaff, Jonathan Simon, Barrie Thorne, Jerry Watts, and Robert Zussman.

was also a ready-made constituency for William Julius Wilson's *Declining Significance of Race*. Similarly, the developing women's movement created a constituency for Chodorow, Kanter, and, above all, *Our Bodies, Ourselves;* the movements of the 1960s created an interest in Tilly's studies of social movements; and the decline of U.S. hegemony increased interest in world-systems analyses.

Emerging, as they did, out of a moment of intellectual and political ferment, many of the other books discussed in this volume did not simply influence sociology, but also gave the field its current shape. Precisely because they have been instrumental in reshaping sociology, it should not be surprising that only about half of the books included on the list are the works of sociologists, strictly defined. Geertz is an anthropologist; Becker, an economist; Said, a literary critic; Foucault was a historian. Braverman and the Boston Women's Health Book Collective worked outside of conventional academic disciplines altogether. Moreover, even many of the books that are the products of sociologists stand on the borders of other fields: Chodorow's *Reproduction,* for example, on the border of sociology and psychology, both Skocpol's *States* and Wallerstein's *World Systems* on the borders of sociology, history, and political science. Indeed, one of the most striking features of the *Contemporary Sociology* list is its interdisciplinary character.

In this sense, the list of most influential books is only a small part of a long-running dispute over the character of disciplinarity. In the long march from the Enlightenment through to the middle of the twentieth century, the pursuit of knowledge came to be organized progressively more around disciplines marked by internally shared paradigms of appropriate methods, questions, and subject matters.[5] For sociology, the key moment in the formation of the discipline, at least in the United States, appears to have come in the final decade of the nineteenth century and the first two decades of the twentieth, with the founding of specialized departments, journals (notably the *American Journal of Sociology*), and the American Sociological Association. Yet as powerful as are the institutional forces of academic departments and professional societies that now rally to defend disciplinary boundaries, it would be a mistake to believe that these boundaries were ever fixed or

---

5. For a stimulating discussion of these issues, see the report of the Gulbenkian Commission (1996).

uncontested. As Connell (1997) points out, the trinity of Marx-Weber-Durkheim did not become entrenched as the basis of the sociological canon until the 1960s. Many prominent sociologists first trained in disciplines other than sociology: Talcott Parsons, David Riesman, and Harrison White, to name only a few.

Even as disciplinary lines were becoming more firmly institutionalized, other forces were undermining them. Since World War II, a number of new developments have challenged the conventional organization of academic disciplines. Area studies — of the Soviet Union, China, Latin America, and elsewhere — came first, probably in response to America's intensified presence in world politics. But area studies were soon followed by a host of other program fields driven by very different constituencies — urban studies, black studies, women's studies, cultural studies, gay and lesbian studies. As a result, key concepts, methods, and orientations tend to migrate across disciplinary lines.

Despite this ongoing process undermining established disciplines — indeed, perhaps because of it — significant elements continue to defend and insist on disciplinary lines. Black studies or women's studies may be accepted, reluctantly, but only on condition that a "core" be maintained. Both those who support and those who contest the "core" recognize the *American Sociological Review* as its exemplar. Gerald Marwell, a former editor, speaks for one significant fraction of the ASA when he says (in an essay included in this volume) that the *CS* list "seems much too political to have been done on the American Sociological Association's dime and with the Association's imprimatur. . . . Is this how we want to be remembered? As a discipline dominated by Geertz and Said and the Boston Women's Collective?" Part of the reason the *Contemporary Sociology* list provoked such controversy was that it constitutes a certification, by one of a disciplinary association's official journals, of the influence, on the discipline itself, of a broad and nondisciplinary set of thinkers.

Although the list of influential books is distinctively interdisciplinary, it both reflects and celebrates the fluidity of boundaries, not their absence. A number of these books, for example, have carved out new connections and thus new boundaries. This is evident not so much in the reshaping of sociology as a whole as in the creation of new subfields. Thus, for example, before the publication of Braverman's *Labor and Monopoly Capital,* there was, to be sure, a sociology of work, a sociology of organizations, a sociology of occupations, a sociology of economics. Braverman did not invent any of these subfields. But his analysis did recast the relationship of each to the others and, in the process, spawned a host of studies around the organizing principle of the labor process. Nor did Kanter's book or Chodorow's by any means invent the sociology of gender but, different as these two books are in other respects, each contributed to the enormous growth of sociological research in the area and gave the field foci it had not previously had.

Some of the books discussed in this volume break the boundaries of subfields in other ways. Skocpol's *States and Social Revolution* is a study of revolution, but its influence, in part through the massive network of Skocpol's students and collaborators, extends to virtually all studies of the state. Similarly, the influence of Said's concept of "Orientalism" extends well beyond the specific literatures discussed by Said himself. Sociology as a whole is not, as it is now practiced, a paradigmatic field. But most of the books discussed in this volume are paradigmatic for the networks of scholars who participate in the very subfields those books helped establish.

The charge to reviewers was not to make a case for a book, but to analyze the character and sources of its influence.[6] The spirit of the volume is perhaps best captured in Barbara Laslett's introduction to her essay on *The Reproduction of Mothering:* Laslett notes that in many conversations over the course of her fifteen-year relationship with Chodorow "there has been mutual critique as well as appreciation" and that her essay "continues in the spirit of those conversations." The essays do not simply venerate or acclaim. As Baehr and O'Brien (1994) argue in their own analysis of sociological canons, "the greatest impediment to a book's elevation is not hostility, but indifference" (88). Because these books are already recognized as milestones in their fields and because many of the reviewers have them-

---

6. Ordinarily, *Contemporary Sociology,* like most academic journals, prefers reviewers who have not yet staked out a position on a book and avoids conflicts of interest. In this case we more or less reversed the rules. If a book is one of the most influential of the past twenty-five years, not to have taken a position on the book bespeaks someone not appropriate to the review (or pathologically cautious). Therefore these reviewers include friends, opponents, students, and rivals of the authors; in the essays that follow, the reader will experience little difficulty distinguishing among these different types of reviewers.

selves played central parts in the critical debates surrounding these books, the essays are as noteworthy for their critical edge as for their celebration of the texts at hand. As a result, the essays contribute to many of the key intellectual debates of the past twenty-five years. For example, Michael Burawoy insists that Harry Braverman's *Labor and Monopoly Capital* is no more than "a classic of its time," denying it the status of an enduring classic, and wonders how "such a simple, even unoriginal thesis [could] transform the field of sociology?" In an essay that mixes praise and criticism, Aldon Morris concludes that "the analytic flaws and political angle of [*The Declining Significance of Race*] were as responsible for the book's success as were its virtues." Christine Williams and Paula England are known as critics of Rosabeth Moss Kanter and Gary Becker. Jeff Goodwin's essay on *States and Social Revolutions* notes that "Skocpol is frequently—and largely ritualistically—cited for one or more ideas that a careful reading of *States* would quickly dispel." Goodwin argues that "at least one path by which one becomes a dominant American social scientist leads through a bog of misunderstanding."

The choice of the seventeen books discussed here as the most influential books of the last twenty-five years constitutes one set of judgments. They are required reading in the sense that a significant part of the discipline takes these books as essential to understanding their projects, their ways of doing sociology. We do not imagine that these seventeen books constitute the only list that could be constructed. We were fascinated by Gans's list of best-selling books and by Cronin's compilation of citations. We would, we suspect, be equally fascinated by efforts to judge and to measure those books—and articles—that have most affected social policy or undergraduate teaching or some other dimension of influence that we lack the wit to imagine. And we would not anticipate agreement about those lists any more than we anticipate agreement about the seventeen books listed here. As Arthur Stinchcombe (1994, 290) has observed, this disintegrated state of sociology may represent an "optimum state of affairs, both for the advance of knowledge and for the expansion of mind of undergraduates." Moreover, as Stinchcombe continues, it may be "better to have disagreement about who is elite in sociology rather than to develop a single dimension of research contribution."

REFERENCES

Baehr, Peter, and Mike O'Brien. 1994. "Founders, Classics and the Concept of a Canon." *Current Sociology* 42 (1): 1–148.

Calhoun, Craig J., and Kenneth C. Land. 1989. "Smelser's *Handbook:* An Assessment." *Contemporary Sociology* 18 (4): 475–77.

Connell, R. W. 1997. "Why Is Classical Theory Classical?" *American Journal of Sociology* 102 (6): 1511–57.

Cronin, Blaise, Gail McKenzie, Lourdes Rubio, and Sherrill Weaver-Wozniak. 1993. "Accounting for Influence: Acknowledgments in Contemporary Sociology." *Journal of the American Society for Information Science* 44 (7): 406–12.

Escoffier, Jeffrey. 1988. "Pessimism of the Mind." *Socialist Review* 18 (1) (January-March).

Guillory, John. [1990]. 1995. "Canon." Pp. 233–49 in *Critical Terms for Literary Study,* 2d ed. Ed. Frank Lentricchia and Thomas McLaughlin. Chicago: University of Chicago Press.

Gulbenkian Commission on the Restructuring of the Social Sciences. 1996. *Open the Social Sciences: Report of the Gulbenkian Commission on the Restructuring of the Social Sciences.* Stanford: Stanford University Press.

Smith, James A. 1981. *The Idea Brokers.* New York: Free Press.

Stinchcombe, Arthur L. 1994. "Disintegrated Disciplines and the Future of Sociology." *Sociological Forum* 9: 279–91.

BEST-SELLERS BY AMERICAN SOCIOLOGISTS
AN EXPLORATORY STUDY

Herbert J. Gans

American sociology's support from the general public, in its taxpayer and other roles, depends in significant part on how informative that public finds sociology, and what uses it can make of the discipline's work. Since one of the many things we do for various sectors of the general public is to inform its reading members through our books and nonjournal articles, this study aims to determine what sociology that general public has read and is reading, and it takes a first cut at answering that question by estimating sociology's best-selling books. The study is about sales, not readership, and this article reports fifty-six titles that have sold over 50,000 copies.[1]

The identification of these titles turned out to be a difficult empirical problem, and discussion of the study must thus begin with a report on methods. What books by sociologists have been read most often by the general public can really only be answered by a readership study among a sample of that public. What I have done instead, and as a very exploratory effort, is to ask a large number of editors at commercial and university presses, and authors, about the sales of sociological books other than texts and classics.

The sales figures I obtained in this fashion were probably dominated in most cases by books sold to undergraduates as supplementary read-

This is a slightly revised and updated version of the article that appeared in *Contemporary Sociology* in March 1997. The study reported in it exists only because of the hard work of staff members of commercial and university presses, and of course authors, who reported their book sales, especially those who went through their royalty files to compile exact figures. I am grateful to all of them, and also to the authors whose book sales did not reach 50,000 copies. They represent the vast majority of all sociologist authors, but I could not include their names and book titles in this article.

1. People may buy books that they do not read, and they may also read books that they do not buy, by borrowing from friends and libraries. Used-book sales are another kind of highly relevant but unavailable datum.

ings, but there is no way to find out from editors or authors how many of their books were bought by members of the general public. Furthermore, most undergraduates, future sociologists excepted, *are* members of the general public. Nevertheless, this is also a study of sociological titles adopted by college instructors. While these instructors chose the titles, I assumed that some picked their supplementary readings to some extent because they thought these stood a better chance of being read than research monographs on the same topic.

For the purpose of this study, I defined sociologists as authors with graduate degrees or teaching affiliations in sociology. In addition, I included social scientists from related disciplines, particularly anthropology, whose books have been virtually adopted as sociological because their concepts and methods are so similar to sociology's, and who are therefore often cited or widely read by sociologists and their students. However, I excluded books by journalists, because while some of their works meet some of our conceptual and methodological criteria and increasingly appear on sociological reading lists, they are not the work of trained social scientists. More important, there is no way to determine what proportion of their often immense sales comes from sociologists, students, or other buyers interested in sociology.[2]

The study was conducted via a brief mail questionnaire sent to editors at all the major commercial and university presses that publish sociologists, and from a similar mail questionnaire sent to sociologist authors I considered likely to have written well-selling books.[3] Both authors and editors were asked to exclude textbooks. I further asked editors not to report on the classic authors, so that sales for the discipline's pantheon of Marx, Durkheim, Weber et al. are also excluded.

I chose both authors and presses carefully from a number of lists, bibliographies, and ASA annual meeting program advertisers, and from nearly fifty years of experience in the discipline, as well as from my knowledge of commercial and university presses.[4] My choices of

2. Of course, the same criticism can be applied to books written by anthropologists, but their sales and readership audience is sufficiently small that they can be included here. Historians, political scientists, economists, and psychologists without any close connection to sociology were not included because they are all members of much larger disciplines than sociology.

3. The questionnaire asked publishers to report up to 8 of their top selling books by sociologists — other than texts or classics. Authors were asked to report the sales of their three to five best-selling works.

4. I also received and used nominations of authors by the editor of this book.

authors were limited to living American (and Canadian) sociologists, which is unfair to, among other people, some foreign authors also read in the United States, as well as to North American colleagues whose work is read mainly overseas.[5]

Altogether, I wrote to 52 presses, of whom 41 responded, and to 55 authors, of whom 43 responded.[6] Twenty-seven, or 52 percent, of the publishers or editors — or their representatives — who responded supplied sales figures. So did 39, or 71 percent, of the authors. Three additional authors responded to an appeal included in the original article to send me eligible titles for an updated table, which was later published in the November 1997 *Contemporary Sociology*. Most of the authors and many of the editors estimated or rounded off sales figures, and the number who could supply exact figures were in the minority.

As the numbers above suggest, authors were on the whole more helpful than editors.[7] In a surprising number of cases, press records were incomplete, particularly for books issued before computerization arrived in the book industry.[8] However, four of the twelve editors who responded without data indicated that company policy required holding sales figures proprietary.[9]

In any case, the findings of the study also reflect the problems of self-reporting — and these problems of self-reporting are numerous and

5. I tried to obtain sales figures for no longer living but popular sociological authors of the last half century, such as Erving Goffman and C. Wright Mills, but was able to do so only for the recently deceased Elliot Liebow, thanks entirely to the persistent efforts of his wife, Harriet, in obtaining the numbers from the publisher. Liebow, although trained in anthropology, was widely read by, and worked mainly with, sociologists.

6. Everyone who did not respond received one reminder. I should note that I received no responses from the big mass-market paperback presses, such as Penguin, that publish sociologists, or from their authors.

7. Sociology editors whom I knew personally or to whom I could write by name were more helpful than other people to whom I wrote, such as sociology editors or social science editors.

8. In addition, some big publishers that bought smaller ones did not get or keep data on the individual book sales of the smaller companies they bought. Moreover, publishers are required by the tax law to retain sales records for only seven years, and some seem to have gotten rid of them after the required period.

9. Some of the editors who failed to answer probably also did so for proprietary reasons, but I find the policy mystifying, since even the best-selling sociologists are not a major source of income, especially for large presses. Just about all the authors who provided no data indicated that they had not saved their royalty statements or were not sent data on the number of books sold, and a surprising number of authors did not look at that number in their statements, although I am sure that some did not respond to my questionnaire because they wanted to keep their book sales to themselves.

obvious.[10] Whenever possible, I made extra efforts to get figures from both authors and their editors, and I practiced some caution by privileging editor figures when these were complete.[11] When respondents offered a range, as many did, I automatically accepted the lower number. Still, I had no reliable way of finding out, from editors or authors, who had accurate sales figures and who was supplying hopeful rather than realistic estimates.[12] Nor could I obtain data from presses or authors who did not respond to my mail questionnaire, my reminder, and my appeal for titles in the original article.

THE FINDINGS

The basic findings of the study are shown in Table 1. Because so many of the numbers I obtained were rounded figures, estimates and even guesstimates, I decided not to report the sales figures I received. Instead, I ranked by numerical intervals — and in order of reported sales — the top sellers for which I obtained data.

I except only two books from my practice of not publishing sales figures. One is the sole title known to have sold over one million copies: David Riesman, Nathan Glazer, and Reuel Denney's *The Lonely Crowd*. That book had already sold one million copies by 1971; by the end of 1995 Nathan Glazer reported (personal communication) that it had sold 1,434,000 copies. The runner-up to *The Lonely Crowd* was Elliot Liebow's *Tally's Corner,* which had sold 701,000 copies through 1995.

Without a readership study of the general public, I can only offer some hypotheses about what kinds of books by sociologists are bought most often — and these are fairly obvious. They are also risky, because

10. In addition, although all authors and editors were asked to report foreign as well as domestic sales, not all did so, although foreign sales are usually small. However, the books of some sociologists who sell well in the United States, e.g., Daniel Bell, Richard Sennett, and Immanuel Wallerstein, are very popular overseas.

11. In the handful of cases for which I had conflicting sales figures from author and editor, I wrote to both, either to try to reconcile the numbers or to determine why they differed.

12. I can only add that I know personally many of the authors I contacted, but I doubt whether that discouraged anyone from hopeful estimating. Likewise, I assume that some editors who lacked complete data also supplied me with hopeful estimates. The immense logistical and other tasks of checking sales figures require a funded study, perhaps by a graduate student interested in making this the subject of her or his dissertation. In that case, however, I hope he or she undertakes a readership study, even if the sample of readers is small.

not only do many books have several themes worthy of note, but also, as every author knows, what authors write is not always what readers read, or even buy to read. Thus, the explicit subject matter of the book is only one factor in understanding the public's interest in sociology.

First, the age distribution of the books on the list reflects the growth in college and sociology enrollments, as well as in the number of sociologists in the last three decades—not to mention the changes in American society. The list includes only one book first published prior to the 1950s—Wiliam F. Whyte's *Street Corner Society*—and three from the 1950s. Fourteen were originally published in the 1960s, thirty-five in the 1970s and 1980s, and three in the 1990s.

Second, all or just about all of the books are jargon-free; whatever their other virtues, they are written in a language that at least educated general readers can understand. As a result, a few authors have several books on the list, and may even have constituencies of their own.

Third, at or near the top of the list are several titles that attract readers, and probably particularly students, from other disciplines. For example, *The Lonely Crowd,* books by Richard Sennett and some others appear on reading lists in the humanities. S. M. Lipset's *Political Man,* like the works of William Domhoff, are among the several books of political sociology that also show up in political science course syllabi.

Fourth, books that try to understand and explain American society as a whole are among the leaders. *The Lonely Crowd* has often been described as portraying the Americas of the 1950s. If decades are actually relevant empirical indicators of anything, their sales figures would suggest that Philip Slater's *Pursuit of Loneliness* and Richard Sennett's *The Fall of Public Man* may have served the same function for the 1960s and 1970s, and Robert Bellah et al.'s *Habits of the Heart,* for the 1980s and 1990s.

That two of sociology's top sellers mention American loneliness in their titles may also be significant. Analogously, that some of the top sellers and a number of other books lower down on the list were at least partly nostalgic for a better American past is probably not accidental either.

Fifth, sociology was among the first disciplines to respond to the country's increased interest in problems of poverty and racial inequality in the 1960s, which surely helps to explain why *Tally's Corner* is second highest on my list, and why William Ryan's *Blaming the Victim* and Lillian Rubin's *World of Pain* are not far behind. Fewer well-

Table 1
*Reported Book Sales, through 1995, Rank-Ordered within Numerical Intervals**

Over 1 Million
D. Riesman, N. Glazer, R. Denney, *The Lonely Crowd,* Yale, 1950

1 Million to 750,000
None

749,999 to 500,000
E. Liebow, *Tally's Corner,* Little Brown, 1967
P. Slater, *Pursuit of Loneliness,* Beacon, 1970

499,999 to 400,000
R. Sennett, *Fall of Public Man,* Knopf, 1977
W. Ryan, *Blaming the Victim,* Pantheon, 1971
R. Bellah et al. *Habits of the Heart,* California, 1985
S. Lipset, *Political Man,* Doubleday, 1960
L. Rubin, *Worlds of Pain,* Basic, 1976

399,999 to 300,000
L. Rubin, *Intimate Strangers,* Harper&Row, 1983
N. Glazer and D. Moynihan, *Beyond the Melting Pot,* M.I.T., 1963
R. Sennett and J. Cobb, *Hidden Injuries of Class,* Knopf, 1972

299,999 to 200,000
G. W. Domhoff, *Who Rules America?* Prentice Hall, 1967
W. Whyte, *Street Corner Society,* Chicago, 1943
F. Piven and R. Cloward, *Regulating the Poor,* Pantheon, 1971
R. Sennett, *Uses of Disorder,* Knopf, 1970
C. Stack, *All Our Kin,* Basic, 1974
D. Vaughan, *Uncoupling,* Oxford, 1986

199,999 to 150,000
H. Gans, *Urban Villagers,* Free Press, 1962
R. Kanter, *Men and Women of the Corporation,* Basic, 1977**
I. Horowitz, *War Games,* Ballantine, 1963

149,999 to 100,000
P. Starr, *Social Transformation of American Medicine,* Basic, 1982
H. Becker, *Outsiders,* Free Press, 1963
K. Erikson, *Everything in Its Path,* Simon & Schuster, 1976
D. Bell, *Coming of Post-Industrial Society,* Basic, 1973
A. Hochschild, *Second Shift,* Viking, 1989
K. Erikson, *Wayward Puritans,* Macmillan, 1966

99,999 to 75,000
T. Gitlin, *The Sixties,* Bantam, 1987
I. Wallerstein, *Africa: Politics of Independence,* Random House, 1961
D. Bell, *Cultural Contradictions of Capitalism,* Basic, 1976
W. Wilson, *Truly Disadvantaged,* Chicago, 1987
D. Bell, *End of Ideology,* Free Press, 1963
P. Blumstein and P. Schwartz, *American Couples,* Morrow, 1983
I. Horowitz, ed., *Anarchists,* Dell, 1964
J. Loewen, *Lies My Teacher Told Me,* New Press, 1995
L. Rubin, *Just Friends,* Harper & Row, 1985
L. Coser, *Functions of Social Conflict,* Free Press, 1956
G. Sykes, *Society of Captives,* Princeton, 1958
J. MacLeod, *Ain't No Making It,* Westview, 1985

Table 1
Continued

74,999 to 60,000
M. Komarovsky, *Blue-Collar Marriage,* Random House, 1962
F. Piven and R. Cloward, *Poor People's Movements,* Pantheon, 1977
G. W. Domhoff, *Higher Circles,* Random House, 1970
I. Wallerstein, *Modern World Systems,* Vol 1, Academic, 1974
N. Chodorow, *Reproduction of Mothering,* California, 1978
R. Sidel, *Women and Children Last,* Viking, 1986
G. W. Domhoff, *Who Rules America Now?* Prentice Hall, 1983
G. Suttles, *Social Order of the Slum,* Chicago, 1968
R. Bellah et. al., *Good Society,* Knopf, 1991
F. Piven and R. Cloward, *New Class War,* Pantheon, 1982
R. Sennett, *Conscience of the Eye,* Knopf, 1990

59,999 to 50,000
G. W. Domhoff, *Powers That Be,* Random House, 1978
W. Wilson, *Declining Significance of Race,* Chicago, 1979
K. Luker, *Abortion and Politics of Motherhood,* California, 1984
R. Sidel, *Women and Child Care in China,* Viking, 1986
S. Lipset, *First New Nation,* Basic, 1963
T. Skocpol, *States and Social Revolutions,* Cambridge, 1979
S. Steinberg, *Ethnic Myth,* Atheneum, 1981

---

* Citations are limited to original publisher and year of publication.
** Sales for paperback edition only.

---

selling books on these subjects have appeared since the 1970s, however, and no book on homelessness made the list.

Sixth, books about the family, children, and friends and other works
that deal with primary groups are as popular as are the courses sociologists teach on these subjects; surely that is one reason why Lillian
Rubin has several books on the list. True, most of the best-sellers are
about larger groups and institutions, as well as macrosociological concepts, but by and large they respond to the audience's interest in specific subjects and political or social issues that had become topical in
previous years — for example, race, ethnicity, and gender.[13]

Seventh, most of the books on the list are not empirical research
reports, but of those that are, ethnographies outnumber depth interview studies and surveys by a considerable margin. This is not surprising since they are apt to be most readable, to emphasize narrative

13. I also expected a correlation with the most frequently taught courses in sociology,
but the number of books about family and marriage and even "deviance" is limited, although many of the best-sellers could fit nicely into courses on social problems and social
stratification.

over abstractions, and to minimize quantitative analyses. Probably the book on the list with the most numbers is William J. Wilson's *Truly Disadvantaged,* but more completely quantitative studies have no chance in this competition; also, most are published as articles, not books.

Eighth, the authors of the two top best-sellers do not hold Ph.D.'s in sociology, but a large number of the other authors do — a pleasant contrast, at least from a disciplinary booster's perspective, to the majority of the authors published in *CS*'s lists of the most influential books.

Ninth, only sixteen of the titles have women as sole or senior authors, several of whom are repeaters with several books on the list; and just two books were written by (the same) black author. However, these and other inequalities — for example, that most authors are associated with elite or other research universities — should not be surprising, even if they are still dismaying.

Tenth, forty-three of the fifty-six books (77 percent) on the list were first published commercially, twelve were issued by university presses — mostly by Chicago and California, and one was published by a nonprofit publisher (the New Press). Ten years from now the commercial/university ratio is likely to be lower. Commercial publishers, particularly those belonging to conglomerates, are already being pressed to produce higher profit rates and may therefore not be allowed to publish as much sociology in the future.[14] Some university presses will most likely add to their sociology lists as a result.

Finally, that I could find only fifty-six books that have sold over

14. One prominent commercial press that had published a number of major sociological titles over the years, BasicBooks, was closed down by HarperCollins in summer 1997, but was then sold to Perseus Books, a venture capital firm that has also acquired or established several other presses. As of this writing (December 1997), Basic has rehired its previous publishing director, announced that it will bring out all 150 of the old firm's titles already under contract, and in a press release looked forward to Basic's "strong future as a bridge between trade books and the academy."

Even so, commercial book publishing continues to confront a generic "midlist" problem that clouds the immediate future of "serious" nonfiction books, such as those published by Basic. The midlist problem is not new, however, and it spans books written by popular writers as well as by social scientists. Books by the latter, including those written by sociologists, are particularly vulnerable since their sales are typically at the lower end of the midlist, even though some, like those discussed in this study, generate further sales when they move to the backlist. As a result, cautious hope for the survival of sociological writing that can reach the general public is justified.

50,000 since the 1940s suggests that the discipline still has a long way to go before it makes a significant impression on the general public. How it can best do so is a subject for another article, but it should not do so by deliberately attempting to publish best-sellers. Sociologists ought to publish intellectually and otherwise useful work, empirical and theoretical, that adds to our own and to the public's understanding of society, and if possible to its improvement as well. If sociologists achieve these goals more adequately, and write more clearly, too, some books will sell more copies, including books like the high-quality and serious ones that crowd Table 1. Equally important, others will be more seminal or influential than now even if they are not best-sellers.[15]

Should sociologists be able to produce more relevant findings and influential ideas about society, particularly American society, we may even be able to attract popular writers, including sociologists, who can report our work to the general public better than we can. The natural sciences have recruited an increasing number of scientists who are serving their fields as popularizers. Meanwhile, part of our informational role is being taken over by talented journalists, although too many of them still write on sociological topics with only a limited understanding of society. The journalists' increasing takeover of what should be our role is a far more serious problem than the scarcity of sociological best-sellers, at least for those of us who believe that sociology must increase its usefulness to the general public if it is to survive as a vital discipline.

15. Still, the books listed in Table 1 include a number of influential titles, including what has arguably been the most influential one of the last decade or more, in sociology and among the sociology-reading public: William J. Wilson's *Truly Disadvantaged*.

2 STATE PROCESSES

HOW TO BECOME A DOMINANT AMERICAN SOCIAL SCIENTIST:
THE CASE OF THEDA SKOCPOL

Jeff Goodwin

STATES AND SOCIAL REVOLUTIONS: A COMPARATIVE ANALY-SIS OF FRANCE, RUSSIA, AND CHINA, by Theda Skocpol. Cambridge: Cambridge University Press, 1979.

Original review, *CS* 9:3 (May 1980), by Walter L. Goldfrank:

States and Social Revolutions marks a leap forward for scholarship in historically-oriented macrosociology, and thus promises to raise the collective stature of the discipline as a whole. . . . It brilliantly dissects a set of sufficiently similar structures, processes, and outcomes. . . . Its major drawback in my view is its tendency toward positivist ahistoricity.

Let me begin by proposing three theoretical conjectures that just might help to explain how *States and Social Revolutions* propelled Theda Skocpol into the front ranks of American social scientists. *Hypothesis number one:* For any book to become widely cited today, let alone to influence how people actually think, it must be reducible to a few general and easily grasped formulations. Many texts are "formulated" in this way, furthermore, not by their authors, but by more or less officially designated readers (call them DRs), including reviewers for academic journals. Books that cannot be formulaically summarized by DRs, accurately or otherwise, are unlikely to generate much discussion, let alone to change minds. Unfortunately, some very brilliant books — many now out-of-print — fall into this category.

The process of "formulation" typically results in simplifications,

My thanks to Mustafa Emirbayer, Drew Halfmann, and Renée Steinhagen for their helpful comments on this essay.

half-truths, and outright errors, particularly when DRs are ill-disposed toward a particular text or (let it be said) a specific author. The more complex the text, moreover, the more simplification is essential if the "formulation" that is a prerequisite of broad influence is to occur at all. Ensuing "discussions" and "debates" about a particular text often build upon these simplifications, half-truths, and errors. Before long, scholars can be influenced by these "debates," or even participate in them, without actually having read (or read closely) the text supposedly at issue; one need simply familiarize oneself with the formulaic summaries and discussions of it that DRs have produced. *Hypothesis number two:* No book can claim to be influential today until large numbers of people who have *not* read it (or have not read beyond its introduction) have very strong opinions about it. In fact, some of the most frequently cited books are, paradoxically, not very widely or closely read at all. Which brings us to *hypothesis number three:* A complex text that, in order to be understood, actually has to be read closely and carefully by large numbers of people, and not just DRs, will never become widely influential.

Whether these hypotheses actually shed light on the intellectual impact of Skocpol's *States and Social Revolutions* (hereafter, *States*) is a matter best left to sociologists of knowledge. Of course, certain postmodernists would claim that there simply are no "misunderstandings" of texts (other than of their own), only *multiple* understandings, none of which should be "privileged." But it seems certain that a good part of Skocpol's eminently deserved fame is actually due to the wide diffusion of several gross misformulations of some key ideas in *States*. (Walter Goldfrank's review of *States* in *Contemporary Sociology*, I hasten to add, was unusually careful and insightful.) Mind you, as a protégé and erstwhile collaborator of Skocpol's, I would be delighted to attribute the broad impact of *States* to the fact that it really is a well-researched, brilliantly argued, carefully crafted, and clearly written book on an important subject. Unfortunately, it would be simplistic to attribute the vast influence of *States,* or of Skocpol, entirely to the many merits of that book. (I have no desire, let me add, to play Skocpol's Wacquant. In any event, she requires no such services — as anyone who has crossed intellectual paths with her can attest!)

The fact is that Skocpol is frequently — and largely ritualistically — cited as a preeminent spokesperson for one or more ideas that a careful reading of *States* would quickly dispel. Partly for this reason, a vast number and remarkably wide assortment of books, articles, and un-published screeds in the areas of political sociology, comparative politics, social movements, sociological theory, and comparative methods are littered with those familiar parentheticals "see Skocpol 1979," "see, e.g., Skocpol 1979," and the like. Citations of particular chapters or pages of *States,* by contrast, are relatively few and far between (see hypothesis number three, above).

Let us examine some of the formulations that are allegedly found in "Skocpol 1979":

1. *Only state institutions matter in explaining how or why revolutions (or political changes generally) occur.* According to this common interpretation of Skocpol's "state-centered" approach, which is taken nearly verbatim from a recent review in *Contemporary Sociology* (Hochschild 1996, 43), *States* propounds a sort of "state determinism." (One scholar has even accused Skocpol of "statolatry"!) Yet the principal argument of *States* is rather more complex and interesting than this: Skocpol argues that the French, Russian, and Chinese revolutions were the result of a *conjuncture* of "(1) state organizations susceptible to administrative and military collapse when subjected to intensified pressures from more developed countries abroad and (2) agrarian sociopolitical structures that facilitated widespread peasant revolts against landlords" (1979, 154). Skocpol's explanation of peasant revolts in chapter 3 of *States,* furthermore, emphasizes the autonomy and solidarity of some, but not all, peasant communities. This explanation may be criticized on a number of grounds, including Skocpol's tendency to neglect local peasant cultures. What cannot be fairly claimed, however, is that only state institutions figure in Skocpol's explanation of peasant revolts or, accordingly, in her explanation of social revolutions. (Dogged by the state-determinist reading of *States,* Skocpol has abandoned the "state-centered" label, describing her more recent work as "historical institutionalist.")

The section of *States* in which Skocpol introduces her theoretical perspective on states, it should also be noted, is entitled "The *Potential* Autonomy of the State." And yet the idea persists that Skocpol's "state-centered" approach presumes that states are *invariably* powerful and autonomous organizations floating above and thoroughly dominating societies (see, e.g., Migdal, Kohli, and Shue 1994, Introduction, ch. 1). This claim is especially ironic insofar as Skocpol emphasizes the *breakdown* of state power as a precondition for the social revolutions that she examines; moreover, her account of the prerevolutionary French and Chinese states emphasizes how dominant landowning classes penetrated and thereby weakened those states in a context of intensified geopolitical conflict. Skocpol could not explain the revolutions that interest her, in short, if she assumed that state autonomy and state capacities were given once and for all.

2. *Ideas and beliefs don't matter in revolutions (or in politics generally).* This formulation is a widespread misunderstanding of Skocpol's self-proclaimed "structuralist" approach, the actual point of which is that the outcomes of complex processes like revolutions cannot be viewed as the self-conscious ideological or political project of any single group of actors — as some scholars, incidentally, continue to argue (e.g., Goldstone 1991, ch. 5). As Skocpol has written elsewhere, "nonintentionalist at the macroscopic level" would have been a more accurate (if rather cumbersome!) label for this claim (1994, 199). In fact, one of the most important contributions of *States* is Skocpol's "conjunctural" approach to revolutions — the idea that revolutions are caused by "separately determined and not consciously coordinated (or deliberately revolutionary) processes and group efforts" (1979, 298 n.44). (Unfortunately, this concise formulation was buried in a footnote.) Nothing in *States*, in any event, suggests that ideas don't matter to people or that Skocpol rejects a priori the potential usefulness of cultural factors in explanations of revolutions or other political processes.

Chapter 4 of *States*, in fact, discusses a number of ways in which political ideologies mattered in the revolutionary conflicts traced out in the second (and largely neglected) half of that book: as forces for cohesion among particular political leaderships; as universalistic creeds that have facilitated joint action by socially diverse actors; as programs for proselytizing and mobilizing specific groups of people; and, not least, as justifications for acting ruthlessly against political opponents, real and imagined. Skocpol might have said much more about these factors than she actually did, and *States* has also been fairly criticized for neglecting what Skocpol (1994, ch. 8) later termed the "cultural idioms" of social groups. Still, the greater emphasis on culture, public opinion, and discourse in Skocpol's more recent work indicates just that: a greater emphasis, not the sort of epistemological break with her earlier work that some have perceived.

3. *A universal, invariant theory that explains social revolutions (or any other social or political process) can be inductively derived*

through comparisons. For every scholar who either draws inspiration from or bemoans, as the case may be, Skocpol's "state-centered" perspective, there seems to be another who claims that she has no theoretical perspective at all. According to the latter view, *States* is an exemplary piece of positivistic or quasi-experimental induction.

In the preface to *States,* Skocpol does celebrate the fact that her initial research into revolutions was not influenced by a close familiarity with (let alone a dogmatic commitment to) any particular theory of revolutions; and she has been downright disdainful of "metatheory" (i.e., theorizing about theory). But it hardly follows that Skocpol is a pure inductivist who imagines that her research is unburdened by *any* theoretical baggage. On the contrary, Skocpol clearly compares cases of revolution in *States* (including several cases where revolutions did *not* occur) in order to develop, test, refine, and (not least) debunk a number of theoretical hypotheses about revolutionary processes. Her method, in other words, is as deductive as it is inductive. (Although it is not deductive enough, clearly, for many Marxist and rational-choice theorists.) Skocpol has explicitly called, in fact, for a "dialectical method" that combines inductive and deductive reasoning (Skocpol 1986).

States, furthermore, does not in any way attempt to derive (inductively or otherwise) the "covering laws" or to formulate a "universal theory" of social revolutions, as many seem to think. Skocpol draws her cases from an analytically delimited universe of "protobureaucratic" agrarian autocracies that had not been colonially subjugated (41); and she explicitly warns that her conjunctural explanation for social revolutions in this particular context cannot be mechanically extended to others (288). This has not prevented a small army of scholars, however, from pointing to this or that case of revolution as supposedly "refuting" or requiring a radical "respecification" of Skocpol's "model." When Skocpol published an account of the Iranian Revolution that differed in several respects from her analysis in *States* (see Skocpol 1982; 1994, ch. 10), some even interpreted this as an unwitting refutation of her own book! This interpretation, however, rests upon an assumption that Skocpol has never made, namely, that all revolutions have the same, invariant causes and can be explained, therefore, by the same general theory.

To be sure, the delimited scope of Skocpol's argument in *States* has not gone completely unnoticed. One notorious review (Burawoy 1989) took Skocpol to task for (among other things) precisely her inability to predict revolutions in a world in which proto-bureaucratic agrarian autocracies no longer exist. This review compared Skocpol's silence about future revolutions with Leon Trotsky's bold prediction in 1906 that socialist revolutions would eventually sweep across not only Russia, but Western Europe as well. The author of this review somehow felt that Skocpol suffered from the comparison, but surely a fairer conclusion would be that scholars (and brilliant revolutionaries) should indeed hesitate to make sweeping generalizations and predictions based on limited data. To paraphrase Tocqueville, revolutions may seem inevitable in retrospect, yet they are almost always unforeseen.

The preceding misformulations served to transmogrify Skocpol's state-centered, structuralist, and comparative explanation of social revolutions that occurred in a particular sociopolitical context into a dogmatic state-determinist, anticultural, and inductivist *Weltanschauung* that she has never articulated. By so simplifying Skocpol's ideas, however, these misformulations undoubtedly facilitated the diffusion of "her" thought to more scholars than would otherwise have been the case. (Some scholars, no doubt, were provoked by these misformulations into actually reading *States*!) Skocpol's "influence" was thereby multiplied: Following the publication of *States,* there have been, to be sure, many interesting discussions and debates about Skocpol's analysis; but there have been even more numerous "discussions" and "debates" about "Skocpol's" analysis. (And, to add to the confusion, the line between the two is of course blurred and indistinct.)

Thus, the case of Theda Skocpol — or, more accurately, of "Theda Skocpol" — suggests that at least one path by which one becomes a dominant American social scientist (see Lamont 1987) meanders, at least in part, through a bog of misunderstanding. One must wonder, in fact, if this is not the only path to academic fame.

REFERENCES

Burawoy, Michael. 1989. "Two Methods in Search of Science: Skocpol versus Trotsky." *Theory and Society* 18:759–805.

Goldstone, Jack A. 1991. *Revolution and Rebellion in the Early Modern World.* Berkeley: University of California Press.

Hochschild, Jennifer L. 1996. Review of *Social Policy in the United States:*

Future Possibilities in Historical Perspective, by Theda Skocpol. *Contemporary Sociology* 25:42–44.

Lamont, Michèle. 1987. "How to Become a Dominant French Philosopher: The Case of Jacques Derrida." *American Journal of Sociology* 93:584–623.

Migdal, Joel S., Atul Kohli, and Vivienne Shue, eds. 1994. *State Power and Social Forces: Domination and Transformation in the Third World.* Cambridge: Cambridge University Press.

Skocpol, Theda. 1982. "Rentier State and Shi'a Islam in the Iranian Revolution." *Theory and Society* 11:265–83.

———. 1986. "Analyzing Causal Configurations in History: A Reply to Nichols." *Comparative Social Research* 9:187–94.

———. 1994. *Social Revolutions in the Modern World.* Cambridge: Cambridge University Press.

HISTORICIZATION OF PROTEST AS A ROUTE TO GENERAL THEORY:
STEPPING BACK TO MOVE FORWARD

Roger V. Gould

FROM MOBILIZATION TO REVOLUTION, by Charles Tilly. Indianapolis: Addison-Wesley, 1978.

Original review, *CS* 9:1 (January 1980), by J. Craig Jenkins:

The book is so important that I would be hard pressed to identify many books that would come higher on my "need to read" list. . . . Nor should repeated use wear off the edges. . . . Those wanting *the* theory of collective action, be it utilitarian or Marxian (or Parsonian for that matter), will be disappointed. But such is the pain of science.

As with most works eventually regarded as seminal, Charles Tilly's *From Mobilization to Revolution* appeared at a time when quite a few people were entertaining similar ideas about protest and how to write about it. Examples include Gamson's comparative study (1975), Michael Schwartz's monograph on the Southern Farmer's Alliance (1976), McCarthy and Zald's eclectic theoretical statement (1977), and Anthony Oberschall's broad-ranging essay on social conflict (1973). These and many other scholars were struggling with a dilemma between, on the one hand, a still prevalent theoretical view of militant protest as a form of social pathology, and, on the other hand, a politically engaged type of research that was directed more toward producing sympathetic case studies than toward generating conceptual insights. As a compromise between sympathy and analytical thinking, the various research efforts that developed into the resource mobilization perspective adopted one premise that collectively destined them all for a thorough thrashing when social science turned discursive: the claim that people who challenge the social order do so for reasons, usually good ones, and that the systematic constraints such reasons impose on action make possible general statements about how protest works. What distinguished resource mobilization thinking from previous and subsequent perspectives was a steadfast focus on the strategic and material nature of social protest: Participants in social movements appeared not as crazed mobs (as earlier writers are, sometimes unfairly, thought to have portrayed them), nor as poet-revolutionaries devoted principally to a symbolic recasting of the social world. In resource mobilization terms, protest is the combined action of groups of people using means defined as illegitimate by existing political institutions to obtain a redistribution of (primarily material) rewards. Social protest is disorderly, in this view, not because a normally functional social system is under strain, but because some members of society are systematically excluded from pressing their demands through orderly means. Disorder is a response to an otherwise unresponsive polity.

That orientation was common to a host of theoretical and empirical studies appearing from the early 1970s onward. *From Mobilization to Revolution,* however, went substantially beyond the archetypical resource mobilization perspective in at least five ways that, together, ensured its legacy to the discipline of sociology. First, it insisted that the goal of research on protest should be the construction of a positive theory, which is to say a relatively abstract conceptual language and a series of logically linked statements about protest cast in terms of the conceptual language. The particular theory sketched in the book was, furthermore, rationalist and, at least in principle, formal: The general statements Tilly offered in the hope that they would become characteristic of theorizing about protest were about costs, benefits, and probabilities of success, and were represented graphically, though without guidance as to how to render the various dimensions (repression/facilitation, organization, power, and so on) operational.

Second, the book urged sociologists to recognize that social movements, as usually discussed in the academic literature, were a particular instance of a broader class of protest behavior Tilly referred to as "collective action."[1] A true theory of protest action would therefore

1. The term "collective action" was already in common use, but it referred to any instance of cooperative behavior by numerous individuals, not just to protest activities. (Indeed,

have to adopt a different unit of analysis, one that would render contemporary social-movement activities comparable with a rich set of alternative forms that could be observed in peasant societies, early modern city-states, traditional monarchies, and the like. Tilly proposed the "contentious gathering" as the common ground on which peasant revolts, Frondes, charivaris, revolutions, and the more familiar social movements of the twentieth century could be compared.

Third, and in the interest of accomplishing the second aim, *From Mobilization to Revolution* posited that the study of collective action, of which the study of social movements should be considered a sub-specialty, should adopt a historical and comparative perspective on the ways in which protest "repertoires" adapt to changing circumstances: If social movements were a form of collective action specific to industrial societies with parliamentary regimes, then any theory of collective action had to confront the question of why different kinds of regimes might be paired with different kinds of mobilization. The existence of the social movement as a kind of political behavior recognizable to members of Western industrial nation-states was a phenomenon to be explained, not a background assumption determining the proper unit of analysis for students of protest. Fourth, seeing social movements as a special case of collective action thus implied a historical examination of the emergence of the social movement along with the modern national state — indeed as a facet of the modern state. Fifth, the broad sweep of scholarship and primary material necessary to achieve these aims required that the study of popular mobilization and contention adopt the form of "big science," with phalanxes of determined researchers entering vast quantities of archival material into computer files containing descriptive accounts along with rigorously codified data on the location, scale, duration, composition, mood, purpose, and outcome of thousands of distinct contentious gatherings from various periods and places.

The impact of *From Mobilization to Revolution* should be seen as in some ways indirect, inasmuch as the study of protest twenty years later looks little like the model Tilly sketched in 1978. It is true that there is a

Olson's classic work in economic theory, which surely rivals Tilly's book in citation frequency, is only peripherally concerned with social protest.) The fact that "collective action" denotes something very different to social-movements scholars, as compared with economists and their rational-choice brethren in sociology and political science, is semantic fallout from the impact of *From Mobilization to Revolution.*

cottage industry in constructing formal models of collective action; that historical research on protest, revolutions, and state-building has an established place in the discipline; and that quantitative studies of contentious events are now pretty common (though they more often pursue the descriptive task of tracking "protest cycles" than the more theoretical project of answering questions about the relationship between repression and political contention). Yet these are separate specialties, most obviously in the sense that very few people write in more than one, but also in the more important sense that scholars writing in one of the sub-areas rarely consider the outputs of the other areas to be relevant inputs to their own. A book on the sociology of revolutions is unlikely to alter social-movement scholars' notions about what they should be writing or thinking about; historical sociologists almost never cite work that models collective action or state-society relations formally; and modelers, whether of the rational-choice bent or not, rarely worry about whether their basic assumptions, let alone their theoretical predictions, correspond to what students of protest have observed in empirical research. Finally, the sympathetic case study, with the movement or movement organization as the unit of analysis, continues to be the modal form of research on present-day social protest; furthermore, these movement-centered studies, when they have a theoretical aim, are now far more apt to concentrate on such issues as framing, identity construction, and cultural dissent than on resources, organizations, strategies, and structural constraints.[2]

In short, the study of social protest does not closely resemble the vision sketched in *From Mobilization to Revolution,* insofar as the current generation of researchers does not seem to be collectively building and testing a grand theory using a broadly coherent, shared empirical methodology. Indeed, the growing interest since the early 1980s in the cultural dimensions of protest, linked as it is to a world-

2. Two qualifications of these generalizations merit mention. First, the statements I have made are truer, I think, in sociology than in political science. Scholars in the latter discipline, perhaps because they are more at home constructing and testing theories about the impact of state action on civil society, appear to be quite interested in the relation between repression and protest, and particularly in contexts that can retrospectively be identified as revolutionary. Political scientists often begin, therefore, with a theoretical model that generates a set of predictions about the form of the repression/protest relation, and then test the empirical predictions using coded records of protest events. Second, it is increasingly common for sociologists to conduct case studies of movements toward which they are hostile. Such studies may, in fact, eventually rival sympathetic accounts in number.

view in which people actively create the worlds in which they live through systems of representation, is at least superficially inimical to the building of grand theory. Anyone arguing that groups who challenge the social order do so principally by articulating moral and practical visions of the world that deviate from previously dominant understandings is unlikely to believe that the actions and utterances of the people he or she studies will conform to general patterns and thus bear out the predictions of a general theory. If protest is first and foremost cultural protest, then the last thing protesters should be expected to do is to confirm anyone's expectations, except in the most general and thus uninteresting ways. Hence the thrashing (noted above) meted out to the resource-mobilization view after "meaning" and "identity" became central concepts in the study of social protest. The clearly defined interests and objectives that need to be identified and considered exogenous if rationalist theories of collective action are to make falsifiable predictions are not to be found in constructivist accounts of how movements (above all the so-called New Social ones) emerge, develop, succeed, or decline.

For sociologists who study protest, *From Mobilization to Revolution* might therefore be said to have been influential more as a lightning rod than as a foundational text. It was more suited for this role than many of its contemporary works because it was unusually clear about what it took to be the "right" and "wrong" ways of studying collective action. (Many authors of synthetic essays shy away from such hardheaded positivist statements, preferring to regard each perspective as contributing valuable insights about a different aspect of the problem. As a discipline, sociology sends very few theories to the scrap heap — and those that are sent do not stay there very long.) A book represented by its author as offering *the* correct perspective, rather than one of several attractive alternatives, is sure to make people uncomfortable. The study of protest has, in response, featured a good deal of work adopting some version of what Clifford Geertz has referred to as the "not on Easter Island" style in anthropology: For almost any generalization some group of scholars has begun to accept as true, there is some case study, somewhere, that claims to refute it. In the case of the social-movements literature, the generalization chosen most often for this kind of challenge is the materialist one: that oppressed groups mobilize (when they manage to mobilize) around issues and interests that can be deduced from their objectively defined material situation.

The lightning-rod metaphor summarizes the short-term impact of *From Mobilization to Revolution,* if twenty years can be considered short-term. There is good reason to believe, however, that its medium- and long-term influence will be different. Whatever the reasons for the discursive turn of the 1980s (and some of those reasons are directly tied to the protest activity of the 1960s and 1970s, above all the weight activists placed on cultural rebellion), it is doubtful that cultural-ist scholarship will permanently discourage sociologists from pur-suing the goal of positing and testing the validity of general — that is, context-independent — propositions about social action, disorderly or not. More likely (and more productively), students of protest will draw the following lesson from the meaning-centered criticisms of books like *From Mobilization to Revolution:* Questions about how and when collective action occurs and/or alters the social order must be an-swered with reference not only to material goods, free time, and state-imposed costs of protest, but also to context-specific ideas about what is just, about what kinds of group memberships — occupational, eth-nic, confessional, and so forth — are most significant, and about what sorts of public actions are most likely to express the sharedness of such ideas.[3] In other words, it will turn out that the demonstration that collective action — like any form of social behavior — is meaning-laden does not necessarily undercut the project of specifying the conditions under which mobilization occurs. Uncovering the processes by which participants in counterinstitutional action actively represent to them-selves and to others what they understand themselves as doing is not a fundamentally different project from the one Tilly proposed in 1978. Instead, it is a central part of that very project — albeit a part that resource mobilization people, Tilly included, did not originally ac-knowledge as central.[4]

3. The fact that conceptions of group identity, ideas about justice and equality, and even about what a person is vary across contexts does not preclude generalization about the role of such conceptions. Rather, a good theory pinpoints precisely those aspects of variation that matter for the phenomenon under study. Theories are bad when they ignore contextual variations that are substantively important given the outcomes they purport to explain, not when they ignore variation as such.

4. Saying that such a development is likely, and saying that it would be a good thing, are obviously quite different assertions. At the same time, it would be nice to think that academic inquiry, however acrimonious it might occasionally become, nonetheless tends on average to move in a direction that most participants — even the ones deemed obsolete by such move-

From Mobilization to Revolution did not transform the study of protest into big science, and this transformation will not take place, if only because large-scale urban riots no longer appear to be a major issue on which policymakers see a need to spend research funds. But it did cement a commitment among at least some students of protest to doing a kind of research that might produce generalizable insights, which in turn could be assembled into a general theory. It also conceptualized the problem of mobilization in a way that made historical research relevant to the project of building such a theory, by treating modern social movements as an instance of a broader class of social phenomena. Finally, by tying the study of social protest to the study of politics, and specifically of the state, the work ensured that sociologists would persist in attending to the strategic aspects of collective action: It is a lot harder to ignore the goal-oriented aspects of activism when the riot police are part of the picture. The materialism of the resource mobilization perspective may have faded, in part because of the culturalist attack on Tilly's work and on that of some of his followers, but the understanding of protest as purposive has not faded, and will not. It is quite possible that protest would not happen without protest songs, but that is one of the main reasons people write them, and that fact shapes what is written.

REFERENCES

Gamson, William A. [1975] 1990. *The Strategy of Social Protest.* 2d ed. Homewood, Ill.: Dorsey.

McCarthy, John, and Mayer N. Zald. 1977. "Resource Mobilization and Social Movements: A Partial Theory." *American Journal of Sociology* 82:1212–41.

Oberschall, Anthony. 1973. *Social Conflict and Social Movements.* Englewood Cliffs: N.J.: Prentice-Hall.

Schwartz, Michael. 1976. *Radical Protest and Social Structure: The Southern Farmers' Alliance and Cotton Tenancy, 1880–1890.* New York: Academic Press.

---

ment—would agree improves the quality of understanding. Radical constructivists might well take issue with me, arguing that inquiry simply changes to suit whatever community of scholars happens to be engaging in it, or the actors at whose pleasure the community of scholars does so.

DISCIPLINE AND PUNISH:
THE BIRTH OF A POSTMODERN
MIDDLE-RANGE

Jonathan Simon

DISCIPLINE AND PUNISH: THE BIRTH OF THE PRISON, by
Michel Foucault. Trans. Alan Sheridan. New York: Pantheon
Books, 1977.

Original review, *CS* 7:5 (September 1978), by Stanley Cohen:

When the intellectual history of our times comes to be written,
that peculiarly Left Bank mixture of Marxism and structuralism
now in fashion will be among the most puzzling of our ideas
to evaluate. . . . Of such "historians" (a description which does
not really cover his method) Foucault is the most dazzlingly
creative.

Toward the end of his 1978 *Contemporary Sociology* review of *Discipline and Punish,* Stanley Cohen wrote that it "must be the most stimulating and revealing history of the prisons and punishment ever written." In some sense this perspective is now dated. Few today would think of *Discipline and Punish* as primarily a book for scholars of punishment. It is more likely to be found on a shelf of philosophy or, if the bookstore is slightly hipper, cultural studies, than in sociology, criminology, or history. A graduate student citing the book in an examination is more likely to expound on its concept "disciplinary power," or on the role of scientific discourses in government, than to talk about the prison, let alone its fate in contemporary society. But Cohen's review was also prescient in its anticipation of how much the book would influence the sociology of punishment. Thus, against the grain of the subsequent years, this essay suggests that Foucault's influence on the sociology of punishment is illustrative of why *Discipline and Punish,* twenty years after its English publication, remains such a compelling model for contemporary sociologists in a variety of substantive fields.

The sociology of punishment has enjoyed a tradition of theorizing out of all proportion to its place in the larger science. Durkheim and de Tocqueville, among others, saw the forms of penal practice as a crucial window into the nature of modern society (see, generally, Garland 1990). Despite this impressive tradition, *Discipline and Punish* has virtually reinvented the field. Few contemporary writers have been able to ignore Foucault's startling way of recounting the place of punishment in the construction of modern life (see Evans 1996 for this point and a spirited effort to get beyond the Foucauldian story of punishment).

When it was published in English in 1977, *Discipline and Punish* offered a stunningly argued, but hardly novel, reversal of the traditional empirical and normative assumptions about modern punishment. It still seemed plausible, in the 1970s, that the modern prison with its quasi-clinical regimes and human science expertise, was an exemplary story of a progressive and humanistic evolution in social consciousness away from the primitive impulse to seek vengeance against the wrongdoer through dungeons and the scaffold. Foucault retold the story as one of the colonization of punishment by the disciplines, a family of techniques for exercising power over individual and assembled bodies with a long history in specialized institutions like the monastery and the military camp. According to Foucault, the emergence of the disciplines as a more general technology of power was marked by the transformation of punishment at the start of the nineteenth century and especially the rapid growth of the prison as the state punishment of choice.

To Foucault, the coming of the prison represented not a reduction but a fantastic extension of state power. The offender was spared the major and minor cruelties of the body, but now was submitted to a more rigorous and comprehensive control over life. Social control abandoned recourse to spasms of spectacular fury in favor of smooth and continuous processes. The widespread dispersal of the disciplines among social institutions was a crucial ingredient, according to Foucault, in the take-off of modern industrial capitalism and democratic politics.

This story was not altogether new. Nietzsche (1956) had long ago described the history of punishment as a central locus for creating the obedient and hard-working last men of nineteenth century European society. Erving Goffman (1961) described the prison as a species of total institutions that played a more general role in the economy of social power than the purposes of punishment might describe. David Rothman (1971) had provided a history of Jacksonian social policy on crime and dependency that reflected important links between the strategy of reformative confinement and the stirrings of democracy and capitalism in post-Revolutionary United States. Likewise Marx, Durkheim, and Weber had all nodded toward the disciplines as important features of modernity. *Discipline and Punish* recast all these themes amid brilliantly interpreted examples (albeit ones ungrounded in any systematic historical framework).

While disputing some or even most of Foucault's substantive claims in *Discipline and Punish,* subsequent scholarship on punishment has been influenced in three directions by the book and its model of research. First, Foucault pointed away from the primacy of the present (realized in the genre of participant observation studies of the '50s and '60s) and toward a blending of historical subjects and ethnographic forms of analysis. Foucault focused for the most part on the last portion of the eighteenth century and the first half of the nineteenth, yet few who read the book missed the salience of the present. His use of historical documents seemed far more akin to the narratives of the ethnographers of social control like Goffman.

Second, Foucault pointed away from a view of the prison as an ideological system operating primarily through representations on the individual and collective imagination, which had become a standard left critique of the penal system, and toward a view of the prison as a surface for the effective exercise of power over individual bodies and groups.

Third, Foucault pointed away from assuming a central role for the state as the key actor in the evolution of punishment and toward a focus on technologies of power developed in state and nonstate settings and circulating among them.

When the first U.S. edition of *Discipline and Punish* appeared in 1977, sociologists of punishment seemed poised to have an influence on public policy and political activism. Starting in the 1960s, "labeling theory" had led many criminologists to reappraise the expansive claims of treatment-oriented penology. A New Left criminology coming out of the United Kingdom and the United States in the late 1960s also succeeded in foregrounding the class content of much of liberal penal ideology. These academic critiques were matched for a time by a wave of prison unrest and the development of popular links between prisoner groups and activists representing disempowered minorities on the outside (Foucault participated in such a nexus in France during the same period). By the mid-1970s judges and state legislatures opened up to legal and philosophical arguments about the penal system. Courts dropped some of their historical deference to penal authority and allowed prisoners through their lawyers to compel officials to explain and rationalize their decisions. A number of states abandoned the indeterminate sentence and the very idea of rehabilitation. Many of these movements responded to precisely the features of disciplinary punishment that *Discipline and Punish* identified: the intrusive demands to penetrate into the subjectivity of the offender; the legal power given to experts to individualize sentences; the deceptive denial of the punitive elements remaining in penal practice. One prominent criminologist even cited Foucault in support of his proposal to restore corporal punishments as a replacement for the prison (Newman 1983).

Almost two decades later, little remains of the radical politics of prisoners' rights or of judicial due process reform. The shift by state legislatures away from rehabilitation has continued, but it quickly leaped over the kind of ethical libertarian position that Foucault's thought might have informed in favor of a massive "get tough" approach that has yet to run its course. The peno-correctional expertise whose role *Discipline and Punish* described so chillingly has continued to lose power. Although recent years have witnessed an unprecedented expansion of imprisonment, with more than three times as many Americans behind bars as in 1977, the prison as a political technology has been transformed. The claims to know the deep truth of the individual have been abandoned, but not the authority to punish, which has increased. The disciplinary focus on normalization of offenders has been replaced by the mission of providing long-term warehousing of populations with little place in the economy (Cohen 1985; Feeley and Simon 1992). Yet the new system shares little of the skepticism about political authority that a Foucault-inspired recasting of penality might have followed.

From this perspective, Foucault's present is no longer ours. The managers of the gargantuan prison system are more likely to be specialists in accounting or systems management than in penology, let alone psychology or medicine. Whereas Foucault portrayed the prison as the cutting edge of the new disciplinary technology of power, today it is the prison that is the recipient of new technologies of power borrowed from business and the self-help movement. More important, Foucault's picture of a society obsessed with the deep truths of the individual, exemplified by delinquents, is increasingly inaccurate in a society that treats individuals as a surplus factor of production and offenders as human garbage to be waste-managed away. But if we are not exactly the disciplinary society that Foucault diagnosed, *Discipline and Punish* remains deservedly influential as a research strategy. The turn to history, the focus on discourse as a material element in institutional systems of power, and a sensitivity to the multiple sources of governance outside the state (and to the way the state itself is capable of exercising power) remain highly productive working principles.

While punishment, even after *Discipline and Punish*, is of only minor interest to most sociologists, the book's influence on that particular field demonstrates its wider influence as a research strategy that moves to fundamental theoretical questions about social order and subjectivity through specific contexts and institutions. The case of punishment fit precisely the metaconcerns that have distracted sociology from dreams of normal science. By the late 1970s, stirred by their readings of Thomas Kuhn (1969) on scientific paradigms, and by both foreign and domestic alternatives to Parsonian social theory, many sociologists found themselves engaged in a discussion about the limits of the scientific model of inquiry. Were human sciences destined to a permanent kind of scientific revolution in which fundamental issues of first principles remained eternally unresolved? If the social sciences required a distinct methodological orientation that wed them to problems of interpretation, where did that leave the ambitions of social science to shape social policy? *Discipline and Punish* galvanized and transformed this discussion for several reasons.

First, it was a book about the relationship between power and social science. Second, Foucault's method was itself a radical form of cultural interpretation that combined features of both structuralism and phenomenology (Dreyfus and Rabinow 1982), the leading methodological alternatives for sociologists seeking a path away from positivism. Third, the story *Discipline and Punish* told reversed the assumptions of the interpretive critique of positivist sciences. According to Foucault, the constitution of an objective science of humanity had as much to do with the deployment of successful techniques of power as it did with better intellectual models. If medicine has established itself as a real science, it was, at least in part, because it has established effective strategies for objectifying human beings. Even as dubious a field as criminology underwent epistemological hardening as it managed to anchor itself in the prison. After *Discipline and Punish* the question of whether a true social science was possible had to be recognized as a fundamentally political question.

Discipline and Punish itself could be read, however, as offering its own rather bald claims to be a kind of scientific theory. Foucault wrote of "disciplinary society." He seemed to be offering a social theory that placed power in the central place that other theories have awarded class struggle or secularization. From this reading, the influence of *Discipline and Punish* has been surprisingly thin. The theory of power, if there is one, has not been widely elaborated or applied. Its critics among social theorists have raised serious questions as to whether Foucault's theory (or what they reconstruct of it) can account for enduring forms of domination.

Far more useful, however, is *Discipline and Punish* as a model for an empirically engaged and politically relevant form of sociology. Foucault was philosophically trained, but *Discipline and Punish* consisted largely of provocative and revealing interpretations of practices and discourses, not highly abstract analytic procedures. Moreover, his account, especially in the era of prison political struggle, had obvious relevance for strategic political thinking, not just vague promises of validating norms. In this sense, *Discipline and Punish* provides an example of what might be called a postmodern version of middle-range theory. As a model for how to gain useful purchase on the present, *Discipline and Punish* offered a license for scholars to operate in the context of specific institutional and cultural fields and a set of methodological tactics for deconstructing policies and institutional programs. Thus it shared something with Robert Merton's (1968) quintessentially influential version of middle-range theory, that is, a commitment to engage practices on the same level practices engage people. Not surprisingly, both strategies emphasize effects rather than ideologies. What Foucault did not share with Merton was the latter's aspiration of accumulating regional explanations into a global one.

Foucault should not be read as rejecting macro frameworks in preference for micro frameworks, but rather as insisting that the same voice not attempt to cover all registers. His works can certainly be stretched into a kind of global social theory, but with results that seem surprisingly thin. Foucault's best work situates itself at the level of particular institutions, and it is here that his insights are sharpest and most effective. It remains to be seen how influential this model of a researcher who is neither a general theorist of societies nor a specialist committed to a specific set of policy topics will be. In that sense, and although he would have rejected the term, his research model is a postmodern one that accepts strategic, if not epistemological, limits to the scope of knowledge.

REFERENCES

Cohen, Stanley. 1978. "The Archeology of Power." *Contemporary Sociology* 7 (4): 566–68.

———. 1985. *Visions of Social Control: Crime, Punishment, and Classification*. New York: Polity.

Beaumont, Gustave de, and Alexis de Tocqueville. 1979. *On the Penitentiary System in the United States and Its Application to France*. Carbondale: Southern Illinois University Press.

Dreyfus, Hubert L., and Paul Rabinow. 1982. *Michel Foucault: Beyond Structuralism and Hermeneutics*. Chicago: University of Chicago Press.

Durkheim, Emile. 1964. *The Division of Labor in Society*. Trans. George Simpson. New York: Free Press.

Evans, Richard. 1996. *Rituals of Retribution: Capital Punishment in Germany*. New York: Oxford University Press.

Feeley, Malcolm, and Jonathan Simon. 1992. "The New Penology: Notes on the Emerging Strategy of Corrections and Its Implications." *Criminology* 30:449–74.

Garland, David. 1990. *Punishment and Modern Society: A Study in Social Theory*. Chicago: University of Chicago Press.

Goffman, Erving. 1961. *Asylums: Essays on the Social Situation of Mental Patients and Other Inmates*. Garden City: Anchor Books.

Kuhn, Thomas. [1962] 1969. *The Structure of Scientific Revolutions*. 2d ed. Chicago: University of Chicago Press.

Merton, Robert K. 1968. *Social Theory and Social Structure*. Enl. ed. New York: Free Press.

Newman, Graeme. 1983. *Just and Painful: A Case for Corporal Punishment.* New York: Macmillan.

Nietzsche, Friedrich W. 1956. *The Birth of Tragedy and the Genealogy of Morals.* Trans. Francis Golffing. Garden City: Doubleday.

Rothman, David J. 1971. *The Discovery of the Asylum: Sound Order and Disorder in the New Republic.* Toronto: Little Brown.

CHARLES MURRAY:
LOSING GROUND, GAINING POWER

Theodore J. Lowi and Gwendolyn Mink

LOSING GROUND: AMERICAN SOCIAL POLICY, 1950–80, by
Charles Murray. New York: Basic Books, 1984.

Original review, *CS* 14:6 (November 1985), by S. M. Miller:

Murray's accusatory book might have gained some attention,
for its own sake; however, a sizable expenditure of public relations money and skill by the conservative Manhattan Institute
has assured extraordinary publicity for the book and its author. . . . Who gets to the public (and social science) limelight
first sets the stage for further debate. Antithesis limps behind
thesis. Getting attention is almost everything in politics and
social science.

Between 1935 and 1965, almost everyone supported the welfare state,
though not everybody was happy with it. Beginning in the 1960s,
defenders as well as critics began to expose its contradictions and limitations. Though conceived to insure democracy, the U.S. welfare state
excluded whole categories of citizens and appeared to tie its most
generous provisions to racial privilege. As this racial stratification
came into political focus, it was inevitable that the scope and legitimacy of the welfare state would be called into question. During the
1960s, the welfare state actually received its harshest criticism from
liberals who hoped to democratize it by opening access and weakening
social controls. Conservatives responded with criticism of the expanded and democratized welfare state that the liberals accomplished.
Their criticism resounded both more widely and more durably, fo-
menting popular resistance to extending to America's poorest citizens
the promise of economic security. The largest and most expensive
arenas of the welfare state have enjoyed broad consensus, notwith-

standing conservative scrutiny (e.g., Social Security). But that consensus did not translate into a ready defense of smaller and less costly welfare programs when conservatives linked them to people of color and called for their repeal (viz., welfare).

Conservative hostility toward welfare first began to mount when administrative and judicial rulings forbade states and localities to deny AFDC grants to poor women of color and their children. The complaints ignited with the Republicans' return to power under Richard Nixon. Nixon's Southern Strategy may have been a strategic response to George Wallace, but its significance can better be appreciated as a supplement to Wallace's rhetorical efforts to tie Washington and welfare together with blacks. Up in arms over affirmative action, the racially redistributive aspects of the War on Poverty, and the redefinition of poverty as a system phenomenon rather than an individual responsibility, recently minted neoconservatives stoked the now-racialized welfare debate. Southern conservatives also joined in, shamelessly embracing "color blind" social policy — but only when it suited them politically and only after three centuries of color-conscious policies that gave Americans so much pain and shame. The revival of the libertarians during the 1970s consolidated a full-scale attack against a state-driven redistribution of wealth — especially to poor single mothers and their children.

Generalized attacks on the welfare state as a whole abounded, but were not successful. They implicated too much and too many. Any attack on the redistributive nature of the welfare state jeopardized the middle class even more than the poor. In addition, most capitalists supported the welfare state, with all its faults, particularly its largest and most expensive parts. Perhaps the best confirmation of the imperviousness of the welfare state to holistic attack was Ronald Reagan's presidential promise to the American people that he would never do anything to weaken the safety net.

Inroads against the welfare state would not be significant until they became more narrowly focused; conservative broadsides against both the welfare state and welfare began to succeed only when they marked America's most economically dependent as black and unworthy. Increment by increment, conservative parsing of poor people's behavior, choices, and values fired public opinion with the power of a social movement. Antiwelfare forces were antistate — but anti- only that part of "the state" that comprises the national government. (State and local governments would be celebrated as the guardians of virtue.) National government meant bureaucracy, and bureaucracy meant heavy-handed regulation and redistribution. Moreover, national government meant the Supreme Court, and the Supreme Court meant civil rights for African Americans. But until policymakers could convert racist assertions into racial factoids, race would remain officially unmentionable in welfare policy discussions.

In 1984, Charles Murray sanitized the racism of antiwelfare discourse by packaging it as social science. Antiwelfare forces enjoyed a real boost with the publication of *Losing Ground,* for it gave them permission to say out loud that social benefits either reward or promote racial misbehavior. This intensified the political isolation of Aid to Families with Dependent Children — both the program and its beneficiaries — while emboldening the majority intent on pulling the plug on women and children who need welfare. *Losing Ground* was the opening shot in a twelve-year war to end welfare, a war that culminated in legislation that all but repealed social provision for poor single mothers and their children. That legislation — the Personal Responsibility and Work Opportunity Act (PRA) of 1996 — bears Murray's imprint. Following Murray's call to repeal social supports for poor people, the PRA rescinds poor single mothers' entitlement to income support. Following Murray's appeal for stronger moral "sticks," the PRA subjects needy mothers to harsh punishments for nonmarital childbearing and childrearing: Mothers of nonmarital children must identify biological fathers, for example, or must expose their intimate lives so that government may do so; failure to comply results in a loss of at least 25 percent of the family's welfare grant, with states having the option to withhold cash assistance altogether. Following Murray's science, the PRA's preamble declares that "marriage is the foundation of a successful society'" and codifies putative correlations between mother-only families, crime, intergenerational single motherhood, and the need for welfare. The Act closes with appropriations for abstinence education — to teach monogamy, chastity before marriage, and sexual inactivity prior to economic self-sufficiency (PL104–193, Section 912).

Although Murray's influence on social science has been negligible, his influence on politics and policy has been historic and paradigmatic. It warrants an effort to explain why. First, of course, was the timing — the chronology and the climate of opinion. The South had all but freed itself of captivity to the Democratic Party. There had been no genuine electoral realignment, but there certainly had been an ideological one. In the early-to-mid-1980s, southern voters kept one foot in the Democratic Party for economic policy (including welfare state policies like Social Security). But they also firmly planted the other foot in the Republican Party as critics of welfare and warriors against crime—both code words, of course, for race. This gave us split tickets and divided government—and Ronald Reagan. Most relevant here, though, is the fact that the dissolution of the Southern Democracy opened a new discursive space where antiwelfare Republicans and antiblack Southerners could meet in opposition to national government.

With *Losing Ground,* Charles Murray defined that space, simultaneously coupling race and state and articulating antipathy to both. Hitting the politically most vulnerable arena of the welfare state—AFDC—he associated its problems specifically with black people, their so-called economic calculus of marriage, and their putatively untutored morality.

The discursive linkage between race, illegitimacy, and welfare did not originate with Murray, of course. From the 1940s into the 1960s, policymakers from Louisiana to Newburgh, New York, devised rules restricting welfare eligibility to marital mothers and children, rules they imposed to limit welfare participation by African American mothers. Twenty years before Murray, Daniel Patrick Moynihan associated poverty and "a tangle of pathologies" with the "matriarchal" structure of black families. Between 1967 and 1974, Congress tested legislative provisions conditioning welfare benefits on the establishment of paternity. And in 1977, Ronald Reagan began his ride to the White House with an attack on morally depraved "welfare queens."

But Murray, more than anyone else, set the terms of discourse about race and welfare. He armed antiwelfare forces with data that seemed to prove their racist claims. He thus helped Americans scratch a great psychological—and political—itch. The single most important achievement of the 1960s civil rights movement and civil rights laws was the shame they taught to white Americans for not having lived up to democratic ideals. Murray, against the backdrop of the Reagan Administration, helped relieve white Americans of their shame.

Why was Murray so successful? One reason is that he led readers into a racially charged syllogism that general audiences found difficult to resist. He went straight to explanation, asking first "Why did welfare fail?" He led his readers to believe that welfare *had* failed by denying them discussion and debate of the prior questions: *Did* welfare fail? In what sense and in what respects or in what parts did it fail? What didn't it do that it was supposed to do? To what degree did it fall short? If welfare was supposed to end poverty, it clearly has failed. But if it was supposed to provide subsistence to single-parent families, as even Murray admits (1984, 18), didn't it accomplish exactly that?

Murray substitutes a discussion of welfare's purposes with a presentation of his premises for welfare reform. This draws the reader into a logical trap. He sucks the reader in even more deeply by appearing to be quite honest and methodical, virtually Aristotelian about his analysis and argument, and almost otherworldly in his good intentions for the poor. Here he is in his own words:

Stripped of the prejudices and the bombast, these . . . are three core premises of the popular wisdom that need to be taken into account:

Premise #1:   People respond to incentives and disincentives. Sticks and carrots work.

Premise #2:   People are not inherently hard working or moral. In the absence of countervailing influences, people will avoid work and be amoral.

Premise #3:   People must be held responsible for their actions. Whether they *are* responsible in some ultimate philosophical or biochemical sense cannot be the issue if society is to function.

The thesis of the chapters that follow is that social policy since 1964 has ignored these premises and that it has thereby created much of the mess we are in. (1984, 146)

Once a skeptical person or an opponent is drawn this far into an argument with what may appear to be preliminaries, it seems also unfair to break off the discussion and insist on a return to a different set of first premises and a different set of rules that should govern the argument. It's contrary to the sense of fair play to start a game and then argue over the rules. It appears so open and honest to lay out one's premises — as though premises are foundations not to be questioned. How often a person loses an argument when making the first concession following an adversary's request to "grant me, just for the sake of the argument. . . ." And if we don't grant it, the argument ends there.

Just ponder the nature of the premises Murray offers. The first premise is the old pleasure/pain principle: "Sticks and carrots work." But others things work, too, such as fear and hope, emotion and reason, honor and dishonor, selfishness and altruism. Besides, for whom do sticks and carrots work? For the wielder? For the recipient? The premise further shunts aside the many occasions when people, not just the poor, don't have a choice and must take the pleasure and the pain as they come. Murray thus entraps his readers into accepting his argument as their own premise. That premise permits only one conclusion: that individual responsibility is removed as soon as the burden of subsistence is lightened. Acceptance of such premises as the substitute for argument creates a readiness to make the desired and predicted moral leap from limited experience and partial data to absolute and unqualified normative certainty.

Murray's influence on the welfare debate also followed from the moral tropes he constructed with his data. The most infamous example of Murray's moralism is his discussion of what he calls "illegitimacy." According to Murray, poverty, crime, and social disorder all hinge on the marital status of mothers at childbirth. In Murray's world, how loving parents are or how desirable relations with particular fathers are matter little. The only thing that counts is the presence or absence of incantations, ceremony, and signatures prior to birth. Murray treats nonmarital childbearing as a morally freighted fact, a morally causal factor. How he decided among moral systems is nowhere explained. It is unlikely that Catholic morality is his yardstick for maternal virtue, for example. Were Murray a Catholic, any children he has with his second wife would be illegitimate, and by Murray's own account the mother of his second family would be responsible for a number of social pathologies. Clearly, Murray didn't have the second families of Catholic middle-class men in mind when he equated nonmarital childbearing with immorality and correlated both with social dysfunction.

Obviously, investing empirical facts (single mothers) with moral attributes (illegitimacy) is an effective debating device, well recognized as an unfair tactic by students of rhetoric. The eminent sociologist Robert Merton, drawing on W. I. Thomas's problem of "defining the situation," recognized this as an opportunity to engage in a kind of moral declension (1955). For example, how does one characterize a man standing with arms folded and eyes fixed unresponsively? "I am firm; thou art obstinate; he is pigheaded." The only solution is keen awareness of the tactic itself, but those who should have known better let Murray and other virtue-mongers get away with it.

Underpinning the normative opinions that Murray parades as logically derived premises is his science. Again, anyone who has ever been involved in public discourse or who has studied the policymaking process will recognize that science works wonders in foreclosing further discussion and ending debate. Even if others mobilize their science to contest yours—as many welfare researchers did after *Losing Ground* made its splash—the discussion usually turns too arcane to shift the grounds of debate (especially when holiness is already on Murray's side).

Murray's claim to science gave his moral argument the ring of truth, not only because he proffered objectivity and empirical verifiability, but most of all because he proffered both so elaborately. This involved mind-numbing explication of the methodologies that others had used in conducting studies or that he had used in reviewing and correlating data. By 1984, millions of people who already believed what Murray had to say welcomed his science as reassurance. But he was not preaching only to the converted. Science was even more important in seducing or silencing (or both) people who continued to support social welfare policies that benefited them but who had no brief for policies designed for poor people, especially poor black people. In the absolute certitude of writing style, trussed as it was with scientific language, Murray extended his influence far beyond folks who already agreed with him. That certitude also hid the shoddiness of his science.

This is not to impugn the government statistics upon which Murray hangs his case. Undoubtedly assembled by well-trained and objective social scientists, the data provide a baseline, scientific empirical referent. But Murray's use of those data fell short. It was merely *scientistic*. It bore all the trappings of science; but it was scientific only in appearance.

Here is our best reconstruction of Murray's science. First, being methodical, he spells out his empirical observations of changes in federal social welfare expenditures:

—Health and medical costs in 1980 were six times their 1950 cost.
—Public assistance costs in 1980 were thirteen times their 1950 cost.

—Education costs in 1980 were twenty-four times their 1950 cost.

—Social insurance costs in 1980 were twenty-seven times their 1950 cost.

—Housing costs in 1980 were 129 times their 1950 cost. (1984, 14)

Note the convenience of these facts. Nineteen Fifty is a marvelously advantageous base year to choose for comparison purposes. For one thing, serious federal spending on health only began with Medicare and Medicaid in 1965. Likewise, national government spent money only at the peripheries of education before enactment of the Elementary and Secondary Education Act of 1965. Moreover, social insurance costs did not increase significantly until the ten years following 1965, when Congress extended coverage to workers in previously excluded occupational categories, broadened the supplemental security income (SSI) program, and indexed certain benefits to the cost of living. Murray's reference to the astronomical increase in housing costs may impress some readers, but has no bearing on the rest of his analysis. Nor does it illuminate anything, since the percentage increase is linked to 1950, which was a close-to-zero base for direct expenditures.

The only potentially bona fide comparison in Murray's enumeration of lamentable increases in public spending is the statistic he supplies for welfare. Unlike health, education, and housing programs, which owed their origins to the social and political dynamics of the 1960s, federal public assistance had been adopted as part of the 1935 Social Security Act. But although a comparison of welfare spending in 1950 and 1980 may be fair, comparison without context or controls is bad science. Of course welfare spending increased: Beginning in the 1960s, welfare became more accessible to more poor people as states lost their prerogative to discriminate against applicants on the bases of "illegitimacy," "substitute fathers," "employability," and various other proxy criteria for race.

The link between Murray's opening observations and his "core premises," rehearsed above, emerges some hundred pages later in an announcement of yet another fact. On the measures of family breakup, nonmarital childbearing, and work outside the home, Murray tells us, things "got worse than they should have gotten" (1984, 135). He admits this is a "hazardous assertion . . . not susceptible to proof" (135). But he proceeds without humility, beginning his explanation for *why* (not *whether*) things got worse in 1959, just as "the civil rights movement is gaining momentum" (135). He then goes on to engage in what he calls role-playing, putting himself on an imaginary panel of experts looking ahead from 1959 to the next decade, in which "we pass sweeping civil rights legislation forbidding all discrimination on the basis of race — in hiring practices, public accommodations, and voting — [and further requiring] businesses and schools to take special measures to recruit Negroes" (136). From the 1959 vantage point, he suggests that one should logically expect the gap between white and black to narrow if not disappear within ten years. Reacting to an imaginary fellow panelist who predicts "what will happen is that the younger generation of Negroes will leave the labor force, form huge numbers of single-parent families, and experience soaring rates of crime and illegitimacy and unemployment," Murray tells us that, in 1959, such a statement would have been treated as complete nonsense.

Virtually all he has to support his causal assertions is post hoc ergo propter hoc — after this, therefore on account of this. In other words, before and after the 1960s, before and after the rise in federal spending on social welfare. The only direct, experimental study he cites from the early 1980s was the "negative income tax" (NIT) study of the effect of a guaranteed income on work and family practices. For Murray, the question was "whether a negative income tax reduced work effort. The answer was yes" (1984, 150). The study reported a 9 percent reduction in labor force participation for husbands, which Murray attributes to bad behavior, discounting the possibility that any significant proportion of that reduction could be attributed to husbands deciding to work outside the home fewer hours each week so that they might increase their time for such worthy pursuits, as helping with the family. Instead he insists that "the reduction . . . *appeared* to have consisted primarily of men who had opted out of the labor market altogether" (151, emphasis added).

Murray pays much more attention to the NIT study's data on wives, for whom the study reported a 20 percent reduction in labor-market work hours. At no point does he explore the extent to which this reduction could be attributed to the demands on women to leave or reduce participation in the labor market in order to take care of their own children in their own homes. So Murray doesn't consider whether the negative income tax could have been considered *pro*-family by making it economically feasible for at least one parent to spend more time on caregiving work.

Perhaps this is because, to Murray and his fellow critics of welfare, caregiving traditionally provided by women is a middle-class virtue; indeed, virtue itself is a middle-class characteristic. The morality of poor women of all races — but especially of women of color — has always been suspect; they can only grope for virtue through work outside the home. The problem, here, is not so much the statistics Murray cites from the NIT study as it is the brazen but unadmitted normative purposes to which Murray puts those statistics. This is a blatant case of scientism rather than science.

By the early 1990s, Murray had more direct and systematic studies available to him — and he drew from them further evidence to shore up his original claims in a journal article published in 1993. However, the studies were inconclusive. Murray confesses this fact at the beginning of his piece, but was undaunted by it. Citing Gary Becker's 1981 book, *Treatise on the Family,* he quotes its conclusion that "the growth of these [welfare] programs in recent years has contributed heavily to the sharp growth in the ratio of illegitimate to legitimate birth rates since the 1960s" (Becker, 97, quoted in Murray 1993b, S234). Murray cites his own 1984 book as confirmation of Becker's point, but then goes on to his confession that "at that time neither Becker nor Murray [*sic*] could point to a body of research directly verifying their rationales for the link. The few studies that had touched on the illegitimacy issue had argued, though inconclusively, that no effect existed" (S234). It is most interesting that none of those contrary, albeit inconclusive, studies was discussed or even cited in Murray's 1984 book. But more important is the way Murray deals with the seven studies that had come out between 1984 and 1993 in his *Journal of Labor Economics* article.

Murray devotes a paragraph or two to each of the seven studies and their findings. He then attempts to draw together the cumulative message of these findings, and he comes up with a curious problem. Three of the studies "found no significant effect of welfare on illegitimacy . . . whereas four did find significant effects" (S238). Now, to ordinary common sense, four out of seven studies on such complex matters as these doesn't sound like a hell of a lot of confirmation. And Murray generously concedes the point with the proposition that "social scientists should come to the data not as a physicist tests a precisely specified theory but as a detective examines the scene of a crime . . . [to] stay intimately close to the data [and] to try to tease out the underlying patterns" (S238). Murray then turns genuinely apologetic about how "the mathematical power of quantitative methods in the social sciences has outstripped the capacity of social scientists to operationalize those models realistically. That is, *political scientists and sociologists in particular are too quick to treat the variables available to them as adequate reifications of the construct they have in mind*" (S238, emphasis added).

But that is precisely what Murray has been doing all along. With phenomena as complex as poverty, family structure, single parenthood, wage work, and family work — and with all of the normative and ideological considerations that can modulate our appreciation of these phenomena — the social scientist must be modest and tentative. All the more so when validation is insecure. When several studies of the same thing, in this case an impressive seven studies, do not consistently and repetitively confirm the same findings, then one must be all the more modest and tentative about their use in larger arguments.

Despite Murray's confessions and concessions on these matters in his journal article, he is guilty in his book of precisely what he advises against in his journal article — of "treat[ing] the variables available to [him] as adequate reifications of the construct [he has] in mind" (S238). Why? Perhaps it is because he is addressing two different audiences — one professional, the other political. Whatever were his objectives and calculations, the fact remains that Murray started with a set of premises that embodied the conclusions he wanted to pursue in his book-length indictment of welfare. He then carefully selected aggregate data that appeared to be consistent with those premises, and then made the enormous moral leap to the normative appeals that would sell the agenda of antiwelfare discourse into the late 1990s. Everyone makes a leap from facts to conclusions, of course; but such leaps, in the hands of responsible authors, are still tied to exceptions, alternative possibilities, and are written much more in the subjunctive. None of this for Mr. Murray. His approach to his readers was not persuasion but force.

The American public may have been assaulted by Murray's scientism, but much of the public also participated in that assault. A kind of academic Rush Limbaugh, Murray excited hostile people, not by enriching their analysis but by confirming what they already believed: that welfare causes illegitimacy and irresponsibility by rewarding both. Murray did not supplant the main themes of welfare politics — race, gender, work, morality — but goaded welfare's opponents to greater vigor and boldness. Who would have thought, as Ronald Reagan began his second term in 1984, that, at the beginning of a Democratic president's second term twelve years later, welfare would have been repealed?

What has been the nature and character of Murray's great influence? Simply put, he deranged reasoned debate about maternal and child poverty by appearing to confirm stereotypes of poor women's behavior. Though researchers either refuted Murray's correlations or paid them little heed, politicians and the public glommed onto them. Antiwelfare politics heated up during the late 1980s, with *Losing Ground* providing grist for advocates of restrictive reforms. By 1988, even Democrats had been seduced by Murray's core assertions: The 1988 Family Support Act imposed stringent paternity establishment and child support conditions on welfare beneficiaries and required states to increase paternity establishment for hospital births.

Within ten years of the publication of *Losing Ground*, Murray's crusade to end welfare altogether was on the verge of victory. In 1993, he issued a final clarion call to antiwelfare forces, warning that "illegitimacy is the single most important social problem of our time—more important than drugs, poverty, illiteracy, welfare or homelessness because it drives everything else" (1993a, A14). Arguing that the increase in nonmarital births among whites would produce a white underclass, Murray predicted that the bad behaviors he associated with blacks would soon spread to white America. This added urgency to his appeal to restore marriage as "the paramount . . . nongovernmental institution to temper and restrain behavior." His central policy prescription: "[E]nd all economic support for single mothers." This became the ambition of Republican welfare reform.

Not only did he supply a language and a legitimacy for the assault on welfare, Murray also supplied the prescription for reform. H.R. 4, the Republicans' first welfare bill after winning control of Congress in the 1994 elections, was a testimonial to Murray's ideas. The bill contained strong sanctions against nonmarital childbearing: a mandatory family cap, denying aid to children born to mothers on welfare; the exclusion of unmarried teenage mothers and their children from cash assistance, with an option to states to withhold housing assistance, as well; and bonuses pegged to favorable illegitimacy ratios achieved by individual states. The measure also included strong sanctions against nonmarital childrearing in its mandatory establishment of paternity and child-support provisions. The bill fell short of Murray's ultimate goal—

repealing all forms of welfare — but nevertheless approached that goal by imposing strict time limits on welfare eligibility.

Some of the 1995 bill's harshest sanctions against nonmarital child-bearing among poor women were eliminated in the bill that became law in 1996: The exclusion of unmarried teenage mothers and their children and the family cap became state options, rather than federal mandates, for example. Nevertheless, out of a morally charged bipartisan discourse that opposed welfare to "personal responsibility" emerged a policy that withdraws the safety net from poor single mothers and children, that punishes single mothers for the structure of their families, and that makes the statutory purpose of welfare policy the restoration of the heterosexual, two-parent, nuclear family (PL104–193, Section 401). *Losing Ground* began the process that culminated in this first major repudiation of New Deal social policy. Even more impressive, it so controlled the terms of debate that by the mid-1990s, even Democratic supporters of the New Deal welfare state conceded Murray's premises about welfare. Like the Republicans, Democrats wielded Murray's sticks against nonmarital childbearing and childraising in their own plans for welfare reform (*Congressional Record*, July 18, 1996, H7907–7974).

Jason DeParle, writing for the *New York Times Magazine* in 1994, guessed that Murray's influence "stemmed from his ability to express through seemingly dispassionate analysis many people's hidden suspicions about race, class and sex. His writings comprise a kind of Michelin Guide to the American underpsyche" (80). Murray improves the point in his own words: "Why can a publisher sell [*Losing Ground*]? Because a huge number of well-meaning whites fear that they are closet racists, and this book tells them that they are not. It's going to make them feel better about things they already think but do not know how to say" (quoted in DeParle, p. 50). By making racism look scientific, Murray laundered our dirtiest instincts.

REFERENCES

Becker, Gary. 1981. *A Treatise on the Family*, 97. Cambridge: Harvard University Press. Quoted in Murray 1993b, S234.

Congressional Record. 1996. July 18. H7907–7974.

DeParle, Jason. 1994. "Daring Research or 'Social Science Pornography'?: Charles Murray." *New York Times Magazine* (October 9).

Merton, Robert K. 1955. *Social Theory and Social Structure.* Glencoe: Free Press.

Murray, Charles. 1984. *Losing Ground: American Social Policy 1950–1980.* New York: Basic Books.

———. 1993a. "The Coming White Underclass." *Wall Street Journal* (October 29), A14.

———. 1993b. "Welfare and the Family: The U.S. Experience." *Journal of Labor Economics* 11: S224–S262.

Personal Responsibility and Work Opportunity Act of 1996. PL 104–193.

3 TOOLS AND FRAMEWORKS

DOING IT OURSELVES

Barry Wellman

SPSS: STATISTICAL PACKAGE FOR THE SOCIAL SCIENCES, by
Norman Nie, Dale H. Bent, and C. Hadlai Hull. New York:
McGraw-Hill, 1970.

No previous *CS* review

THE CALCUTTA REVELATION

This volume's presentation of influential books for sociology is mostly
concerned with weighty tomes discussing world-historic subjects. By
contrast, I believe that the most influential books have been those that
have empowered sociologists through precept or example. That is why
I propose the *SPSS* manual (Nie, Bent, and Hull 1970) as our most
influential book, for it was the *SPSS* statistical package that in the early
1970s revolutionized how sociology was done.[1]

It was only in Calcutta in 1986 that I fully appreciated how empowering the *SPSS* revolution has been. Social networks had brought
me to Calcutta. I had been corresponding with Suraj Bandyopadhyay's
research group at the Indian Statistical Institute. As I was going to be in
India for the World Congress of Sociology, why not come to the ISI and
work together?

At a small workshop, I showed my techniques for analyzing personal community networks by means of linking information about the

My thanks to David Armor, Arthur Couch, Michael Schwartz, and Philip Stone, who
taught me to use the computer for both quantitative and qualitative analysis at Harvard's
Department of Social Relations in the mid-1960s, to Bev Meyrowitz/Bev Wellman, who
spent many hours at Harvard and Toronto helping me keypunch and consoling me when the
runs did not work after twelve-hour turnaround, and to Joanne Daciuk, who recently shared
her memories of *SPSS* with me.

1. Early users will recall that the original blue *SPSS* manual (and the subsequent maroon
manual, 1975) also were weighty tomes. Fortunately, there was only a single volume at that
time. Today, there are too many.

characteristics of network members and their ties (Wellman 1992). "No problem!" I announced in breezy AmeriCanuck, "*SPSS* or *SAS* can do this easily."

The Indian sociologists looked stricken, a Maalox cum Imodium moment. "We do not have *SPSS* or *SAS*," they said wistfully. Because of strained relations with the United States, American computer technology or software was not readily available in India.[2] Instead, the ISI had a Russian-made mainframe computer with a Russian operating system and statistical package. Only a few initiates at the computer center knew how to work the system: a Marxian cum Weberian instance of the overbureaucratization of statist societies. To do one statistical analysis on the computer, ISI members had to queue for weeks and plead for the attention of the priestly group serving the mainframe. If they got a command wrong or wanted to do another analysis, they went to the back of the queue again. Hence, only very crucial or large analyses were done on the computer. The researchers did most analyses by hand or by calculator, with the help of assistants.

THE *SPSS* REVOLUTION

My epiphany was the unlikely product of the wisdom of Norman Nie (the "father" of *SPSS*) and of Harold Garfinkel (the maven of making the taken for granted visible). Jointly, their spirits guided my appreciation of how user-friendly statistical packages had enabled social scientists to become masters of our own analyses. Such packages have enabled us to do our own computer-based statistical analyses instead of being forced to rely upon high priests of the Great Machine. We no longer have to queue and beg experts who possess the rare knowledge of how to get a user-unfriendly statistical package to work. Instead, we are now routinely able to do complex analyses from a number of perspectives instead of talking about complex processes but measuring only simple relationships. We can easily check a variety of alternative causes and correlates, and we can view endless perspectives of our

2. A rapprochement between the United States and India has changed this situation. Whatever new dependency relationship this entailed, American software is now available.

data. We revel in our post-P(e)arsonian ability to try dozens of complex procedures, to view things in ten different ways, to obsessively clean and reweight data, to transform the intractable, to hunt down pesky residuals, and to apply once obscure statistical tests with exotic-sounding names.

I focus on *SPSS* because it was the first widely implemented, easy to use, reasonably comprehensive package. To be sure, there were earlier ones such as *BMD* (whose company has recently been bought by *SPSS*), *Osiris* (at the University of Michigan) and *Data-Text* (which I helped code a bit at Harvard in the mid-1960s). Indeed, I use *SAS* now because it has been more network-analysis-friendly. But *SPSS* came to the social sciences well before *SAS,* and it was *SPSS* that first proliferated in the developed world's computer centers. It was *SPSS* that made the revolution and that remains the most user-friendly of the main packages. Undergraduates at the University of Toronto now use it early in their first statistics course, easily doing the kinds of analyses that senior Indian scholars had been blocked from doing a decade earlier.

I do not want to commit the "presentist" fallacy of asserting that no statistical analyses were done before statistical packages became available. Soon after coming as a new graduate student to Harvard in 1963, I was taken to the basement of Emerson Hall to view with awe the very countersorter that Samuel Stouffer had used. In my mind's eye, I could see the statistical analyses of *The American Soldier* (1950) dropping into the sorter pockets in front of me. I was even initiated into the priesthood and learned how to rewire this very same machine all by myself. Of course, folks like Sam Stouffer and Paul Lazarsfeld did wonderful work using counter-sorters, but they were rare giants. In those precomputer days, most people could do only limited analyses using counter-sorters and other IBM machines. Now, we do not have to be giants. We can be ordinary people, using statistical packages to play with data and examine hundreds of analytic possibilities.

THE COSTS OF REVOLUTION

Every revolution has its victims. This one has had several, brought forth by *SPSS*'s triumph. Not only did *SPSS* become a tool for empowerment, it fostered a worldview:

1. SPSS has made statistical analysis so easy that theory and common sense have sometimes fallen by the wayside.

I have no doubt that Lazarsfeld and Stouffer would have happily embraced statistical packages, but I am also confident that they would have urged the careful specification of variables and relationships beforehand. With statistical packages and multivariate routines, it is easy to pour a heap of variables into the regression and stir wildly to see what sticks to what. Many spurious and silly things have come out of such stews.

2. SPSS tilted the sociological playing field so much toward statistical analysis that other modes of inquiry, such as fieldwork, have become neglected.

Because quantitative analysis became much easier than the qualitative analysis of texts, it became much more popular. Moreover, it became the only prevailing orthodoxy in almost all major research universities. Inevitably, students came to believe that quantitative procedures were the best, and perhaps the only, road to the truth. Until recently, there have been no easy ways to do computer-based analyses of field situations. When I used *The General Inquirer* in the 1960s (Stone et al. 1969), I needed six months of preparatory work and produced only frequency counts of concept categories. *Data-Text* never implemented the latter part of its name and remained only a statistical package until it was supplanted by the more widely usable *SPSS* in the 1970s. The result has been that fieldwork has remained hard and imprecise, generally requiring lots of transcribing and hand sorting of notes. A cursory look at sociology journals and books shows that the balance has swung much more to statistical analysis since statistical packages proliferated in the 1970s.

Many qualitative analysts suspect a quantitative plot against them. Be that as it may, it is clear that the current orthodoxy of statistical analyses is related to their greater ease of use and the greater availability of quantitatively coded data sets. It is only very recently that microcomputer textual analysis packages such as *Nud. ist* have arrived to help those working with transcripts and other texts (Miles and Huberman 1994; Weitzman and Miles 1995). *Nud. ist* 4.0 now links with *SPSS,* and the *SPSS* organization introduced *TextSmart* 1.0 in

1998 to capture the meaning of open-ended survey responses. We are starting to have the kinds of powerful hybrid analyses that *Data-Text* promised thirty years ago.

3. The proliferation of statistical packages led to survey research perspectives dominating sociological research.

SPSS was born and raised at the National Opinion Research Center, a survey shop par excellence. Surveys are almost always based on a random sample whose very essence is that each individual must be treated as a separate unit of analysis, or else the sample would be biased. Yet as soon as the unit of analysis becomes the discrete individual, crucial information is lost about the structure of the social system in which this person is embedded. The very assumption of statistical independence, which makes standard statistical analyses so powerful, detaches individuals from social structures and forces analysts to treat them as parts of a disconnected mass. This "methodological individualism" (Coleman 1958, 28) has shifted analyses away from looking directly at social structures and social processes to efforts that try to infer structure and processes from the cross-classified, aggregated characteristics of analytically disconnected individuals. Each record—which usually means each individual—is treated as a separate entity consisting of variables measuring discrete social characteristics (e.g., age, socioeconomic status, attitudes). Yet aggregating each person's (or organization's) characteristics independently obscures or destroys structural information. "Individuals do not act randomly with respect to one another. They form attachments to certain persons, they group together in cliques, they establish institutions" (Coleman 1964, 88).

Of course, sociologists try to infer something about social systems from the multivariate analysis of individual-level data. But analysts taking this approach can only study social structure indirectly by organizing and summarizing numerous individual covariations. Analysts are forced to neglect social properties that are more than the sum of individual acts and concentrate on the attributes that discrete individuals possess. They cannot directly study flows of information or other resources; discover clusters, cleavages or overlapping networks; or reveal underlying role structures. One partial solution is to use social network analytic programs, such as *UCINet,* to analyze structure, but such programs lack the statistical firepower of mainstream packages such as *SPSS*. Another partial solution is to use hierarchical linear modeling, available in the *HLM* package for multivariate analysis.

COLLATERAL POSSIBILITIES

Despite such caveats, the statistical-package revolution has been good for sociology, expanding our scope and empowering our efforts. What we started has spread to other fields, so much so that I was startled to read in an article about market-research "data mining" (talk about being atheoretical!) in *PC AI* (a magazine for computer scientists interested in artificial intelligence): "I suspect that undergraduates new to other disciplines (economics, business, and sociology, for example) could use other features of *SPSS* to great advantage" (Schmuller 1996, 31). When I emailed him, the statistician-author was unaware that sociologists had ever heard of *SPSS,* and he was astonished to learn that we had been there and done that more than twenty-five years ago.

I do not want to be snobbish: The attention of the marketing mavens may augur the integration of statistical packages into office suites. This may lead to future creative linkages of statistical packages with other tools, such as those for graphical or textual analysis. Already, the development of statistical packages (including *SPSS* and *SAS*) for microcomputers has liberated sociologists from their thirty years of dependence on central computing centers.

Although the *SPSS* manual and those for other statistical packages have been the most influential books for sociology, there have also been other empowering books. Among my other candidates for consideration would be:

Hubert Blalock's *Social Statistics* (first edition, 1960), an exemplar of the sociologically minded statistics books that clearly told recent generations of sociologists what to do with *SPSS.*
Blalock's *Causal Models in the Social Sciences* (1971), and Peter Blau and Otis Dudley Duncan's *The American Occupational Structure* (1967). In tandem, they disseminated the lore of nuanced multivariate analysis.
S. D. Berkowitz's *An Introduction to Structural Analysis* (1982) for its integrated presentation of social network analysis.
Barney Glaser and Anselm Strauss's *The Discovery of Grounded Theory* (1967), which showed how to do qualitative analysis systematically.

Charles Tilly's *The Vendée* (1964), which showed how to use a sociological perspective to interview the past.

And as an article-writing book reader, I would love to see a compilation of influential journal articles for each substantive field as well as for sociology in general.

Choosing influential books is a nice game because the fun is more in the playing than in the outcome. I have taken a stand here in favor of empowering tools as the most influential sociological development in recent decades. Which is more important? The findings or the tools that enabled us to make them—and many more? Which should we celebrate more? Copernicus's sixteenth-century hypothesis of the solar system or Galileo's seventeenth-century invention of the telescope that enabled scholars to understand it clearly? It is an unresolvable dialectic between knowing what to look for and knowing how to find something. But if pressed, I would vote for the toolmakers because they give us the eyes to see things.

REFERENCES

Berkowitz, S. D. 1982. *An Introduction to Structural Analysis*. Toronto: Butterworths.

Blalock, Hubert. 1960. *Social Statistics*. New York: McGraw-Hill.

———. 1971. *Causal Models in the Social Sciences*. Chicago: Aldine Atherton.

Blau, Peter, and Otis Dudley Duncan. 1967. *The American Occupational Structure*. New York: Free Press.

Coleman, James. 1958. "Relational Analysis." *Human Organization* 17: 28–36.

———. 1964. *Introduction to Mathematical Sociology*. New York: Free Press.

Glaser, Barney, and Anselm Strauss. 1967. *The Discovery of Grounded Theory*. New York: Aldine.

Miles, Matthew, and A. Michael Huberman. 1994. *Qualitative Data Analysis*. 2d ed. Thousand Oaks: Sage.

Nie, Norman, Dale H. Bent, and C. Hadlai Hull. 1970. *SPSS: Statistical Package for the Social Sciences*. New York: McGraw-Hill.

Schmuller, Joseph. 1996. "Statistical Modeling Takes Off: SPSS Advanced Statistics 6.1." *PC AI* 10 (September): 28–31.

Stone, Phillip J., Dexter Dunphy, Michael Smith, and Daniel Ogilvie. 1969.

The General Inquirer: A Computer Approach to Content Analysis. Cambridge: MIT Press.

Stouffer, Samuel, and Associates. 1950. *The American Soldier.* Princeton: Princeton University Press.

Tilly, Charles. 1964. *The Vendée: A Sociological Analysis of the Counterrevolution of 1793.* Cambridge: Harvard University Press.

Weitzman, Eben, and Matthew Miles. 1995. *Computer Programs for Qualitative Data Analysis.* Thousand Oaks: Sage.

Wellman, Barry. 1992. "How to Use SAS to Study Egocentric Networks." *Cultural Anthropology Methods* 4(2): 6–12.

GEERTZ'S AMBIGUOUS LEGACY

Ann Swidler

THE INTERPRETATION OF CULTURES: SELECTED ESSAYS, by Clifford Geertz. New York: Basic Books, [1973] 1993.

Original review, *CS* 4:6 (November 1975), by Elizabeth Colson:

His anthropology is an art, not a science. To a very large extent therefore his work does not provide a model for other anthropologists or sociologists of lesser talent to follow, since he proceeds from an intuitive grasp of what is important and reaches his conclusion with a flourish that conceals the tedium of the procedures.

Well before *The Interpretation of Cultures* (hereafter, *TIC*) was published, Clifford Geertz had already changed the way we study culture. Indeed, the heart of *TIC* is a collection of beautiful essays, published between 1957 and the mid-1960s, that provided a new theoretical vocabulary for studying culture and a new understanding of what that enterprise involves.

First, Geertz clarified the object of cultural study: not hidden subjectivities or whole ways of life, but publicly available symbols (Keesing 1974). Second, Geertz developed a rich theoretical language for analyzing culture. Beginning with the 1957 "Ethos, World View, and the Analysis of Sacred Symbols," and culminating in 1966 with "Religion as a Cultural System," Geertz asked how particular symbols become real for particular groups. (The very different ways symbolic realities become real and the different kinds of realities they create has been a continuing preoccupation, in "Ideology as a Cultural System" and the later "Art as a Cultural System" and "Common Sense as a Cultural System" [collected in Geertz 1983]). Geertz's answer is that "sacred symbols," and especially ritual actions, generate an "ethos" — an emotional tone, a set of feelings, "moods and motivations" — that simultaneously make the religious worldview seem true and make the ethos seem "uniquely realistic," given that kind of a world. This theoretical formulation seems to explain how symbols, or meanings embodied and enacted in symbols, generate experiential realities that in turn make the symbols real. This is how "man" can be "suspended in webs of significance he himself has spun" (5 [all page numbers from *TIC*]).

Other important essays in *TIC* dealt with such issues as the incompleteness of "human nature" without culture to organize action and experience ("The Impact of the Concept of Culture on the Concept of Man"), different conceptions of the continuity of human personality in different cultures ("Person, Time, and Conduct in Bali"), the resurgence of ethnic particularisms in the new nations ("The Integrative Revolution: Primordial Sentiments and Civil Politics in the New States"), and the problem of when and why ritual practices break down or fail ("Ritual and Social Change: A Javanese Example").

Despite the theoretical and conceptual advances of these earlier essays, the greatest impact of *TIC* came from the two essays that bracketed them — the introductory essay, "Thick Description," and the concluding essay, "Deep Play: Notes on the Balinese Cockfight." Whatever their generalizing theoretical impulse, the earlier essays now marched under the banner of "interpretation," as contrasted with "explanation." The polemical title suggested a rejection of general theorizing about culture and a rejection even of broad comparative claims about why cultures differ. Geertz argued that "culture is not a power, something to which social events, behaviors, institutions, or processes can be causally attributed; it is a context, something within which they can be intelligibly — that is thickly — described" (14). The analysis of culture is "not an experimental science in search of law but an interpretive one in search of meaning" (5).

The enormously influential essay "Deep Play" became a new paradigm for how to study culture: Focus on a single event, symbol, or ritual, such as the cockfight, and "thickly" describe it in the context of all the other symbols, social arrangements, sensibilities, and concepts in terms of which it has "meaning." This demonstration of a new kind of practice in cultural study sent a tidal wave across the disciplines by showing how to take a piece of culture — a ritual, a tall tale, a performance, a symbol, or an event — and treat it as a "text." By placing the text in a context of all the other meanings, experiences, practices, or ideas that shed light upon its meanings, the interpreters of a text could find a way to explicate the sensibility of other times and places, the meanings that organized popular culture, or the conceptual structures that lay behind great literary works. Liberated from the rigors of explanation and able to take as a focal text any piece of the social world, great or small, historians (Robert Darnton, Natalie Davis, Lynn Hunt, and many others), literary critics (Stephen Greenblatt), and even policy analysts (Judith Innes) were freed to put culture center stage.

We may see some of the strengths and weaknesses of the interpretive/textual approach by seeing what *TIC* liberated scholars from. For anthropologists, a Geertzian approach meant liberation, first, from standard, comprehensive ethnography. Second, the Geertzian focus on culture as important in itself provided a way out of the battle among reductionist theories. Rather than having to explain why matrilocal or patrilateral societies produced one kind of birth ritual or another, or why myths had a particular structure, or what function some practice served, anthropologists could focus on a set of symbols, practices, or rituals and their meaning. The detailed description of kinship structure, myths, or rituals could be jettisoned, or, rather, these could be reintroduced in much less systematic ways as part of the interpretation — the thick description — of particular "texts."

In literary criticism, which had always studied texts, and which indeed provided the model for the kind of "semiotic" analysis Geertz was advocating, Geertz ironically showed the value of putting texts back into their social and historical "contexts." But this approach to textual analysis radically redefined what that context might be. Rather than locating a great work in the major intellectual currents of its day, seeing it as a vehicle for the expression of interests, ideas, or literary influences, Geertz's method allowed a text to be related to whatever other particular texts seemed to illuminate it. So even obscure folk culture can reveal the "semiotic structure" of a culture and thus shed light on underlying structures in a literary text. And any text — the most engaging, exotic or ordinary, high or low, obscure or well known — can be the entry point for understanding the meanings that animate a cultural system.

In history, first and foremost, Geertz's work legitimated taking seriously popular culture, the culture of subordinated groups, and the symbols and discourse even of major political events. Historians were also freed from focusing on events, or on such hard realities as birth rates, marriage patterns, or material life. The ability to focus on particular, even obscure texts, and then to ask what they revealed about the larger complex of meanings within a society, meant that historians could focus not only on popular rituals, but also on little-known, unusual, or even bizarre events, examining them for what they reveal about deeper cultural patterns in a society. The loosening of the strictures on how central, how repeated, or how institutionalized a practice needs to be to serve as a text allowed a historian like Natalie Zemon Davis to move from studying well-institutionalized ritual practices like *charivari* to studying the single episode of the disappearance and "return" of Martin Guerre. Robert Darnton moved from studying the influence of popular belief and practice on major social transformations (the influence of mesmerism on Enlightenment thought, or the influence of book censorship on French political thought) to using particular engaging, but often atypical, events or stories as texts that reveal the whole structure of meanings available in a historical era.

Geertz's revolution has also met substantial resistance. In anthropology there is by now an enormous critical literature (see Shankman 1984; Asad 1983; Biersack 1989; Parker 1985; Wikan 1992). Some argue that interpretation is insufficient, that Geertz provides no criteria for an adequate interpretation, and that interpretation is substantively inferior to explanation. Geertz has also been attacked for exoticizing the peoples he studies, making them seem foreign and incomprehensible so that their texts require elaborate "interpretation." And he has been taken to task for neglecting or actively obscuring power, domination, conflict, historical change, and the colonial context of the societies he studies. He has also had to face the increasing resistance in anthropology by "natives" to being "translated" at all, their insistence that indigenous understandings are privileged.

These are not, however, quite the issues that have been (or necessarily should be) of greatest concern to sociologists. Rather, sociologists can benefit from a critical assimilation of Geertz at his best. We certainly need a better understanding of the status of "interpretation" as an enterprise and of the relation between interpretation and explanation (see Swidler and Jepperson 1994). We also need to confront a question Geertz and his imitators ignore: What about the selection of texts? Is every text equally important? Or is there some implicit claim analysts make in choosing a text—perhaps simply that that text was indeed meaningful to a particular group of persons in a particular time and place? What about "contradictions" among texts? Geertz's implicit assumption of a unified semiotic system appears plausible as long as the analysis focuses on a single text and arrays other meanings around it; but the assumption breaks down if groups participate in multiple practices that have varying underlying meaning systems.

Where does the interpretive enterprise lead by itself? If we only want to "translate" from another culture to our own, what makes any particular instance of translation of more general interest (Alexander 1987)? Geertz's forays into other cultures certainly are of broader interest, and not, I think, primarily because we are eager to understand the particular meanings that animate Javanese, Balinese, or Moroccan life. Rather, Geertz's analyses are important because they develop an important set of new concepts, and even some theories and explanations, that have not been as fully exploited as they could be.

We might begin by returning to Geertz's analysis of the interaction of ethos, world view, and ritual experience. The question of how different orders of reality intersect, and how different kinds of realities become true (or remain more or less provisionally true) under differing circumstances, seems one of the most critical a serious sociology of culture might address.

Second, sociologists might follow up Geertz's interest (in "Internal Conversion in Contemporary Bali" and, later, in *Islam Observed* 1968) in how societies deal culturally with the challenges of modernity. Geertz builds on a basically Weberian understanding of rationalization, but he sees it as an enormously complex, self-contradictory, sometimes paradoxical process.

Third, students of culture would also do well to take the notion of "deep play" (a theoretical idea, if ever there was one) more seriously. In "Deep Play," Geertz is not only exploring the meanings of the Balinese cockfight. He is also asking what makes some cultural performances, some cultural experiences deeper, more intense, more gripping than others. This is the beginning of an analysis of why some rituals, texts, or symbols generate more meaning than others do. Geertz explores how tension, uncertainty about the outcome, balanced opponents, and the ability to symbolize (and sublimate) significant social tensions make some cockfights deeper, more exciting, and more satisfying than others.

Barely breaking the surface of Geertz's essays, but there, nonetheless, lurks the question of whether and in what sense cultures are really "systems" after all. He recognizes that multiple kinds of realities can abide side by side. He also occasionally addresses great clashes of meanings, when people's cultural assumptions don't mesh, and when culture itself is a source of sometimes violent conflict. If cultural coherence is itself variable, Geertz's work provides a starting point for studying this variation.

Geertz's polemical stands — in favor of interpretation and against explanation, for description over theory, and against all general theory — are red herrings. They have distracted us from the depth and originality of his own theorizing. Sociology has not faced a crisis of confidence like that of anthropology; and sociology has always had a stronger commitment to both theory and explanation. Perhaps, then, sociologists will be able uninhibitedly to assimilate and find real nourishment in the rich filling of Geertz's interpretation-sandwich.

REFERENCES

Alexander, Jeffrey C. 1987. *Twenty Lectures: Sociological Theory since World War II*. New York: Columbia University Press.

Asad, Talal. 1983. "Anthropological Conceptions of Religion: Reflections on Geertz." *Man* 18: 237–59.

Biersack, Aletta. 1989. "Local Knowledge, Local History: Geertz and Beyond." Pp. 72–96 in *The New Cultural History*, ed. Lynn Hunt. Berkeley: University of California Press.

Geertz, Clifford. 1968. *Islam Observed: Religious Development in Morocco and Indonesia*. New Haven: Yale University Press.

——. 1983. *Local Knowledge: Further Essays in Interpretative Anthropology*. New York: Basic Books.

Keesing, Roger M. 1974. "Theories of Culture." Pp. 73–97 in *Annual Review of Anthropology* 3. Palo Alto: Annual Reviews, Inc.

Parker, Richard. 1985. "From Symbolism to Interpretation: Reflections on the Work of Clifford Geertz." *Anthropology and Humanism Quarterly* 10 (3): 62–67.

Shankman, Paul. 1984. "The Thick and the Thin: On the Interpretive Theoretical Program of Clifford Geertz." *Current Anthropology* 25 (June): 261–79.

Swidler, Ann, and Roland L. Jepperson. 1994. "Interpretation, Explanation, and Theories of Meaning." Paper presented at the American Sociological Association Annual Meetings, Los Angeles (August).

Wikan, Unni. 1992. "Beyond the Words: The Power of Resonance." *American Ethnologist* 19 (August): 460–82.

SOCIOLOGY'S OTHER POSTSTRUCTURALISM

Craig Calhoun

OUTLINE OF A THEORY OF PRACTICE, by Pierre Bourdieu.
Trans. Richard Nice. Cambridge: Cambridge University Press,
[1972] 1977.

Original review, CS 9:2 (March 1980), by Arthur W. Frank III:

The contribution of Bourdieu's work is that in producing a better grounded structuralism, he accomplishes the practice of a
more scientific Marxism. . . . The European idiom of Bourdieu's
writing should not distract North American sociologists from its
extraordinary importance as a theory of method.

Pierre Bourdieu (1988) has described one of the central motivations
behind his intellectual work as a determination to challenge misleading
dichotomies. This is nowhere more manifest than in the work that first
made him famous in English language sociology, and which remains
perhaps his single most influential, *Outline of a Theory of Practice*.[1]
Outline attacks many problematic dichotomies, but has gained its enduring influence most of all from its challenge to the opposition of
structure and action.

The idea of transcending this dichotomy was not a new one in sociological theory; indeed, it gave shape to Talcott Parsons's first book,
The Structure of Social Action. But Bourdieu's effort was both original
and compelling. It caught, moreover, the rising demand for an attempt
to integrate structure and action that followed the successive crises of
first Parsons's own functionalism and then a Marxism that had split
into structuralist and voluntarist camps.

Outline did not achieve the instant English-language fame of some

---

1. Bourdieu in essence rewrote *Outline* in his later, but less widely read, *Logic of Practice* (Stanford: Stanford University Press, 1990).

of Bourdieu's later work. *Distinction,* for example, burst on the Anglophone scene in a 1984 translation and helped immediately to spark the renaissance of the sociology of culture as well as a thriving subfield of cultural studies of stratification. Bourdieu's writings on education and the reproduction of social inequality quickly became well known in education studies. Partly because it is a more difficult book, *Outline* attracted readers gradually. Combining empirical studies of the Kabyle, an Algerian people, with complex theoretical reflections, it was hard to categorize by subfield. But it was also key to making Bourdieu's reputation in social theory and sociology in general. By the 1980s, it found its way into the standard syllabi for graduate courses in contemporary sociological theory.

Outline also had a substantial indirect influence on English-language sociology, even before translation. Most prominently, Bourdieu's work helped shape Anthony Giddens's intellectual framework, and later readers picked up Bourdieu's ideas and terms — like structuration — from Giddens, without always knowing their source.

Outline spoke to a desire for theory that made sense of the stability of social organization without succumbing to the conservatism of much functionalism, and that made sense of human agency without relying on highly cognitive accounts of intentions. It presented human action as deeply situated in social contexts and cultural patterns, without reducing it to either. It also helped that, despite a good translation, the text was sufficiently oblique in style that it could be read — at least superficially — with approval by English-language theorists of starkly contrasting orientations. While some (especially in anthropology) took it as a direct extension of Lévi-Strauss's structuralism, doing more to accommodate practical action, others took it to be an attempt to open Marxism up to more cultural analysis. By the later 1980s, James Coleman was assimilating Bourdieu's concept of cultural capital to Gary Becker's notion of human capital. Bourdieu was widely criticized as an economic reductionist, asserting like rational choice theorists that selfish motives underlay all human action. Yet he was equally taken up as a standard-bearer for cultural and ethnographic approaches stressing situated interpretation of social action. Some of the clash of receptions was apparent when Coleman drew Bourdieu into a jointly organized conference (Bourdieu and Coleman 1991). *Outline* was the key book through which all these impressions of Bourdieu were formed (though various of his empirical studies of cultural patterns outstripped its influence among less theoretically inclined readers). This contributed to some of the misunderstanding, because the political and critical dimensions to Bourdieu's analyses were relatively unclear in *Outline* — especially to English-language readers.

Since the book was originally written some years earlier in French, this context of reception was not exactly its context of production. The dichotomy that rent the French intellectual scene and that shaped Bourdieu's own initial orientation opposed the structuralisms of Lévi-Strauss and Althusser to the ego-centric existentialism of Sartre.[2] If forced to choose, Bourdieu was clearly on Lévi-Strauss's side (though not that of Althusser), but in *Outline* he combined classic structuralist analyses of the Kabyle with a developing critique of structuralism's cognitivist neglect of practical knowledge, its more general objectivism, and its inability to turn that objectivist gaze on itself in order to provide an adequate account of its own scientific standpoint. Like Foucault's work of the same period (*The Order of Things* and *Archaeology of Knowledge*), *Outline* offered both one of structuralism's high points and important movement beyond it. For all of his influence in anthropology and general fame, Lévi-Strauss had not been widely read in American sociology. This made *Outline* both more difficult for many readers to assimilate and more valuable as a critical introduction to some of the achievements of structuralism (that is, of French cultural structuralism, as distinct from various acultural or purely sociological accounts of social structure, like Peter Blau's later work).

Bourdieu is of approximately the same generation as Jacques Derrida and Michel Foucault. He became an intellectual superstar somewhat later than either, however, and translation of his major works lagged substantially behind translations of theirs. Bourdieu also focused more on institutionally based research and teaching, less on the conference circuits of celebrity. Taken up by literary and cultural theorists (and then by anthropologists, historians, and others, but not very widely by sociologists) Derrida and Foucault became key exemplars of a movement called (much more in English than in French) "poststructuralism." Bourdieu's work shared much in inspiration and context with this intellectual current (especially with Foucault, despite Bour-

2. Though published in 1972, *Outline* was largely written before 1968 and is not the work in which to find Bourdieu's response to the events of that year or the late '60s intellectual conflicts more generally. For that, see *Homo Academicus*, trans. Peter Collier (Stanford: Stanford University Press, 1988).

dieu's early personal connection to Derrida, a classmate at the École normale superieur). But Bourdieu has seldom been understood as a member of this intellectual generation, and *Outline* has not figured as prominently in English-language poststructuralism as the work of Derrida or Foucault. The others learned more of their structuralism from Lacan and Althusser, significantly, while Bourdieu avoided both — and the politics associated with both — siding with Lévi-Strauss.[3] But perhaps the most important reason why Bourdieu has not figured prominently in poststructuralism, even though it is important to situate *Outline* in that context, is that Bourdieu was unrelentingly sociological in his analyses, focused on both directly interpersonal relationships and systematic patterns of social organization, while the dominant approach of poststructuralists made little room for the social. Likewise, however much Bourdieu's analyses in *Outline* revealed the limits of agency, the misrecognition of actors (and analysts) who thought they had perfect autonomy, he did remain concerned — politically as well as sociologically — with accounting for practice, and even while he challenged subjectivism (like Sartre's), he refused to join the common poststructuralist attack on the idea of action (and responsibility for action) as such.

Structuralist analyses were commonly static, and therefore commonly opposed to accounts of process.[4] In the Manichean opposition of structuralism to existentialism, Parisian intellectuals of the 1960s tended to cede individuals, action, and especially personal experience to the latter (thereby declaring the latter unscientific). As Althusser famously put it, individual persons were not of analytic significance in themselves, but rather were simply the "bearers" of structure. From early in his work in Algeria, Bourdieu found it crucial to analyze both the recurrent processes through which ways of life were enacted and the more linear processes of historical change. Above all, Bourdieu sought to show how structures were reproduced through the very actions by which individuals sought to achieve their personal ends. *Outline* was his first major theoretical statement of this approach, and this was a crucial basis of its early influence.

Partly because many English-language readers had previously been

3. On structuralism as an intellectual movement and the roots of what outside France is commonly called poststructuralism, see François Dosse (1997).

4. Foucault's structuralist histories thus stress ruptures between statically conceived epochs more than processes, whether of change or flux.

exposed to Bourdieu's early writings on the French educational system, *Outline* was at first read largely as a "reproduction theory." The power of Bourdieu's accounts of how individual actions were recuperated into the reproduction of structure (recalling Merton's classic evocation of the unintended consequences of purposive social action) was readily grasped. The other side of Bourdieu's analytic approach was less fully appreciated. But Bourdieu equally made structure dependent on action and in so doing provided an opening for studying how changing material conditions (e.g., the monetarization of the Kabyle economy) could change the way cultural processes played out in the realm of individual action.

In order to address action, Bourdieu drew on a largely Anglo-Saxon language of strategy and recovered with new meaning the old term "habitus." It was the language of strategy, first and foremost, that suggested to many American readers an affinity to rational choice theory (which Bourdieu has strenuously denied; see Bourdieu and Wacquant 1992). This repelled at least as many who objected to what they saw as excessive economism and instrumentalism as it attracted others who saw the possibility of developing a culturally richer approach to strategic action. Whether filtered through rational-choice thinking or not, part of the impact of *Outline* has been to show in the tradition of Marcel Mauss's analysis of "the gift" how apparently nonstrategic or disinterested actions in fact can be understood as resulting from actors' interests, even when those actors are not consciously aware of this motivation. Bourdieu sought to demonstrate how the "strategy" inhered not simply in conscious intentions (a fallacy at once cognitivist and subjectivist) but in the situation and in the whole being of the actor.

This is where habitus comes in. Notoriously difficult to pin down, the term means basically the embodied sensibility that makes possible structured improvisation. Jazz musicians can play together without consciously following rules because they have developed physically embodied capacities to hear and respond appropriately to what is being produced by others, and to create themselves in ways that others can hear sensibly and to which others can respond. Or in Bourdieu's metaphor, effective play of a game requires not just knowledge of rules but a practical sense for the game.[5] Bourdieu's account of this dimen-

---

5. The notion of "sense" carries, in French as in English, both cognitivist and bodily connotations: to "make sense" and to "sense something." When Bourdieu rewrote and

sion of "tacit knowledge" is one of the most fruitful to have been offered, all the more so because he related this to bodily *hexis* (picking up the Aristotelian concept). Bourdieu showed culture as embodied, not just thought, and this alone could have ensured a considerable influence for *Outline*.

But the point was even more basic (and more sociological). Bourdieu emphasized that habitus was not just a capacity of the individual, but an achievement of the collectivity. It was the result of a ubiquitous "collective enterprise of inculcation." The reason why "strategies" could work without individuals being consciously strategic is that individuals became who they were and social institutions existed only on the strength of this inculcation of orientations to action, evaluation, and understanding. This was a matter not only of socialization, conceived in the neutral manner of much sociology, but also of power and of interested interaction. Inculcation took place in families differently endowed with cultural capital, for example, and thus blessed some children with advantages in performing various social roles. It was for this reason too that struggles over classification — over naming, taxonomies, categorization of people and the things of the world — figured so importantly for Bourdieu. Bourdieu showed that the classificatory schemes basic to structuralist analysis were not simply objective, as a static account would imply, but the products of interested struggle among social actors (albeit seldom explicit). The most fundamental social changes had to appear not only as changes in formal structures but also as changes in habitual orientations to action. Bourdieu sought thus to overcome the separation of culture, social organization, and embodied individual being that was characteristic of most existing sociology. In this, his most important American forebear was Erving Goffman, with whom he spent time early in his career, and it is surprising that this connection did not achieve more recognition in the early reception of *Outline*.

Outline has been most influential among those who seek to analyze the interplay between cultural and social structure and social action. If

---

slightly expanded *Outline* in the late 1970s — about the time it was first becoming known in English — he chose the French title *Le sens pratique*. This second version of *Outline* (which has never been comparably influential or as widely read as it deserves) has the English title, *The Logic of Practice*, which sacrifices one side of the double meaning.

others of Bourdieu's works have helped to create the sociology of culture as a subfield, *Outline* has played a major role in bringing cultural analysis back into the center of sociological analysis in general. In encouraging the attempt to see both actors (and therefore actions) and institutions as shaped by cultural schemas (to borrow Sewell's recent term), it also opens up the possibility of analysis of the way in which those schemas are shaped in struggle. This is the larger task to which Bourdieu's account of "symbolic violence" speaks; it has already been put to use in a variety of more specific analytic contexts. *Outline* also foreshadowed Bourdieu's development of the concept of cultural capital, and more generally the theory of how different forms of accumulated resources may have different effects, and may be converted. In one related sense, however, *Outline* may have misled readers. Bourdieu's sociology is aimed largely at an account of power relations, and especially of the many ways in which power is culturally produced, reproduced, and manipulated. Partly because of the heavy emphasis on strategizing language, this is not as manifest in *Outline* as in some of the rest of Bourdieu's work.

The influence of *Outline* remains large partly because it appears (along with the overlapping *Logic of Practice*) as the most important of the relatively few general and synthetic statements Bourdieu has offered of his "theory" (a label he doesn't like). The rest of his publications range across a wide variety of empirical objects of analysis, from museum and literature to kinship, class, Algerian workers, and French higher education. *Outline* is not a cure for the common fragmented reading of Bourdieu, but it does go some way toward showing what is central to his perspective and situating many of his key concepts in relation to broader theory. In a sense it explicates and provides a rationale for what Brubaker (1992) has described as Bourdieu's sociological *habitus,* his characteristic mode of improvising in empirical analysis.

REFERENCES

Bourdieu, Piérre. 1988. "Vive la crise! For Heterodoxy in Social Science." *Theory and Society* 17 (5): 773–88.

Bourdieu, Piérre, and James S. Coleman, eds. 1991. *Social Theory for a Changing Society.* Boulder: Westview Press; New York: Russell Sage Foundation.

Bourdieu, Piérre, and Loïc Wacquant. 1992. *An Invitation to Reflexive Sociology.* Chicago: University of Chicago Press.

Brubaker, Rogers. 1992. "Social Theory as Habitus." Pp. 212–34 in *Bourdieu: Critical Perspectives,* ed. C. Calhoun, E. LiPuma, and M. Postone. Chicago: University of Chicago Press.

Dosse, François. [1991] 1997. *Structuralism.* 2 vols. Minneapolis: University of Minnesota Press.

4 APPROACHES TO THE ECONOMY AND ECONOMIC PROCESSES

GARY BECKER ON THE FAMILY:
HIS GENIUS, IMPACT, AND BLIND SPOTS

Paula England and Michelle J. Budig

A TREATISE ON THE FAMILY, by Gary S. Becker. 2d ed. Cambridge: Harvard University Press, 1991.

Original review, *CS* 22:2 (March 1993), by Debra Friedman:

Reading this book from cover to cover is a trial. Little attention is paid to the writing, and to absorb the power of the analysis, the reader must come to the book as a student who is ready to submit to a master teacher. This is not a scholarly book in the usual sense, but rather a cross between a reference volume and an encyclopedia, in which Gary Becker's mind and work are the universe from which knowledge is drawn. Combined with the tone of certainty and finality that is the mark of much high economic theory, the book is a bitter pill. But swallow it we must.

Gary Becker's genius is his ability to apply neoclassical economic theory to topics seen as not susceptible to economic reasoning and as outside "the economy," such as crime, demography, the family, habits, and addictions. This is surely why he received the Nobel Prize for Economics in 1992. What is infuriating about his work is that, despite having broadened the economic model in ways that provide an opening for such considerations, he completely ignores unequal power in social life, or the unequal happiness and suffering it engenders.

We focus here on Becker's *Treatise on the Family*, published first in 1981, and reissued in a second enlarged edition in 1991. We first characterize the whole body of Becker's work, with an eye to where he deviates from usual neoclassical assumptions and where he toes the line. Then we outline basic arguments of *Treatise*, especially those pertaining to gender differentiation. Next, we discuss the impact of the work

We thank Nancy Folbre for comments on an earlier draft.

in the social sciences and law. We conclude with our view of the book's virtues and blind spots.

ECONOMICS ACCORDING TO BECKER

Becker considers topics usually ignored by economists, broadens or relaxes some assumptions economists conventionally make, but holds unwaveringly to the rationality assumption, which he considers the most valuable core of the rational choice perspective (Becker 1996, 155–56). Four common assumptions in neoclassical economic theory are that individuals are rational, that they are self-interested, that tastes are exogenous, and that interpersonal utility assumptions are impossible.

Becker unflinchingly retains the rationality assumption. This assumption implies that people do not violate logic in their preferences. For example, rational actors have transitive preferences (if one prefers A to B and B to C, then she or he prefers A to C). It also implies that people make decisions based on logically correct inferences from the information they have about which means will lead to which ends. Rationality allows optimizing.

But what the rational optimizer will do is unclear unless we know what she or he wants. The usual assumption is self-interest, often construed narrowly by economists to mean selfish pursuit of material goods (or the money to buy them).[1] But the self-interest assumption, if construed broadly, only implies that people optimize their own utility, not that their wants are only material or that they ignore others' well-being. Becker adopts this broader view of self-interest: "I have tried to pry economists away from narrow assumptions about self interest. Behavior is driven by a much richer set of values and preferences. . . . The analysis assumes that individuals maximize welfare as they conceive it, whether they be selfish, altruistic, loyal, spiteful, or masochistic" (1996, 141).

Economists generally assume that tastes (preferences) are exogenous (i.e., they must be explained by variables causally prior to those in the economic model) and unchanging. If tastes are assumed stable, then changes in what we choose must be due to changes in our income or the relative prices (including opportunity costs) of various choices.

---

1. A formal way of putting the assumption of selfishness is that individuals' utilities are independent of each other — i.e., that A's utility is not affected by B's utility.

Whether Becker retains this assumption of exogenous and unchanging tastes is at first glance unclear. His famous 1977 paper with George Stigler, "De Gustabus Non Est Disputandum" defends this assumption. The rough translation of the title is that "there is no accounting for tastes." It is one of the ritualistic phrases economists invoke frequently as if to remind each other of a fundamental truth.[2] But Becker's recent work on addiction and habit discusses changing tastes. When we say someone is addicted to heroin, don't we mean his tastes have been altered by using heroin, causing him to want it more than previously? Indeed, his most recent book, a collection of previous essays, is titled *Accounting for Tastes* (Becker 1996). This suggests that he has changed his position.

However, it is not so simple. As he explains in the new book (Becker 1996, 3–23), he believes that preferences for specific commodities (e.g., apples, listening to classical music, marriage to a particular partner) can change over time in response to an individual's social connections or consumption experiences, because either of these may increase one's propensity to appreciate the specific items. For example, having parents who expose one to classical music may allow one to learn to appreciate it. Many things may be habit-forming. In this sense, Becker thinks tastes are endogenous and can change. However, what he still sees as exogenous and unchanging is an "extended utility function," which specifies, for each individual, the way in which social connections and past consumption experiences determine how much utility will be gained from various combinations of specific commodities. This is a bit different from the standard economists' notion of a utility function that simply consists of one's preferences, rank ordered (i.e., to say I have more of a taste for chocolate than vanilla is to say chocolate increases my utility more than vanilla).

Becker appears to retain the assumption that interpersonal utility comparisons are impossible. He never concludes that social arrangements (e.g., traditional marriage) provide unequal utility to the persons involved. This suggests that he shares the assumption that utility is so inherently subjective that we can never know when one person has more of it than another, so we can never say that, overall, some arrangement is more beneficial to one group than another.

---

2. It has a similar ritualistic status to the saying "there is no free lunch" (meaning that *someone* always pays for it, even if it was free to the person eating it).

BECKER'S *TREATISE ON THE FAMILY*

Many credit Becker as the founder of "the new home economics." Major tenets of the new home economics are that economic theory applies to decisions made in households as well as in formal markets, and that households are sites of production. Becker's *Treatise* collects many of his papers that contribute to the new home economics.

Becker sees the household as a factory. What is produced there? Children are reared into adults who become paid workers and adult members of families; "reproduction" is just another form of production. Many goods and services are produced for the adults as well—meals are made, clothes are sewn and laundered, rooms are cleaned, entertainment is provided.

When Becker analyzes production in the household, economists' usual assumptions of rationality and optimization are fully in force. Households optimize utility. But whose utility? What if the members disagree? Becker posits considerable altruism in families, especially of parents to children, and a "single family utility" function. His "rotten kid" theorem says that if a family contains one adult altruist, then even a selfish ("rotten") child or spouse will be induced to behave altruistically toward the family because the altruist will redistribute away from "rotten" family members to discourage selfish behavior. Thus, as long as there is one true altruist, everyone will behave *as if* they are altruistic.

So how does a married, heterosexual couple with children organize their productive activities? Will they have any division of labor, or will they each be employed part time with all household tasks shared? Becker argues that the division of labor is efficient in the household, just as in the factory. People learn fewer specialized tasks better than many general tasks, and division of labor takes advantage of different comparative advantages. Couples have traditionally divided labor such that women did childrearing and household work (possibly combined with some employment) while men worked full time in the market. But why divide labor *according to sex?* Assuming that couples divide labor to optimize productive efficiency, he invokes a combination of biology and socialization to explain why sex-based specialization achieves this. In the second edition of the book he concedes that employment discrimination might also be a factor.

In Becker's view, a family considers the value (in terms of meeting the family's needs and wants) of what each person could produce at home versus the value of what can be bought for the wage she or he could command in paid employment. Who will do what is decided by comparative advantage. Women, Becker says, are biologically advantaged in childrearing. Only they can breast feed, and he suspects that women are biologically advantaged in other aspects of childrearing as well. He does not argue that women are biologically advantaged for other household work, but notes that childrearing is efficiently combined with housework. Thus women may specialize in household production, not because women are less productive in market work, but because men are less productive in childrearing.

Specialization also develops because men receive higher wages, so the family's gain from an hour of male employment is greater than from an hour of female employment. The higher male wage could result from sex discrimination in employment, although he discusses this little. This is surprising in one sense, because Becker's earliest contribution to economics was a book on race discrimination (Becker 1957). Another reason men often have higher wages is they are more continuously employed. Insofar as people learn on the job, job experience can be seen as an investment in human capital. But why would men have more experience-based human capital in market work? Sometimes this is because in the past the couple specialized with the husband doing the market work, itself explained by either biology or market discrimination.

An important yet subtle aspect of Becker's argument is often missed: Even small initial differences in comparative advantage can lead to large later differences (Becker 1991, 4). Small initial differences in wages between husbands and wives, perhaps because of discrimination, or small initial biological advantages of women in childrearing cause a division of labor early on. This initial division of labor further increases the husband's productivity and wage in the market through on-the-job learning, and further increases women's household productivity through learning-by-doing at home. Thus, what was only slightly more efficient right after marriage is the hands-down choice twenty years later if efficiency is the criterion.

Becker admits that prior socialization influences how spouses divide labor by sex. Parents often invest more in sons' market-relevant human capital, and more in daughters' household-relevant human capital (e.g., learning to cook, clean, and care for children). He ties these differential investments back to biological differences via a type of "statistical discrimination" by parents. In this view, sex differences in average ability on various traits are biologically produced. But some individuals have traits atypical for their sex. Since parents cannot identify atypical children early on, it is more efficient (a priori) to invest in children according to the average biological advantage for their sex. Thus, Becker brings gendered socialization into the story, but he does so in a much less comprehensive way than sociologists do. Parents teach children sex-typical skills, but only because of a biological predisposition of women to be better at childrearing. Moreover, the socialization of a child affects the sex division of labor in their adult household only indirectly through different skills developed. There is no room in his account for couples who decide that she, rather than he, should stay home with the children simply because that's what everyone else does, nor for parents who teach only boys about cars and only girls about cooking, simply following social convention. He only uses explanations based on either socialization or biology when they are consistent with the touchstone of efficiency in production.

Women's employment has increased dramatically in this century in all industrial nations. Becker explains this two ways. First, his demographic analysis argues that fertility declined with economic development because the costs of children increased and the benefits parents get from children declined. Benefits declined because children no longer work on the family farm, and costs increased in part because modern economies require that, to be successful, children must be educated. Thus, even though income goes up with development, which should have meant that parents could "afford" more children, fertility decreased because people invested more in the human capital of each child. Quantity of children was traded for quality. The decline in fertility decreased the need for women's childrearing labor at home, which encouraged employment. Also, the wage rate available to women increased as the overall productivity of the economy raised wages in general, which pulled more women into employment by raising the opportunity cost of being a full-time homemaker. Yet, even in families where women are employed, it is often part time or sporadic. Becker attributes this to the efficiencies of the sex-based specialization discussed above.

Becker argues that women's increased employment can account for the increase in divorce and the decrease in marriage rates. He sees the gains in productive efficiency from specialization as a major motivation for marriage. Since women's employment reduces specialization, it reduces the gains from marriage, thus making marriages less popular and less enduring.

Becker argues that the longer the marriage endures, the less likely partners are to divorce. This is because "marriage-specific" investments increase the value of the current partner relative to a new partner. Investments are "marriage-specific" to the extent they produce benefits reaped only if one stays in the current marriage. Examples of marriage-specific investments are learning to deal with and possibly even enjoy a partner's idiosyncrasies, or bearing and rearing children.

Becker recognizes that women who make the marriage-specific investments of child rearing are vulnerable to a lower standard of living if they divorce. Becker thinks of marriage as a long-term contract that is broken by divorce. He argues that the state responds to this problem by securing for women and children at least some of what is due them from men under the contract, by prohibiting divorce in some circumstances, by requiring husbands to pay alimony or child support, or through welfare programs that substitute for men's earning. Such policies may increase women's willingness to make investments in child-rearing, because they reduce the associated risk (Becker 1991, 15–16, 374–76).

THE IMPACT OF BECKER'S TREATISE

The impact of Becker's *Treatise on the Family* has been enormous, not only in economics, but in law and in the social sciences more generally. The Social Science Citation Index showed that the book was cited in 103, 114, and 142 articles, respectively, in 1993, 1994, and 1995 (in the wide array of social-science–related journals covered by the index). Even before receiving his 1992 Nobel Prize, and before the 1991 edition could have been cited, *Treatise* was cited 73 times in 1990 and 67 in 1991. The book has both stimulated and infuriated scholars of the family.

Many citations to the book appear in generalist journals in economics and sociology, in law review articles, especially articles on family law, as well as those on the new field of law and economics, pioneered by Posner (1972). Legal writers have applied Becker's ideas in multiple areas of law; some examples include tort law (Croley and Hanson

1995), divorce law (Reagan 1992), poverty law (Cahn 1994), tax law (McCaffery 1994; Kornhauser 1987), and criminal law (Posner 1985). In the social sciences, citations to Becker's *Treatise* appear in journals on the family dominated by sociologists (such as *Journal of Marriage and the Family*), in demography journals, and in labor economics journals (such as *Journal of Human Resources*). It is often used as the standard citation to refer to the whole corpus of the "new home economics." What accounts for the large impact across disciplines?

First, the book is at least somewhat accessible to noneconomists. Unlike most economists, Becker writes books as well as technical articles.[3] While many of the chapters contain mathematical proofs, most of the arguments are presented in verbal logic that one familiar with core neoclassical ideas can follow.

The book's power lies mainly in presenting one integrated theoretical perspective to illuminate many questions about the family. Needless to say, this imperialistic move on behalf of rational-choice theory has evoked defensive responses from sociologists defending their turf. It is often the standard citation for neoclassical predictions on the family, whether an author is confirming a prediction or using it as a "straw person" to juxtapose to a preferred perspective. It is cited equally by authors arguing against its view and by those supporting it.

Becker generates hypotheses about polygamy, assortative mating, the marriage rate, fertility, women's employment, the sex division of labor in marriage, the sex gap in pay, investments by parents in their own and their children's human capital, bequests by parents to children, divorce, intergenerational mobility, and state regulation of marriage and divorce. *Treatise* seems to beg for research supporting or refuting the integrated perspective presented; it typically proceeds by generating implications of the theory, presenting little empirical evidence to support the assertions, and reviewing others' research quite selectively. It thus created a demand for tests of its predictions.

The family is a "hot" topic in the academy and elsewhere, in part because such dramatic change is going on — increases in premarital cohabitation, nonmarital births, divorce, and families with step-parents.

---

3. Economics is a discipline in which writing articles featuring mathematical proofs is the highest status activity. As an economist friend explained to one of us, tongue in cheek, "Real economists don't write books, like 'real men don't eat quiche'."

Most commentators see something terribly wrong—but whether the solution is a defense of the traditional sex-differentiated family or feminist proposals for more egalitarian families—is a subject of great debate, and what the role of the state should be is hotly contested.

The rise of feminist scholarship, driven mainly by the increased representation of women among researchers, has also increased scholarly interest in the family. Women are not well represented among economists, but their numbers have reached high levels in some other social sciences. For example, in 1990 20 percent of Ph.D.'s in economics were granted to women, compared to 49 percent in sociology (National Center for Educational Statistics 1993). Women are disproportionately interested in studying the family, and pointing out the patriarchal nature of the family has been a central feminist insight. Even those feminists not entirely hostile to economic theory (e.g., England and Farkas 1986; England and Kilbourne 1990; Folbre 1994) have attacked Becker's claims about the advantages of the traditional family, reminding readers that the traditional family is also patriarchal and can hurt women.

Conservative commentators were also drawn to the book. Those who advocate traditional families found in the book a way to legitimate this goal in terms of something that has high status in American discourse: "economic efficiency." This is most pronounced in the legal literature. Polsby (1995) argues that traditional families (defined as employed husband and housewife) should be encouraged by public policies: we should end welfare (which allows women to support children without husbands); end no-fault divorce; end the implicit "marriage penalty" in the tax system that makes taxes higher for a married couple than for the same two people if they were not married; and allow housing discrimination against nontraditional families. Becker's reasoning has stimulated some prowoman legal proposals, such as a defense of alimony for homemakers (Epstein 1995) and the argument that women should get more than half of the property in the event of divorce (Reagan 1992). But the motivation is less to give the homemaker a just compensation for her work than to provide incentives for women to be married, stay-at-home moms by lessening the risk of this marriage-specific investment. All this interest in the family has probably increased the impact of the book.

Becker's *Treatise* has also increased the respectability of research on the family, especially within economics, where it was suspect. There is an element of "Nixon goes to China" here. Just as it took a hawkish, anticommunist president to reopen our relations with China without a deluge of criticism, it may have taken someone at a prestigious economics department known for its neoclassical orthodoxy (Becker has been at the University of Chicago for years) to get the "new home economics" taken seriously. Arguably the real founder of the new home economics was Margaret Reid, who published *Economics of Household Production* in 1934. Yet it is Becker rather than Reid who is usually credited, despite the fact that she, too, was a full professor of economics at the University of Chicago for years.[4] This suggests that the economics profession was only going to take this "feminine" topic seriously if the messenger was a man, and a high-status one at that. Perhaps the fact that he never draws feminist policy implications from his work has helped.

A CRITICAL EVALUATION OF BECKER ON THE FAMILY

We applaud the one sense in which Becker is a good feminist. He recognizes that productive work is done in the household and that it is part of the economy. He sees that childrearing is an investment in children's human capital that increases their adult productivity in both the market and the household. We find these points obvious, but they have typically been ignored by economists.[5]

Beyond this, Becker has done little to illuminate, and much to obfuscate, gender-related dynamics. The problem, simply put, is that he doesn't notice male dominance in the family. In his world those who

4. Reid tried to measure the economic contribution of household production to the national economy. In 1951 she joined the economics department at the University of Chicago, where she served until 1961. She was a colleague of T. W. Schultz, Milton Friedman, Franco Modigliani, and Gary Becker, all of whom won Nobel Prizes in economics. In his 1985 Nobel lecture, Modigliani credited her with contributing to the development of the life-cycle permanent-income hypothesis (which states that consumption is affected not just by present income but by knowledge of one's future income trajectory), usually attributed to Friedman. Strangely, Becker's *Treatise* does not cite her work. (On Reid's contributions, see the special issue of *Feminist Economics* in Fall 1996, especially Yi 1996.)

5. It would be consistent with his view of the household for him to have joined those feminist economists (e.g., Folbre and Wagman 1993) who have argued for including some measure of the value of what is produced in the household to national accounts that measure gross domestic product. As one advocate of this change put it to us, "his silence on the issue has been deafening."

have resources to distribute in the family are altruistic.[6] He has an explicit doctrine of "separate spheres" in which people are selfish in markets and altruistic at home (Becker 1981, 1991). One wonders how he squares this with the prevalence of wife-battering all over the world. We believe that some degree of both altruism and selfishness exists in all social relations, so that he has overestimated the altruism in the family and underestimated group solidarity (a kind of selective altruism) in markets.

It is a common complaint against economists that they ignore power. Economists generally don't think that either party to a market exchange has power over imposing costs (prices) on the other because market competition prevents this. However, when there is no market with a large number of competitors (e.g., monopoly), neoclassical theory admits the relevance of power. Game theory, rather than supply and demand, is seen as the relevant theoretical tool. By this reasoning, if we want to know if husbands have power over their wives (or vice versa), we have to ask whether, after marriage, partners are still facing competitive market forces of the marriage market. It is a bit like asking whether, after taking a job, either an employer or employee is still subject to the competitive pressures of the market.

From the perspective of economic theory, there is a very clear answer: The more either party has made investments that are specific to this relationship, the more both parties are in a situation of "bilateral monopoly." After relationship-specific investments in marriage, there is no other partner as "trained in" to one's particular needs. And of course no other partner would be the coparent of whatever children the couple has had. Thus, there is no comparable partner on the external "marriage market," and so neither spouse is fully competing with other potential spouses their partner could leave them for. This makes both more likely to stay in the marriage, but it also means that power will affect distribution of gains to marriage; the situation is now game-theoretic, even by strict neoclassical reasoning.

The odd thing about Becker's ignoring power in the family is that some features of the family recognized by his own analysis meet this

---

6. Even fairly orthodox critics of his "rotten kid" theorem have shown that the conclusion that the altruist can induce a selfish spouse or child to act as if s/he were altruistic holds only to the extent that the altruist controls resources to be distributed (Ben-Porath 1982; Pollak 1985). We sense that a male benevolent dictator who uses power only for altruistic purposes is the underlying image for his model, despite his claims of gender neutrality.

strict neoclassical litmus test for the applicability of notions of power. Recall that Becker speaks of women's childbearing and -rearing as a marriage-specific investment, whereas a man's "general" investment in earning power yields benefits to him that he keeps regardless of whether he stays in a marriage. Recall also that Becker is not oblivious to the fact that women (and children) usually experience a large drop in income upon divorce. Thus, he had theoretical tools and empirical observations in place that would have allowed him to see how specialization in the family lessens women's bargaining power in marriage. The argument he could have made runs like this:

Couples bargain over how things (money, goods, leisure) will be distributed. Game theory (which assumes selfish actors) sees one's bargaining power affected by "threat points." The better one's alternatives for utility outside the relationship (relative to one's utility in the relationship), and the worse one's partner's alternatives outside, versus inside, the marriage, the harder one can afford to bargain. This is because the better the alternatives outside the relationship (relative to inside), the less one would lose if insisting on a better deal within the marriage drove the other person to divorce. And the worse one's alternatives outside the marriage, the more likely one is to "give in" to avoid a divorce. Even if we believe in some altruism in marriage, to whatever degree spouses are selfish, this model is relevant.

Women are in a vulnerable situation, threat-point-wise, in traditional marriages. Because they have been the ones at home with children, they have less job experience, which lowers what they could earn if they suddenly had to support themselves and their children. Men take their earning power with them in case of a divorce — so the very investments they have made during the marriage also help them if they leave. Because both spouses know that the homemaker has much to lose if the marriage breaks up, she gets less of what she wants when there is a disagreement than she would if she had better alternatives outside the marriage. (This reasoning is developed in England and Kilbourne 1990. Economists proposing models of marital bargaining include Sen 1990; McElroy 1990; McElroy and Horney 1981.)

This view that earning power leads to more power in marriage fits sociological evidence (reviewed in England and Kilbourne 1990); employed wives have more leverage than nonemployed wives in marriage, and relative earnings of spouses affect relative power. The assumption that most people would prefer to do less housework and might use power to this end, is consistent with the finding that relative wages affect household work such that the higher A's earnings relative to B, the less housework A does (Ross 1987; Brines 1994; Presser 1994).[7] Effects of relative earnings on hours of household work could also be predicted by Becker's notion that comparative advantage determines which kind of work (market or household) each spouse will spend the next hour of work in. However, his model does *not* predict that women's lower wage causes them to work more total hours (when household and market work are added together) than men and thus to have less leisure. Yet research often finds that women have less leisure, and that relative wage rate predicts housework *net* of hours of market work. This is better explained by seeing men's higher wage leading to higher marital bargaining power than seeing it as based on productive efficiency.

But not all male power flows from men's higher earnings. The game-theoretic view of marital power suggests that anything that affects how well women can fare outside marriages improves their "threat points" in marriage. How well single or divorced women fare varies importantly across nations, depending on how well child-support obligations are enforced, how generous the social safety net is (much more generous in Europe than in the United States), whether women inherit land (crucial for Third World peasant women), and the frequency of remarriage for women with children.

Social norms or "gender display" also affect marital power. The research on housework cited above, while showing effects of relative wages, also shows that women do much more of the housework than can be explained by wage disparities. The tradition that housework is women's work dies hard. We would have thought that Becker's interest in endogenous tastes — specifically the inertial role of habits — would

---

7. Although we think that existing evidence largely supports the notion that earnings yield power in marriage, we also think more research is needed here. Many of the studies comparing the marital power of homemakers and employed women are quite old and rather inadequate in statistical modeling and controls. In the studies showing that one's earnings relative to one's spouse's decrease one's housework, there is some evidence of nonlinearity. For example, Brines (1994) shows that when women's earnings become virtually the sole support of men, the curve reverses and men's housework declines, as if either the husband or wife (or both) thinks he needs to do less housework to shore up his sense of masculinity. Finally, some evidence from research on wife battering is entirely inconsistent with this view, showing higher rates of husband to wife violence where women have higher (not lower) relative earnings (McCloskey 1996).

have provided an opening for him to look at how gendered displays and patriarchal power become habit-forming for men. But he did not move in this direction.

If Becker had pursued the question of power he would have concluded that the traditional family has disadvantages for women that probably outweigh any gains from efficiency. This kind of an analysis leads many feminists to endorse more egalitarian marriages, with equal participation by men and women in the relationship-specific investments of childrearing and in the development of earnings. Women's relative earnings would be increased by policies that reduce sex segregation in training and jobs, as well as "comparable worth" policies that challenge the lower wages paid to women in occupations that require as many skills, although different ones from those needed for "male jobs" (England 1992).

But, so far, women's greater access to earnings has also increased divorce. Our interpretation is that the male role is so resistant to change that women are more able to leave marriages than to change them in ways that require men to share previously "womanly" responsibilities. To use Albert Hirschman's famous terms, "exit" seems to be dominating "voice" as the alternative to "loyalty" when women gain more marital power. Thus, in many societies, just as women are gaining access to earnings, increases in divorce and nonmarital births are leading women and children to fewer shares in men's earnings. There is no society where child-support enforcement and the social safety net comes close to making up for the male earnings lost when marriages break up or never occur, although the gap is greater in the United States than Europe.

Thus, there is a deep paradox about the results of female empowerment on women's and children's access to money and other resources. Increases in women's relative earnings increase women's marital power, and they help children in two-parent families, if we are to believe the evidence from poorer nations that resources under female (versus male) control are more likely to be spent on children (Blumberg 1989; Dwyer and Bruce 1988). Children who do not live with their fathers also do better the higher their mothers' earnings. However, by increasing divorce, on net, women's higher earnings indirectly reduce women's and children's access to men's earnings. Recent U.S. research shows that living in any alternative to a two-parent family does have adverse effects on a number of socioeconomic outcomes for children

(McLanahan and Sandefur 1994), much of this from loss of income, but some of it from disruptive effects of moving after divorce and from reduced parental supervision. Thus, female empowerment may make things better for children for both the group of children living with their father and the group not doing so — but increasing the number in the second group relative to the number in the first may, in net effect, disadvantage children. Of course, if women's earnings were to increase even more, maybe the net effect wouldn't be negative.

The big policy question is whether to push even harder for female empowerment or return to (or stay with) the specialized traditional family, which is patriarchal. Becker makes few policy recommendations, but is easily read as favoring the latter, and he has certainly not spoken out for female empowerment. Most feminists want women to have the options of not marrying and of having egalitarian marriages, and thus favor continued focuses on women's political power and access to education, property, and earnings. This may lead to fewer durable marriages temporarily, or even permanently, but in the long run people may adjust to egalitarian marriages, and the access of women and children to men's earnings may again increase. Concern about the feminization and juvenilization of poverty stemming from the decreased durability of marriage leads feminists to call for policies to collectivize some of the costs of children, recognizing that children are public goods (i.e., we all benefit when they grow up to be productive workers, good parents, and contributing citizens). Folbre (1994) presents cogent arguments in these directions, with which we agree.

These are the dilemmas Becker could have illuminated had he recognized the role of power in the family. It is now up to others to turn the new home economics in a more interdisciplinary and gender-sensitive direction.

REFERENCES

Becker, Gary. 1957. *The Economics of Discrimination.* Chicago: University of Chicago Press.

——. 1981. "Altruism in the Family and Selfishness in the Market Place." *Economica* 48: 1–15.

——. [1981] 1991. *A Treatise on the Family.* Cambridge: Harvard University Press.

——. 1996. *Accounting for Tastes.* Cambridge: Harvard University Press.

Ben-Porath, Yoram. 1982. "Economics and the Family—A Match or Mismatch? A Review of Becker's *Treatise on the Family.*" *Journal of Economic Literature* 20: 52–64.

Blumberg, Rae Lesser. 1988. "Income under Female versus Male Control: Hypotheses from a Theory of Gender Stratification and Data from the Third World." *Journal of Family Issues* 9 (1): 51–84.

Brines, Julie. 1994. "Economic Dependency, Gender, and the Division of Labor at Home." *American Journal of Sociology* 100: 652–88.

Cahn, Edgar S. 1994. "Reinventing Poverty Law." *Yale Law Journal* 103: 2133–55.

Croley, Steven P., and Jon D. Hanson. 1995. "The Non-Pecuniary Costs of Accidents: Pain and Suffering Damages in Tort Law." *Harvard Law Review* 108 (8): 1785–1917.

Dwyer, Daisy, and Judith Bruce. 1988. *A Home Divided: Women and Income in the Third World.* Stanford: Stanford University Press.

England, Paula. 1992. *Comparable Worth: Theories and Evidence.* Hawthorne, N.Y.: Aldine de Gruyter.

England, Paula, and George Farkas. 1986. *Households, Employment, and Gender: A Social, Economic, and Demographic View.* Hawthorne, N.Y.: Aldine.

England, Paula, and Barbara Kilbourne. 1990. "Markets, Marriages, and Other Mates: The Problem of Power." Pp. 163–89 in *Beyond the Marketplace: Rethinking Economy and Society,* ed. Roger Friedland and A. F. Robertson. Hawthorne, N.Y.: Aldine de Gruyter.

Epstein, Richard A. 1995. "Two Challenges for Feminist Thought." *Harvard Journal of Law and Public Policy* 18(2): 331–47.

Folbre, Nancy. 1994. *Who Pays for the Kids?* New York: Routledge.

Folbre, Nancy, and Barnet Wagman. 1993. "Counting Housework: New Estimates of Real Product in the U.S., 1800–1860." *Journal of Economic History* 53(2): 275–88.

Kornhauser, Majorie E. 1987. "The Rhetoric of the Anti-Progressive Income Tax Movement: A Typical Male Reaction." *Michigan Law Review* 86(1): 465–523.

McCaffery, Edward J. 1994. "The Uneasy Case for Wealth Transfer Taxation." *Yale Law Journal* 104(2): 283–365.

McCloskey, Laura. 1996. "Socioeconomic and Coercive Power within the Family." *Gender & Society* 10: 449–63.

McElroy, Marjorie B. 1990. "The Empirical Content of Nash-Bargained Behavior." *Journal of Human Resources* 25: 559–83.

McElroy, Marjorie B., and Horney, Mary Jean. 1981. "Nash-Bargained

Household Decisions: Toward a Generalization of the Theory of Demand." *International Economic Review* 22 (2): 333–49.

McLanahan, Sara, and Gary Sandefur. 1994. *Growing Up with a Single Parent: What Hurts, What Helps.* Cambridge: Harvard University Press.

National Center for Educational Statistics. 1993. *Digest of Educational Statistics.* Washington, D.C.: U.S. Government Printing Office.

Pollak, Robert A. 1985. "A Transaction Cost Approach to Families and Households." *Journal of Economic Literature* 23 (2): 581–608.

Polsby, Daniel D. 1995. "Ozzie and Harriet Had It Right." *Harvard Journal of Law and Public Policy* 18 (2): 531–36.

Posner, Richard. 1972. *Economic Analysis of Law.* Boston: Little, Brown.

———. 1985. "An Economic Theory of the Criminal Law." *Columbia Law Review* 85 (6): 1193–1231.

Presser, Harriet B. 1994. "Employment Schedules, Gender, and Household Labor." *American Sociological Review* 59 (3): 348–64.

Reagan, Milton C., Jr. 1992. "Divorce Reform and the Legacy of Gender." *Michigan Law Review* 90 (6): 1453–94.

Reid, Margaret. 1934. *Economics of Household Production.* New York: J. Wiley & Sons.

Ross, Catherine E. 1987. "The Division of Labor at Home." *Social Forces* 65: 816–33.

Sen, Amartya. 1990. "Gender and Cooperative Conflicts." In *Persistent Inequalities: Women and World Development,* ed. Irene Tinker. New York: Oxford University Press.

Stigler, George, and Gary Becker. 1977. "De Gustabus Non Est Disputandum." *American Economic Review* 67: 76–90.

Yi, Yun-Ae. 1996. "Margaret G. Reid: Life and Achievements." *Feminist Economics* 2 (3): 17–36.

EMOTION MANAGEMENT AS EMOTIONAL LABOR

Lynn Smith-Lovin

THE MANAGED HEART: COMMERCIALIZATION OF HUMAN FEELING, by Arlie Russell Hochschild. Berkeley: University of California Press, 1983.

Original review, *CS* 13:2 (March 1984), by T. J. Scheff:

It's been said recently that the seventies were the decade of cognition, and the eighties will be the decade of emotion. A book like this one could help bring about such a change.

Of five excellent monographs that ushered in the decade of emotion (Denzin 1984; Heise 1979; Hochschild 1983; Kemper 1978; Scheff 1979), Arlie Hochschild's study of Delta flight attendants had the greatest influence. Its central concepts — feeling rules, emotional labor, surface and deep acting — define the modern sociology of emotion for many nonspecialists and are featured in most sociological research on emotions. After almost fifteen years of scholarly research on emotion, however, one is struck by how pervasive — but how shallow — *The Managed Heart*'s influence has been.

The pervasive impact is due partly to Hochschild's decision to put the theoretical work that underlies the study into four appendixes. She made the book as readable as possible and communicates mainly by example. It's an engaging technique, and accomplishes one of the chief requirements of an influential book: It was read and talked about by a large scholarly community outside of her specialty. Sociologists who could not penetrate the mathematical sophistication of Heise's affect-control theory (1979) or the specialized language of Denzin's phenomenological approach (1984) embraced Hochschild's insight that emotions were governed by feeling rules and controlled through culturally guided management. *The Managed Heart* permanently changed the way that its readers viewed its phenomenon of interest. Before, we viewed the smiling faces of service workers as a pleasant *lagniappe* of an economic transaction; after, we see them as an element of the worker's job. Furthermore, we see a parallel between the type of effort required to present that public face and the emotion management required of people in low-power positions everywhere in nonwork life.

To have a deep, restructuring impact on the discipline, however, a work must have three other characteristics. First, it must introduce a theoretical framework that allows us to view the social environment in a new, fruitful way. The framework must provide both insight and a source of new research questions. Second, it must provide a blueprint for developing researchable problems — a strategy for generating evidence that is relevant to the theoretical questions. Third, the ideas and methods must fall on fertile ground. That is, the intellectual climate must be ready to move into the domain that is opened by the work.

Hochschild was lucky on the third score (although one could argue that she put a great deal of work into creating her own good fortune). Sociology, psychology, anthropology, and the related social science disciplines all began a major swing away from the cognitive emphasis of the '60s and '70s into a greater concern with affect and emotion about the time that *Managed Heart* came out. The new developments in the sociology of emotion first reached an open scholarly forum in 1975 (although the actual work was begun much earlier and probably has its roots in the intellectual climate of the 1960s). Hochschild (1975) published her first treatment of feeling rules in an edited collection of feminist theory; Collins (1975) discussed the ritual production of emotion in his book *Conflict Sociology;* and Scheff organized the first session on the sociology of emotion at the 1975 American Sociological Association meetings in San Francisco. The ASA Section on the Sociology of Emotions was formed in the late '70s to institutionalize the intellectual trend.

The questionable part of *Managed Heart*'s legacy comes from the first and second criteria — the fit between the theoretical problems that it posed, the data generated to deal with them, and the subsequent research legacy generated by the scholarly community. Hochschild does not spend much time in her main text on definitional or theoretical issues. She defines emotion as "a sense, like the sense of hearing or sight" (Hochschild 1983, 17). Such statements work well for giving the casual reader a gut-level feel for how she views the concept. But the scholarly community needs a bit more. In the first two appendices (especially 218–29), she clarifies her theoretical position in the context of classic literatures from Darwin to Goffman to Freud. It is clear that Hochschild has a strong sense of emotion as a basic response to events that occur in the social environment, and of their function to signal the implications of those events for the self experiencing the emotion. She emphasizes cultural resources and constraints that govern the interpretation of emotion, but it's clear that for her there is something visceral and unprocessed *there* to interpret.

Many of the people she has influenced have missed this important point. Hochschild often is viewed as the leader of the social constructionist school in the sociology of emotions, and *Managed Heart* as its classic statement. The main text is impressionistic enough to allow for many interpretations (and its emphasis on management puts culture in the central role), but the appendixes make clear that Hochschild takes a more mixed, inclusive approach. She is against the organismic view only to the extent that it would have totally "wired in" emotions, without room for social interpretation (a position so extreme that hardly anyone would embrace it these days). She finds the purely social, situational view of Goffman useful for analyzing display, but thinks that he has lost the self that is experiencing the performance. Her discussion of the "signaling function" of emotion, while it comes from Freud, is highly compatible with structural symbolic interactionist views (e.g., Heise 1979) and Kemper's (1978) social interactional theory. Hochschild, like Heise and Kemper, recognized that social events give rise to spontaneous emotion in a way that signals their import for the individual; only then does she proceed to detail how these spontaneous emotions can be transformed through emotion management.

Perhaps what led scholars to pick up on the cultural, constructionist aspects of *Managed Heart,* but to ignore its more basic substrate of emotion experienced as a sense or signal, is the fact that Hochschild does not develop any analytic framework for how events (and how the person interprets them) give rise to emotions. In the second appendix, she produces charts that relate emotion names to some dimensions of social interaction — what I want/like, what I have/see I have, what I approve, the causal agent of the event, and the relation of the self to the causal agent. This theoretical structure is strangely akin to Kemper's (1978) framework, where emotions are determined by gaining or losing status and power. Since Hochschild's statements about the sources of emotions are buried in the appendixes, her readers have concentrated on the management of emotions and neglected the emotions themselves. Kemper has sometimes been reviled as a deterministic organismic positivist, while Hochschild is seen as a hard-core constructionist; but if one reads Hochschild's appendixes as well as the main text, it is clear that their positions are much closer than this.

Hochschild's methods in *The Managed Heart* reinforced the (sometimes questionable) images that her readers formed of her ideas. In the first section of the book, "Private Lives," she lets people tell their own stories. Her data are composed of undergraduates' accounts of times that they thought their emotions were problematic and how they tried to manage them. In the second, "Public Lives," her better-known participant observation study of Delta flight attendants and their training in emotion management techniques illustrates how emotion management can be transformed into paid labor. She attended classes for the flight attendants, talked with participants at several levels, and generally immersed herself in the lives of her subjects. A very sketchy set of conversations with bill collectors attempted to illustrate that emotion management is not always in the direction of suppressing negative emotion; although flight attendants have to suppress anger, the bill collectors have to suppress sympathy. Clearly, these data are better equipped to illustrate aspects of the manipulation of cultural symbols surrounding emotion than to ascertain the source of basic emotional experience (i.e., what is aroused and needs to be managed). The labeling of Hochschild as a social constructionist concerned mostly with culture may have more to do with her evidence than with her theory or her research questions.

In a sense, *Managed Heart* was a profoundly exploratory book. It searches through rich, vivid accounts of people's emotional lives for hints about how those lives are shaped by their social environment. Hochschild generates many interesting research questions from these accounts and gives a lively commentary on how she thinks these things work. What the book does not provide is much systematic evidence for those ideas. This may sound like a harsh statement, but systematic evidence is not usually an exploratory, generative study's strong suit; nor should it be. The more serious problem, in my view, is that

Hochschild doesn't give us much sense of *how* to answer these questions she has raised.

Let's take a few examples. List the major points that Hochschild would like to make in the book:

1. People actively manage emotions by controlling their display (surface acting) and by manipulating their thoughts and experiences (deep acting) to make their feelings correspond to norms (feeling rules).

2. Some occupations require emotion management as a condition of employment (emotional labor).

3. Emotional labor jobs are more common in service work, in middle-class work, and in women's work.

4. Emotion management as labor alienates workers from their true feelings by destroying the emotions' signal value about the self's relationship to the social environment. (A value judgment that runs strongly through the book is that this deleterious effect is more vile when it is created for profit by a capitalist employer than when created by interpersonal power dynamics in marriage or other relationships.)

5. Middle-class parents socialize their children for emotion management more than working-class parents do, to prepare them for emotional labor jobs.

6. Women are socialized for (and do more) emotion management because of their emotional labor jobs. When men have emotional labor jobs, their higher status buffers them from some of its effects.

Although Hochschild's work is often cited as establishing all of these propositions, in fact she only generates a substantial show of evidence for the first and second. She uses the loose content analysis of the undergraduates' open-ended responses and her observations of the Delta flight attendants to establish that something like emotion management does occur, and that it is an aspect of some (at least two) jobs.

Many researchers, intrigued by Hochschild's ideas, have tried to follow in her path to study these propositions. For example, researchers have studied the occupational socialization and emotion management among medical students (Smith and Kleinman 1989), nurses (Smith 1988), and supermarket checkers (Tolich 1988). These participant observation studies of single occupations can only repeat the same insight that Hochschild originally had (which is much less striking the second or third time around) — the fact that people do emotion management for work. Many a graduate student has used a single-group observational study to argue that he or she is generating evidence on one of the other propositions; some faculty mentors may let them get away with it, but few journal reviewers will.

To move beyond the mere existence of emotion management and emotional labor to study social structural sources of their variation (propositions 3, 5, and 6) and to study the psychological effects of this labor (proposition 4) would require a very different type of research. Hochschild hints at this in her third and fourth appendixes: In the third, she informally chooses occupations that she thinks will be high on emotional labor and analyzes their sex composition; in the fourth, she lists the socialization practices in the middle or working class that she thinks would lead to different emotion management styles in those two populations. To generate evidence about propositions 3, 5, and 6, we need comparative studies that cover larger parts of the occupational and class structure — something that's difficult to do with participant observation methods. Even the accumulation of evidence across multiple studies is unlikely, if people choose to study only groups that are presumed to have extensive emotional labor (as opposed to those who do not). Studying one cell of a table can tell you only so much.

It may be even harder to generate evidence about Proposition 4. In *Managed Heart,* we read about conversations with a therapist who has treated flight attendants for sexual problems; the implication is that the blunting of the attendants' emotional signal function through their emotional labor has created these problems. That's quite a leap. How do we know that women in occupations requiring less emotion work don't have the same rate of these sexual problems? To study whether emotional labor had serious psychological effects would demand not only variation in the independent variable (the amount of emotion labor required in one's job), but also careful measurement of the dependent variable. It would be a daunting task to assess this type of emotional distress in a wider population, although specialists in mental health might show us the way.

The reason that I characterize *Managed Heart*'s influence as pervasive but shallow is that it has alerted us to some potentially important concepts, given us some interesting propositions, but not shown us the way to generate meaningful evidence about them. As a result, we use Hochschild's words a great deal and try to mimic her vivid, compelling descriptions. But we haven't advanced beyond her initial, exploratory insight — emotional labor exists — to find out more about how it is related to social structure. These questions were the sociological core of her book, what made it a classic in the *sociology* of emotion. The work would have had a deeper influence if it had showed us a path to travel to generate a cumulative corpus of research on these problems. As it is, the ideas seem to be absorbed as catchwords in a literature that uses them frequently, but usually continues doing research that would have been done in a similar way without *Managed Heart*'s publication. The sociology of emotion has influenced sociological social psychology, the study of culture, and the study of mental health, but has done so mainly through its influence on how they talk about their problems. It has generated little evidence about new phenomena. It appears that *Managed Heart* will be absorbed into the literature, rather than transforming it.

REFERENCES

Collins, Randall. 1975. *Conflict Sociology: Toward an Explanatory Science.* New York: Academic Press.

Denzin, Norman K. 1984. *On Understanding Emotion.* San Francisco: Jossey-Bass.

Heise, David R. 1979. *Understanding Events.* New York: Cambridge University Press.

Hochschild, Arlie R. 1975. "The Sociology of Feeling and Emotion: Selected Possibilities." In *Another Voice: Feminist Perspectives on Social Life and Social Science,* ed. M. Millman and R. M. Kanter. New York: Anchor.

———. 1983. *The Managed Heart: Commercialization of Human Feeling.* Berkeley: University of California Press.

Kemper, Theodore D. 1978. *A Social Interactional Theory of Emotions.* New York: Wiley.

Scheff, Thomas J. 1979. *Catharsis in Healing, Ritual, and Drama.* Berkeley: University of California Press.

Smith, Pam. 1988. "The Emotional Labor of Nursing." *Nursing Times* 84: 50–51.

Smith, Allen C., III, and Sherryl Kleinman. 1989. "Managing Emotions in Medical School: Students' Contacts with the Living and Dead." *Social Psychology Quarterly* 5 (1): 56–69.

Tolich, Martin. 1988. "Doing Emotion Work: The Similarities and Differences between Manual Supermarket Checkers and Hochschild's Airline Flight Attendants." Paper presented at the Pacific Sociological Association, Las Vegas, Nevada.

MODELS OF INFLUENCE

David B. Grusky and Kim A. Weeden

OPPORTUNITY AND CHANGE, by David L. Featherman and
Robert M. Hauser. New York: Academic Press, 1978.

Original reviews, *CS* 9:1 (January 1980), by Charles Mueller,
Joan Huber, Keith Hope, and Herbert Gintis. From the reviews
of Joan Huber and Keith Hope:

Featherman and Hauser have provided a valuable replication of
a major inquiry. By choosing to revive the analysis of mobility tables they have posed in acute form the problem of the relation
between mobility and status-attainment research (Hope, 11).
    The book is long and, like the Bible, it contains statements
that will please readers of a plethora of persuasions. . . . The
careful and detailed description of the findings makes summarizing a real chore—every empirical nugget is honed and po-
lished in a dazzling display of methodological virtuosity
(Huber, 5).

Like many disciplines, sociology often asks that its scholars complete
analytic tasks for which they have no formal training, thus obliging
them either to proceed as novices or, more rarely, to crash-train in the
required skills. The present exercise is a case in point; that is, insofar as
our charge is to characterize the consequences of a single event (i.e.,
a book publication), one might reasonably conclude that historical
rather than sociological methods are most appropriate. We accordingly lead off our review by attempting a thought experiment of the
sort favored by some historians. In a series of follow-up analyses, we
also devise and evaluate formal models of influence wielding, with our
principal objective being to distinguish the true effects of *Opportunity*

    The research reported herein was supported by the Stanford University Dean's Research
Fund. We are grateful to Dan Clawson, David Featherman, and Robert Hauser for helpful
comments and advice.

and Change (hereafter, *O&C*) from those of the larger academic, social, and political context in which *O&C* is embedded. The latter exercise might be regarded as sociological in spirit, since it formalizes the causal forces at work and interprets the influence of *O&C* through the lens of these forces.[1]

We begin, then, by asking how the field of stratification would have evolved in the absence of *O&C*. The rules of play for such counterfactual exercises are poorly defined; most notably, the task of assessing influence is complicated when functional equivalents are allowed or presumed to emerge, since the reviewer is then obliged to speculate about when (or whether) these equivalents would appear and how the discipline would likely receive them. We clearly have no choice but to ignore all such complexities and simply assume that excising *O&C* would not unleash reactive or compensating forces in the discipline (e.g., the emergence of equivalents). If the foregoing assumption is accepted, the following seven pathways of influence suggest themselves:

1. The most obvious "*O&C* effect" is of course the revitalization of mobility analysis. After years of neglect, the publication of *O&C* and related pieces (e.g., Hauser 1978) ushered in a new era of tabular mobility research, much as *The American Occupational Structure* (Blau and Duncan 1967; 1978; hereafter, *AOS*) introduced and popularized status attainment research.

2. This development had the further effect of legitimating categorical representations of the class structure rather than the vertical socioeconomic scales favored in *AOS*. If "class models" were thereby reinvigorated, it should also be stressed that *O&C* relied on conventional Census Bureau categories and therefore had a largely conservative influence on the development of class models.

3. In their analyses of racial stratification, Featherman and Hauser followed in large part the analytic example set by Blau and Duncan, but they also advanced and elaborated this framework by distinguishing Hispanics explicitly and thus moving beyond simplistic black-white dichotomies (see ch. 8). The research of Marta Tienda, Matt Snipp, and many others can be seen as building on this example.[2]

---

1. We have perforce glossed over current controversies and debates regarding the usefulness of sociological methods in understanding single cases or events (see, e.g., Lieberson 1998; Ragin 1998).

2. If *O&C* were somehow excised from the academic landscape, we suspect that an equivalent "pioneer" analysis of Hispanics would probably have emerged in its place, given

4. The O&C project provided an early and influential prototype that assisted scholars in replicating AOS elsewhere. In many respects, O&C was a more important template for replication than AOS, since most of the replicate studies in other countries were planned and implemented concurrently with O&C.

5. The log-linear models that O&C popularized were subsequently applied to diverse research areas (e.g., assortive mating, educational mobility, sex segregation, response consistency, geographic mobility). The influence of O&C was, in this regard, twofold; namely, it not only contributed to the diffusion of log-linear models in general, but it also spawned a small industry of spinoff research applying levels models in particular.

6. The main conceptual contribution of O&C was the development of an elaborated theory of postindustrial change (esp. ch. 5). The resulting framework, emphasizing as it does institutional sources of change, went well beyond prior work (e.g., AOS) that treated "universalizing forces" in abstract form without specifying the social institutions through which such forces might be realized. This institutional approach provided the conceptual underpinnings for much subsequent work on stratification trends.

7. The most important influence of O&C may nonetheless be stylistic rather than substantive. Indeed, while some skeptics question whether O&C made any conceptual contributions at all (e.g., Gintis 1980; Huber 1980), it is rather more difficult to dispute that O&C provided an influential model of disciplined and systematic research that served, if only stylistically, as the prime exemplar of "Wisconsin research" for generations of scholars. The main features of this approach are (a) a willingness to ransack data for whatever they may reveal (Huber 1980); (b) an insistence that all interpretation be closely substantiated by analysis; and (c) a commitment to attend to operational details that, while seemingly minor, have the (presumed) potential to materially affect results and conclusions.

In the present context, such stylistic influences have motivated us to supplement our own commentary with quantitative evidence, albeit of an indirect sort. We have proceeded by searching the *Social Science Citation Index* for articles that cited O&C (between 1979 and 1996)

---

that ongoing demographic and political changes rendered simple black-white classification systems increasingly untenable.

and then coding the citations in these articles by year, subject, and context.[3] The resulting citation counts suggest that *O&C* disproportionately influenced research on mobility, attainment, and race (see Figure 1). Moreover, when compared to such classics as *The Declining Significance of Race* (Wilson 1978; 1980) and *States and Social Revolutions* (Skocpol 1979), we find that *O&C* very much holds its own with respect to total citation activity (see Figure 2).[4] The influence of *O&C* falls short, however, of the more spectacular standard set by *AOS*, not merely in terms of total citation activity but also with respect to the shape of the trend line and the implied "staying power" of *O&C*. As revealed in Figure 2, the take-off period for *AOS* citations stretched over ten years, whereas that for *O&C* lasted at best four years. By contrast, the trend lines for Wilson (1978; 1980) and Skocpol (1979) are slightly less steep during the first four years (relative to the *O&C* trend line), but the subsequent tailing-off in citation activity is also less pronounced.

What, then, limited the influence of *O&C* and produced the declining citation activity in Figure 2? Although many competing accounts might be adduced, we are persuaded by such standbys as (a) the discipline values replication less than "breaking new ground" (Mueller 1980, 4); (b) the social indicators movement, which was the principal impetus behind *O&C*, had fallen into academic and political disfavor by the early 1980s; (c) the status attainment tradition had likewise outlived the usual half-life of academic movements and was vulnerable to backlash and revisionism; (d) the all-male analyses of *O&C* quickly dated the study and precluded it from contributing to the burgeoning field of gender stratification;[5] (e) the period covered by *O&C* (i.e., 1962–1973) predated the rise of the black underclass and hence lent itself to a more optimistic assessment of African American progress than was justifiable or fashionable in the post-*O&C* period; and (f) the

3. We will provide on request a more detailed discussion of the data collection and coding procedures.

4. The counts in Figure 1 pertain to the total number of citations, whereas those in Figure 2 pertain to the number of articles in which these citations appear. Although *O&C* was cited 969 times between 1979 and 1996, some of these citations appeared in the same article; and, consequently, there are only 479 articles in which citations to *O&C* can be found. The corresponding counts for Wilson (1978; 1980), Skocpol (1979), and Blau and Duncan (1967; 1978) are 555, 695, and 1,430 respectively.

5. Although Featherman and Hauser opted for an all-male sample (thereby following the lead of *AOS*), women did nonetheless enter the analysis as wives of the sampled men.

Figure 1: Citation Counts by Subject

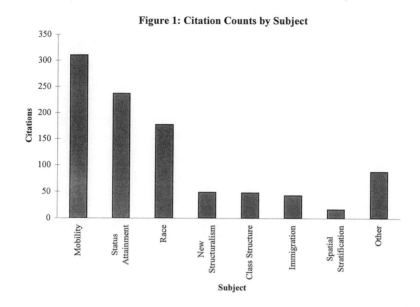

Figure 2: Trends in Citation Activity

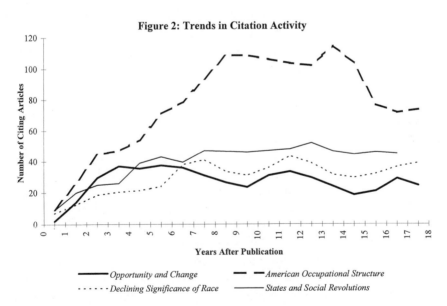

NOTE: The data were smoothed with a 2-year moving average.

Figure 3: Full Model of Influence

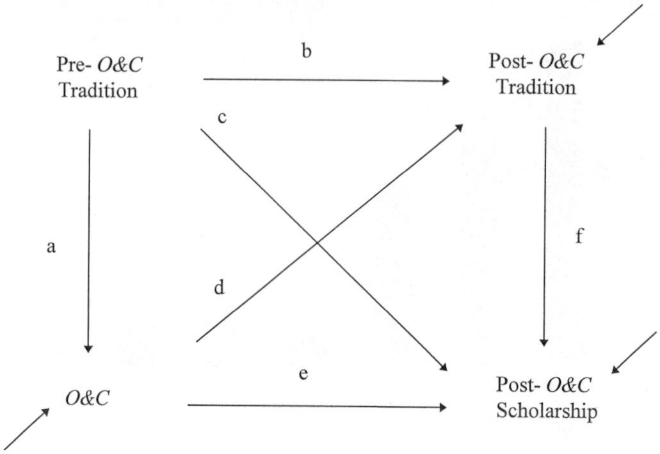

prose in *O&C* is relentlessly descriptive and lacking, therefore, in sweeping generalizations of the sort that generate much controversy and influence. The latter consideration is arguably the most important one. Indeed, the long-standing recipe for academic fame and influence involves combining sweeping claims and incendiary statements with more careful qualifiers, thereby generating the requisite controversy while also protecting the authors from charges of irresponsibility. The prose in *O&C*, which is consistently and irritatingly careful, violates this fail-proof formula.

The foregoing discussion of *O&C*, standard though it may be, is nonetheless unsatisfying, and not merely because the evidence on which it rests falls far short of the Wisconsin standard. It is also troubling that we have not distinguished the influence of *O&C* from that of the larger scholarly traditions (i.e., "paradigms") that *O&C* both reflected and created. There is surely good reason to believe that scholarly production is reactive not merely to individual classics but also to more encompassing traditions and conventions (Kuhn 1962). The model of Figure 3 allows us to frame a series of questions that address this potentially complex relationship between *O&C* and its academic context:

1. To what extent was *O&C* innovative and agenda-setting rather than reflective of a pre-existing tradition? Although Featherman and Hauser obviously stood on the "shoulders of giants," their work also

undermined and supplanted the *AOS* paradigm on many fronts. This conclusion implies that the left-hand residual in Figure 3 may well be large.

2. If *O&C* is partly derivative (as might be expected of a replicate study), was subsequent scholarship more strongly influenced by this pre-existing tradition than by *O&C* itself? The task of reviewing *O&C*, when taken seriously, obliges us to distinguish its true effects (i.e., paths d and e) from the continuing influence of the larger tradition from which it flowed (i.e., paths b and c).

3. Was the accumulation of Featherman-Hauser research so substantial by the late 1970s that *O&C* was effectively crowded out by its sister publications? The "pre-*O&C* tradition" of Figure 3 includes, of course, a large body of earlier Featherman-Hauser scholarship, much of which was quite influential and hence capable of squeezing *O&C* out of its natural citation niche.

4. Did *O&C* exert its influence indirectly through the creation of a new post-*O&C* scholarly tradition (see paths d and f)? As Kuhn (1962) noted long ago, most authors no doubt wish to establish a new paradigm, but not necessarily one that is fast moving and hence quickly overshadows their own work. There is clearly great variability in the rate at which sociological paradigms fill out and change; indeed, some subfields never progress much beyond their canonical works, whereas others generate more transitory classics that are rapidly supplanted by the very work they inspire.

It is easier to pose these questions than to answer them. Once again, the only quantitative evidence at our disposal is *O&C* citation data, but now we are interested in the character and context of these citations rather than simply the raw counts themselves. We have thus distinguished standard solitary citations of *O&C* from those that are targeted, illustrative, or seriatim (see Figure 4 for definitions).[6] In the following discussion, we assume that solitary or targeted citations indicate the singular influence of a canon, whereas seriatim or illustrative citations give priority to the larger undergirding tradition (see Goodwin 1998 for related comments). We are well aware that such interpretations are eminently contestable. Indeed, our discussion of *O&C* effects will also rely heavily on our qualitative understanding of the

---

6. The unit of analysis in Figure 4 is the citation itself (rather than the article in which the citation appeared).

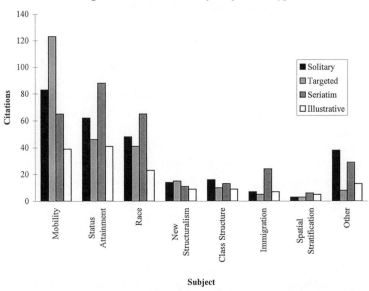

Figure 4: Citation Counts by Subject and Type

NOTE: We define a solitary reference as a standard citation of a single source (Featherman and Hauser 1978), a targeted reference as a citation including a specific page, range of pages, or chapter in *O&C* (Featherman and Hauser 1978, 147-50), a seriatim reference as a standard citation of multiple sources (Blau and Duncan 1967; Featherman and Hauser 1978; Hout 1988), and an illustrative reference as a citation preceded by "e.g." (e.g., Featherman and Hauser 1978).

field, if only because citation practices are obviously more complex than the preceding typology allows.[7]

The available evidence, such as it is, suggests that the direct *O&C* effect (i.e., path e) is strongest within the mobility subfield. The path-breaking work of Goodman (e.g., 1972) laid the foundation for all log-linear models of mobility, yet the role of *O&C* in popularizing and diffusing such models appears to be substantial. Moreover, the levels model introduced in *O&C* clearly broke from prior approaches in creative ways (i.e., path a is weak), and the resulting analytic framework assumed a near-hegemonic hold on the field, one that was repeatedly challenged in the 1980s (e.g., Hope 1981; MacDonald 1981; Jones 1985; Kim 1987) but never truly broken. The large number of

7. We suspect that citation practices are affected by such extraneous factors as "house-specific" editorial policies and the purely idiosyncratic styles of authors, reviewers, and copy editors.

solitary and targeted references to $O\&C$ (see Figure 4) testifies to this strong direct effect on the mobility literature. At the same time, the *Citation Index* reveals heavy citation activity for various spinoff articles published before 1978, thus suggesting that $O\&C$ was by no means the exclusive inspiration for early converts to log-linear analysis.[8] Although $O\&C$ was the flagship of the larger Featherman-Hauser project, it faced stiff competition from precursor publications that assumed a prominent position in the pre-$O\&C$ literature and were not easily supplanted thereafter.

The log-linear modeling that $O\&C$ popularized was of course elaborated and extended by an active post-$O\&C$ research literature. As noted by Yamaguchi (1995), the resulting log-linear tradition quickly took on a life of its own, so much so that fifteen years later Hauser (personal communication) bemoaned the endless analysis and reanalysis of mobility tables and the consequent inattention of scholars to the mediating processes through which reproduction and mobility occur. The sibling analyses that Hauser (1987) subsequently published can be viewed in this context as a partly successful effort to reintroduce the discipline to alternative modes of analysis. We therefore suspect that the direct effects of $O\&C$ are gradually weakening; indeed, insofar as Featherman and Hauser have lost control over the research literature they spawned, the effects of $O\&C$ may be increasingly mediated through a post-$O\&C$ tradition.

The contribution of $O\&C$ to the status attainment literature was less fundamental. As shown in Figure 5, a trimmed three-variable model probably suffices here, since the publication of $O\&C$ did not in this case substantially alter research practice and convention. The model in Figure 5 implies that $O\&C$ borrowed heavily from a pre-existing research tradition, that a new $O\&C$-inspired paradigm failed to emerge, and that any stylistic similarities between $O\&C$ and contemporary research are spurious.[9] The citation counts of Figure 4 reveal that, as predicted, seriatim and illustrative references to $O\&C$ occur disproportionately relative to what prevails in the mobility do-

---

8. The citation counts for such articles as Hauser (1978), Hauser et al. (1975), and Featherman, Jones, and Hauser (1975) are 102, 79, and 120 respectively.

9. The model of Figure 5 represents our argument in admittedly extreme terms. While $O\&C$ did not break new ground in the modeling of attainment processes, it did introduce an elaborated version of the "industrialism thesis" (Kerr et al. 1960) that proved to be quite influential.

Figure 5: Trimmed Model of Influence

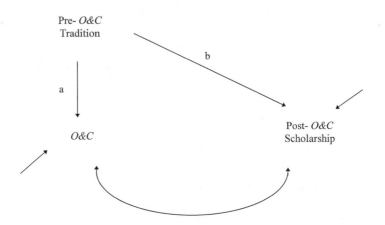

main. This evidence suggests that attainment scholars treated *O&C* as exemplary of a more encompassing research tradition. If the citation count is accordingly less impressive, it is undoubtedly because *O&C* did not introduce attainment scholars to new models, methods, or concepts, all of which have the potential to generate more citation activity than the mere presentation of empirical results (which, by contrast, can quickly become dated). As is well known, Featherman and Hauser made important contributions to the development of path analysis (e.g., Bielby, Hauser, and Featherman 1977), yet these methodological advances were not featured in *O&C* itself.

As an instructive contrast, we next consider the contribution of *O&C* to the sociological study of minority employment, attainment, and mobility. The influence of *O&C* was complicated here by the emergence of a new post-*O&C* paradigm that emphasized the rise of a minority underclass and was otherwise less upbeat in tone than *O&C*. To some extent, this post-*O&C* paradigm gained force because of a real deterioration in African American life chances (in some domains), but as always the usual forces of academic revisionism were also involved, with the work of Wilson (1978; 1980) serving as the principal catalyst underlying the reaction. The results reported in *O&C* were, in this sense, relegated to the academic sidelines, since they neither mobilized a large body of follow-up studies nor inspired a countervailing revisionist movement. The preceding argument again finds support in Figure 4; that is, when scholars of race and ethnicity did cite O&C, they opted disproportionately for seriatim citations and hence minimized the distinctiveness of O&C (see Figure 4). It follows that paths d and e in Figure 3 are both likely weak.

We could readily elaborate similar models for other research domains, but we have undoubtedly tried the patience of our readers. The skeptic might indeed suggest that the foregoing is all so much useless formalism. In our defense, such formalism at least has the merit of obligating reviewers to attend to competing accounts, whereas past practice simply privileges "great book" formulations without any serious consideration of more sociological alternatives. This practice arises, in part, because of the personal benefits accruing to those who are generous in attributing influence, yet it hardly helps matters that the field offers so little in the way of alternative models of influence and influence wielding. In the present case, our models imply that the net effect of O&C was moderately strong within the race and attainment domains, but far stronger among scholars whose passion lies in analyzing mobility tables. It is impressive for a replicate study to rise above the natural constraints of the form and become so influential in a core domain of quantitative sociology.

REFERENCES

Bielby, William T., Robert M. Hauser, and David L. Featherman. 1977. "Response Errors of Black and Nonblack Males in Models of the Intergenerational Transmission of Socioeconomic Status." *American Journal of Sociology* 82: 1242–88.

Blau, Peter M., and Otis D. Duncan. 1967. *The American Occupational Structure.* New York: Wiley.

———. 1978. *The American Occupational Structure.* 2d ed. New York: Free Press.

Featherman, David L., and Robert M. Hauser. 1978. *Opportunity and Change.* New York: Academic Press.

Featherman, David L., F. Lancaster Jones, and Robert M. Hauser. 1975. "Assumptions of Social Mobility Research in the United States: The Case of Occupational Status." *Social Science Research* 4: 329–60.

Gintis, Herbert. 1980. "The American Occupational Structure Eleven Years Later." *Contemporary Sociology* 9: 12–16.

Goodman, Leo A. 1972. "Some Multiplicative Models for the Analysis of

Cross-Classified Data." Pp. 649–96 in *Proceedings of the Sixth Berkeley Symposium on Mathematical Statistics and Probability.* Berkeley: University of California Press.

Goodwin, Jeff. 1998. "How to Become a Dominant American Social Scientist: The Case of Theda Skocpol." Pp. 31–38 herein. First published in *Contemporary Sociology* 25 (1996): 293–95.

Hauser, Robert M. 1978. "A Structural Model of the Mobility Table." *Social Forces* 56: 919–53.

———. 1987. "A Note on Two Models of Sibling Resemblance." *American Journal of Sociology* 93: 1401–23.

Hauser, Robert M., Peter J. Dickinson, Harry P. Travis, and John M. Koffel. 1975. "Temporal Change in Occupational Mobility: Evidence for Men in the United States." *American Sociological Review* 40: 279–97.

Hout, Michael. 1988. "More Universalism, Less Structural Mobility: The American Occupational Structure in the 1980s." *American Journal of Sociology* 93: 1358–1400.

Hope, Keith. 1981. "The New Mobility Ratio." *Social Forces* 60: 544–71.

Huber, Joan. 1980. "Ransacking Mobility Tables." *Contemporary Sociology* 9: 5–8.

Jones, Frank L. 1985. "New and (Very) Old Mobility Ratios: Is There Life after Benini?" *Social Forces* 63: 838–50.

Kerr, Clark, John T. Dunlop, Frederick H. Harbison, and Charles A. Myers. 1960. *Industrialism and Industrial Man.* Cambridge: Harvard University Press.

Kim, Jae-On. 1987. "Social Mobility, Status Inheritance, and Structural Constraints: Conceptual and Methodological Considerations." *Social Forces* 65: 783–805.

Kuhn, Thomas S. 1962. *The Structure of Scientific Revolutions.* Chicago: University of Chicago Press.

Lieberson, Stanley. 1998. "Causal Analysis and Comparative Research: What Can We Learn from Studies Based on a Small Number of Cases?" Pp. 129–45 in *Rational Choice Theory and Large-Scale Data Analysis,* ed. Hans-Peter Blossfeld and Gerald Prein. Boulder: Westview Press.

MacDonald, K. I. 1981. "On the Formulation of a Structural Model of the Mobility Table." *Social Forces* 60: 557–71.

Mueller, Charles W. 1980. "Introduction to Review Symposium on *Opportunity and Change.*" *Contemporary Sociology* 9:4.

Ragin, Charles C. 1998. "Case-Oriented Research and the Study of Social Action." Pp. 158–68 in *Rational Choice Theory and Large-Scale*

Data Analysis, ed. Hans-Peter Blossfeld and Gerald Prein. Boulder: Westview Press.

Skocpol, Theda. 1979. *States and Social Revolutions.* Cambridge: Cambridge University Press.

Wilson, William J. 1978. *The Declining Significance of Race.* Chicago: University of Chicago Press.

———. 1980. *The Declining Significance of Race.* 2d ed. Chicago: University of Chicago Press.

Yamaguchi, Kazuo. 1995. "Editor's Introduction to the Special Issue on Log-Linear and Log-Multiplicative Models." *Sociological Methods and Research* 24: 3–6.

A CLASSIC OF ITS TIME

Michael Burawoy

LABOR AND MONOPOLY CAPITAL: THE DEGRADATION OF
WORK IN THE TWENTIETH CENTURY, by Harry Braverman.
Foreword by Paul M. Sweezy. New York: Monthly Review Press,
[1974] 1976.

Original reviews, *CS* 5:6 (November 1976), by Douglas Dowd
and by Dale Tomich. From Dale Tomich's review:

Braverman's decision not to deal with the subjective side of the
transformation of work and the reconstitution of the working
class is particularly lamentable. . . . Despite these limitations,
however, the great virtue of Braverman's book is that he puts
labor as a living activity at the center of his analysis. . . . *Labor
and Monopoly Capital* will remain an essential starting point for
new research for some time to come.

There are two types of classics: those we remember and those we
forget. Those to which we return again and again stand out as sources
of continuing inspiration. They are sufficiently profound to endure and
sufficiently multivalent and multilayered to sustain new interpretations. Such works are rare. More usual are classics whose impact is
singular and therefore more ephemeral. They transform a field but are
then absorbed and transcended. Harry Braverman's *Labor and Monopoly Capital* is of the latter kind. It brought together and recon-
figured both stratification theory and industrial sociology, reverber-
ating into political sociology. But it is no mecca to which we make
continual pilgrimage. Its contributions have become conventional wisdom, the field has moved on.

Its charm and appeal lay in its simplicity: Braverman argued that
the history of capitalism was marked by the progressive degradation

Thanks to Dan Clawson for his helpful suggestions.

of work, in which management expropriated control from workers through deepening the division of labor, particularly the division between mental and manual labor, what has come to be known as "the deskilling hypothesis." How could such a simple, even unoriginal thesis transform the field of sociology? As is always the case, timing is of the essence. *Labor and Monopoly Capital* appeared in 1974 when core areas of sociology, battered by the storms of the 1960s, were atrophying and Marxism was resurgent.

Industrial sociology and stratification theory had entered a double impasse: a *subjectivism* that focused exclusively on responses to given structures and an *ahistoricism* that took those structures as natural and unchanging. Marxism restored structure and history in new theories of development and of the state, and, with Braverman, the renaissance turned to the core of Marx's own work — the labor process and class structure.

Associated with Baran and Sweezy and the group around *Monthly Review,* Braverman used his own experience as a skilled metal-worker as a lens to interpret the transformation of the American class structure. He was not an academic and would have written the book irrespective of the resurgence of Marxism, but it was the latter that gave it such a positive reception. Already beleaguered by their association with "structural functionalism," stratification research and the sociology of work were particularly ripe for new beginnings.

The field of stratification emerged in the 1950s from interest in the value consensus underlying occupational hierarchies. Sociologists demonstrated a remarkable convergence in the way people of all advanced capitalist nations ranked the prestige of occupations, and this became the basis of a *transhistorical* scale of socioeconomic status. Stratification research focused on the inter- and intragenerational transmission of occupational status. Mobility studies became the rage, taking as given the existing structure of empty places through which people moved. Here lay the *subjectivist bias* — mobility as *adaptation* to a fixed, agreed-upon order.

Braverman stood stratification theory on its head by focusing exclusively on the supposedly pregiven order, that is, on the occupational structure itself. Capital accumulation leads to deskilling, polarizing mental and manual labor in all spheres of work, white collar as well as blue collar. *A dynamic hierarchy based on work replaced a fixed hierarchy based on status.* Individuals are no longer conceived of as mobile atoms, moving through a socioeconomic space, but are stripped of agency to become "effects" of the positions they hold.

Braverman laid the basis for the resurgence of objectivist theories of class structure—the most celebrated being that which Erik Olin Wright has elaborated over the last twenty years. Where Braverman collapsed ownership into control, Wright separated the two dimensions to reveal a series of "contradictory class locations" that stood between the major three classes—capital, labor, and self-employed. Wright asked "What is middle about the middle-class?"—a problem Braverman's polarization thesis elided. Wright did not build into his class framework any teleology. Indeed, on examining Braverman's hypothesis, he showed that shifts in the sectoral composition of the economy could reverse any tendencies toward deskilling within sectors. The simple polarization thesis does not work. Braverman himself had recognized that the rate of birth of new skilled occupations counteracted, even if it did not overwhelm, progressive deskilling. Herein lay the first task of the research program Braverman initiated—to develop a more refined theory of the labor process to account for the trajectory of class structure.

The shift from status attainment to class structure depended upon a Bravermanic transformation of industrial sociology. As a distinct discipline, industrial sociology was born in the famous Western Electric studies, conducted before and during the Depression by Elton Mayo and his colleagues. They examined worker productivity and asked why workers did not conform to managerial expectations—why they "restricted" output. After painstaking investigation they concluded that workers were possessed of an irrational plant culture and therefore could not comprehend managerial economic rationality. Elton Mayo inaugurated the school of human relations research that focused on how best to reshape that culture so as to adapt workers to work. Challenging this view, plant ethnographies found *managerial irrationality*—poor organization of work or badly designed incentive systems—to cause workers to rationally restrict their output.

Whatever their differences, both sides viewed output restriction as a matter of *subjective orientation* rather than irreconcilable interests. Braverman transposed the debate by turning from output restriction to the production of surplus value. He asked: How was capital so successful in extracting effort from workers? Instead of workers adjusting to work, he examined how work was imposed on workers to compel them to deliver just what management needed. In his account, therefore, workers were neither rational nor irrational but, instead, were stripped of all subjectivity. They became objects of labor, appendages of machines, another instrument of production, executors of managerial conceptions.

If industrial sociology suffered from subjectivism, organization theory, which superseded it, reveled in ahistoricism. The interest in output restriction reached its peak during the Second World War and in the 1950s. With economic growth, interest waned, and industrial sociology was absorbed into organization theory, which pursued claims applicable to all organizations, whether firms, hospitals, schools, armies, or prisons. Against this tradition *Labor and Monopoly Capital* restored history and the specificity of capitalism. It popularized the concept of *labor process,* which signified a break with both industrial sociology and organization theory, and a shift to structure and history.

Early studies in the new "labor process" paradigm recapitulated Braverman's focus on deskilling in the examination of the trajectory of specific occupations. But critical studies quickly emerged to counter Braverman's reduction of labor control to the expropriation of skill. Edwards, for example, introduced a typology of labor controls that emerged sequentially from the nineteenth century to the present: personal control, technical control, and, finally, bureaucratic control.

Pluralizing the strategies of control raised questions about Braverman's treatment of managers. For him management was a black box that simply transmitted market pressures into the expropriation of control. Research has moved into the *managerial labor process* to study conflicts between factions and levels of management, or how managers choose labor-control strategies or manage one another out of jobs. Another area of elaboration lay in the service sector. In focusing on deskilling, Braverman missed the specificity of the service work — the way managers use customers to control workers.

With every new research program come new challenges. Labor-process theory suffered from an objectivist bias. Andrew Friedman began the necessary corrective work by arguing that deskilling was not always to management's advantage, and in certain high-trust occupations it was better to grant workers "responsible autonomy." As many studies demonstrated, labor control was not only about constraint but also about eliciting consent to managerial goals. The workplace becomes an arena of struggle for shaping subjectivities — it becomes an arena of politics that constructs and mobilizes different identities, not just worker identities but also gender and racial identities, harnessed to managerial interests.

Restoring the subjective moment of work and its regulation creates a conceptual space to study worker opposition to management, something Braverman relegates to the margins of history. Following E. P. Thompson, labor historians set about documenting artisanal struggles against deskilling. Workplace ethnographies documented everyday forms of resistance on the shop floor, from gossip and tea breaks to walkouts and strikes. Rick Fantasia developed this theme most completely, bringing social-movement theory to the workplace. Studies of the labor process in the state sector showed how clients and workers can mobilize together for their common interest.

State socialism provided unexpected corroboration of the importance of work in shaping struggle and at the same time corroborating Braverman's deskilling thesis. Precisely because it is *not* capitalism, deskilling leads to chaos on the shop floor. Endemic supply uncertainties of the socialist economy called for improvisation and workplace autonomy, *reskilling,* if you will, which in turn gave workers space to create class solidarity. These peculiarities of the socialist labor process underlie the periodic working-class revolts in Eastern Europe from 1956 all the way to 1991.

One can elaborate *Labor and Monopoly Capital* by problematizing assumptions about the objective character of work, the subjectivities of workers, the strategies of managers, the omnipotence of profit. But how does its analysis help us understand class structure today? During the last twenty years we have become ever more conscious of the global dimensions of production. Early studies of the international division of labor gave Braverman's thesis a geographical twist — transnational labor processes were divided between processes of conception concentrated in advanced capitalism and processes of execution concentrated in the labor reservoirs of the periphery. From here it was a short step to the analysis of "commodity chains" in which surplus transfer and appropriation along the chain affect the form of work organization at each node. Increasingly, these nodes are seen not as single firms but as synergistic networks of firms, or "industrial districts." In this view, class structure is simultaneously globalized and localized.

Others have taken a more radical tack and argued that Braverman's theory of deskilling marked a period of mass production that has been superseded. A "second industrial divide" ushers in a world of custom-made goods in which demand-side constraints enter production, calling for a labor process of flexible specialization and a multiskilled labor force. Industrial sociology once more resurrects an incipient utopia within capitalism, a "yeoman democracy" that gives pride of place to the holistic, multivalent, fulfilled worker. Here a dose of Braver-mania would do no harm.

Braverman helped to redefine sociology by restoring structure and history. Even those who still study mobility are compelled to take into account changes in the occupational structure, while those who study workers cannot ignore the transformation of work. However, *Labor and Monopoly Capital*'s absorption into mainstream social science has taken its toll. Its critical moment has been sacrificed. We have lost sight of "The Degradation of Work in the Twentieth Century." Braverman's point of departure was the craftworker who obtains fulfillment through the creation of objects first conceived in the imagination. His point of conclusion was the vision of an alternative future, a socialism that would not restore the craftworker but would instead recombine conception and execution at the collective level to forge a classless society based on democratic planning. This double critique from the standpoint of a vanishing past and a utopian future easily disappears in a welter of scientific "explanation." Moreover, the eclipse of materialist critique opens the door to idealism — structure dissolved into a linguistic construction, and history reduced to narrative. Experience becomes discourse, oppression becomes talk about talk.

The domestication of critique and the interpretive turn coincide with the separation of intellectuals from the working class. *Labor and Monopoly Capital* described the eclipse of the *industrial* craftworker, but it could as well have been about the eclipse of the *intellectual* craftworker who unites the academy with the working class, who resists the intense professionalization of the university, who refuses to package the lived experience of workers for scholastic consumption. Once an artisan, now an organic intellectual, Braverman strove to refute his own thesis, to be an exception to his own laws. And here lies Braverman's crowning and lasting achievement: As a product of the unity of mental and manual work, *Labor and Monopoly Capital* proclaimed itself against the very tendencies it so persuasively described.

WHAT'S GENDER GOT TO DO WITH IT

Christine L. Williams

MEN AND WOMEN OF THE CORPORATION, by Rosabeth Moss
Kanter. New York: Basic Books, 1977.

Original reviews, *CS* 7:3 (May 1978), by Michelle Patterson and
Donileen R. Loseke, and by Lillian B. Rubin. From the review by
Lillian B. Rubin:

Rosabeth Moss Kanter's *Men and Women of the Corporation* is a
finely crafted book—a scholarly, carefully documented, superbly
reasoned presentation of the structural basis of inequality in
corporate life. . . . For anyone who seeks a better understanding of how our modern organizational world works, *Men and
Women of the Corporation* will be must reading for a long time
to come.

Nearly twenty years after its publication, Kanter's *Men and Women of
the Corporation* receives around one hundred citations per year and
remains one of the most influential books in U.S. sociology. I have written a great deal about this book, mostly about the tokenism thesis —
Kanter's claim that the proportional representation of any group in an
organization determines the status and power of that group (Williams
1989, 1995). In fact, my dissertation proposal was originally titled
"Men and Women of the Corps," referring to the two case studies I had
selected to assess this thesis: women in the U.S. Marine Corps and men
dancers in the corps de ballet. (I later substituted nursing for ballet
dancing, regretfully giving up the best title I've ever written.)

I am convinced that Kanter was wrong about tokenism. When men
enter predominately female jobs they do not face the same discrimination and differential treatment that women face in "male" jobs.

Although being a token does seem to impede women's progress in nontraditional jobs, men benefit from male advantages built into organizations, whether they are tokens or not.

But Kanter's analysis of tokenism is only a small part of *Men and Women of the Corporation*. The goal of the book was to challenge well-worn assumptions about the naturalness and inevitability of gender differences. Kanter sought to demonstrate that gender differences in work performance, which were commonly attributed to the different personality traits of men and women, are actually the by-products of organizational structure. Much like Wilson's *Declining Significance of Race* challenged the importance of race as key to understanding the contemporary status of African Americans, *Men and Women of the Corporation* argued that gender per se does not account for women's disadvantaged status in the workforce.

To grasp the importance of this argument, *Men and Women of the Corporation* has to be put in historical context. Prior to Kanter, the sociology of women (like the sociology of everything) was dominated by structural functionalism and subsumed within the study of "sex roles." From this perspective, any differences in the work behavior of women and men are believed to stem from their different socialization experiences: Girls are socialized to be expressive, and boys, instrumental. Thus, if women become secretaries and not executives, that is because they have expressive personalities, which happen to be very well suited to the demands of the secretarial role. When women move into predominantly male jobs, according to structural functionalists, they usually fail to reach the top because they lack the instrumental traits needed for these jobs. Consequently, they either segregate into lesser paying "feminine" specialities that draw on their expressive traits (like pediatric medicine or family law), or they jeopardize their advancement by prioritizing their family lives over their careers.

To Kanter, this was all backward: Most women work in predominantly female jobs not because they have feminine personalities; rather, they display "feminine" characteristics because they are locked into dead-end, powerless, low-paid jobs. She argued that men stuck in these same jobs would be just as likely as women to display stereotypically feminine traits. Furthermore, she maintained that when women manage to escape the female job ghettos and obtain better jobs, they usually do not fare as well as the men in these higher positions because the women are subjected to token dynamics, including stereotyping and other forms of discrimination. The job maketh the woman.

Kanter based these conclusions on an in-depth study of Indsco, her pseudonym for a multinational industrial supply corporation. Kanter spent five years as a consultant, participant observer, and researcher at Indsco while working on this book. She attended meetings, conducted attitude surveys, analyzed corporate documents, and interviewed managers, salespeople, secretaries, and managers' wives. Kanter locates her project in relation to sociological theory (including the works of Durkheim, Marx, Simmel, and Weber), and she draws on experimental research on small group behavior to bolster her claims. As a workplace ethnography, *Men and Women of the Corporation* is unsurpassed, and it should be on the essential reading list of all sociologists who study work and organizations. It richly documents a bygone era of large corporations on the brink of the computer revolution, TQM, and downsizing. For these reasons alone, *Men and Women of the Corporation* merits its status as a sociological classic.

But the main contribution of *Men and Women of the Corporation* is to the sociology of gender. This book almost single-handedly debunked several widespread, pernicious stereotypes about employed women. (The works of Cynthia Fuchs Epstein are also very important in this regard.) Prior to Kanter's study, women who were reluctant to apply for promotions were believed to suffer from "fear of success"; Kanter countered that low aspirations are a strategic response to blocked opportunities, which happen to be characteristic of jobs where women are concentrated. Similarly, women in management were widely believed to manifest the "Queen Bee Syndrome," jealously guarding their token status among men by refusing to mentor other women. Kanter demonstrated how this behavior is a rational reaction to the extreme performance pressures suffered by anyone in a token position. And to those who maintained that women workers were naturally more emotional, gossipy, and detail oriented than men, Kanter responded that each of these attributes is a consequence of the peculiar reward structure found in predominantly female occupations; women do not bring these attributes with them to their jobs.

Men and Women of the Corporation also had a significant impact on the development of theory and research on sexual harassment, though the book was written before "sexual harassment" entered the legal and sociological lexicons. One of the most frequently cited lines in he book is "power wipes out sex" (200). In this passage, Kanter is attributing the problems faced by women in management to their relative powerlessness. If women had the same ability as men to mobilize resources, she argues, then they would exhibit the same "masculine" traits as the powerful men, and the fact that they are women would become irrelevant. This basic idea was expanded to define sexual harassment as a product of unequal power, not an inevitable outcome of heterosexual men and women working together in organizations. This "power" perspective continues to dominate research on sexual harassment. Barbara Gutek (1985), a leading researcher in this field, also drew upon Kanter's theory of tokenism to explain the sexual harassment of women in nontraditional occupations, arguing that because their numerical rarity makes gender their salient feature, they are treated as sex objects rather than workers.

Men and Women of the Corporation also made (and continues to make) a significant impact on the sociology of gender for theoretical, methodological, and political reasons. Kanter's insistence that individual gender differences are not the cause of occupational gender inequality resonates strongly with a dominant strand of feminist sociology, often called the "minimalist" or equality perspective (Epstein 1988). This view emphasizes that men and women are essentially the same, attributing any differences detected in the attitudes and behaviors of the two groups to their different social locations. The book lends itself very well to the empirical methods of research favored by many sociologists. Although Kanter based her claims on qualitative research, many of her propositions can be assessed with quantitative variable analysis. The book appeals to many feminist scholars because of its refreshing optimism about the prospects for social change. Kanter argues in *Men and Women of the Corporation* that gender differences could be all but eliminated if corporate policies promoted the equal distribution of men and women in every occupation, and if all workers were given opportunities for advancement and empowerment.

But despite its many important contributions to the sociology of gender, a key problem of the work, and the focus of many subsequent advances in feminist scholarship, is *Men and Women of the Corporation*'s limited success in addressing a central, unresolved paradox, sometimes referred to as the "sameness-difference" paradox: If it is true that men and women are the same, then why do organizations sort men and women into different roles? Kanter maintains that organizations themselves are gender-neutral: The slots they create for workers follow a bureaucratic logic that is independent of gender. Although ideologies of gender may be overlaid onto an existing division of labor as a form of legitimation, the division itself is not gendered in her view (see also Acker 1990). But if men and women are the same, and organizations are gender-neutral, then why are women hired for some jobs and men for others? Why does occupational gender segregation even exist?

Kanter cannot adequately answer this question because, in her determination to prove that women are not to blame for their low occupational achievement, she ends up denying any role to individual agency in her theory of organizational behavior. Although she acknowledges that some men do discriminate against token women, she attributes this behavior (which she calls "boundary heightening") to men's superior positions in organizations. If women monopolized the top positions, then they would be just as sexist as men, according to her theory. But once again, this begs the question, Why are men in the most powerful positions in organizations?

It is very interesting that at about the same time Kanter's book appeared, another book in this "most influential books" collection also made its debut: Nancy Chodorow's *Reproduction of Mothering*. In contrast to *Men and Women of the Corporation,* Chodorow's book gave a central place to individual subjectivity in explaining the persistence of gender inequality in society. Chodorow examined how differences in men's and women's early childhood socialization produce differences in men's and women's unconscious emotional needs and relational capacities, which in turn promote sexist attitudes in men, and the gender division of labor in the home.

Not surprisingly, just as Kanter was faulted for denying a role for individual agency, Chodorow has been frequently criticized for underplaying the role of social structure in causing gender differentiation, as Barbara Laslett points out in her review of *The Reproduction of Mothering* in this collection. Indeed, these two books represent opposing poles in the sociology of gender, which Paula England and Irene Browne (England and Browne 1992; Browne and England 1997) have labeled the "external constraint" versus the "internalization" models: One side argues that gender differences are imposed on individuals by outside social forces, and the other maintains that men and women shape society according to their gender-differentiated needs and desires.

In the past decade or so, several significant steps have been made toward reconciling these two extreme positions. In an important essay, "Bringing the Men Back In" (1988), Barbara Reskin made a compelling case that sexist men in organizations use their power intentionally to constrain opportunities for women. This paper, and her subsequent work with Patricia Roos (1990), emphasize the linkages between men's agency and social structure in the reproduction of gender inequality in organizations. Joan Acker (1990) also has contributed a great deal to resolving this agency-structure impasse by indicating how organizational structure itself can be gendered. According to Acker, organizations are not gender-neutral hierarchies filled in by ungendered workers; instead, new jobs typically are created with a particular, gendered worker in mind, and workers often act on the basis of their perceived collective interests as men or women.

Unlike the earlier works of Kanter and Chodorow, these new approaches in the sociology of gender and organizations situate their conclusions in concrete historical and cultural circumstances. Instead of asking, "Are men and women the same or different?" scholars are now asking, "Under what circumstances are men and women treated the same or differently?" There is also a great deal of interest today in how men and women reproduce gender differences in interaction (e.g., West and Zimmerman 1987), and how they resist gender differentiation (e.g., Connell 1987; Lorber 1994). The new emphasis on context highlights the ways in which race, class, and sexual orientation shape the process of gender differentiation in organizations (e.g., Glazer 1991; Glenn 1992; Woods and Lucas 1993). A more nuanced picture of the dynamic interplay between social structure and agency is emerging, one that is sensitive to differences among women and differences among men.

But none of these advances in our understanding of gender at work would have been possible without *Men and Women of the Corporation,* which marks an important transition point in the feminist revolution in sociology. Because of this exceptional study, sociologists no longer consider gender solely a property of individuals. In challenging the taken-for-granted assumption that men and women are "different," Kanter laid the foundation for understanding how "gender" is produced by work organizations.

REFERENCES

Acker, Joan. 1990. "Hierarchies, Jobs, Bodies: A Theory of Gendered Organizations." *Gender & Society* 4 (2): 139–158.

Browne, Irene, and Paula England. 1997. "Oppression from Within and Without in Sociological Theories: An Application to Gender." *Current Perspectives in Social Theory* 17: 77–104.

Connell, Robert W. 1987. *Gender and Power: Society, the Person and Sexual Politics.* Stanford: Stanford University Press.

England, Paula, and Irene Browne. 1992. "Internalization and Constraint in Theories of Women's Subordination." *Current Perspectives in Social Theory* 12: 97–123.

Epstein, Cynthia Fuchs. 1988. *Deceptive Distinctions.* New Haven: Yale University Press.

Glazer, Nona. 1991. "Between a Rock and a Hard Place: Women's Professional Organizations in Nursing and Class, Racial, and Ethnic Inequalities." *Gender & Society* 5: 351–72.

Glenn, Evelyn Nakano. 1992. "From Servitude to Service Work: Historical Continuities in the Racial Division of Paid Reproductive Labor." *Signs* 18: 1–43.

Gutek, Barbara A. 1985. *Sex and the Workplace.* San Francisco: Jossey-Bass.

Lorber, Judith. 1994. *Paradoxes of Gender.* New Haven: Yale University Press.

Reskin, Barbara F. 1988. "Bringing the Men Back In: Sex Differentiation and the Devaluation of Women's Work." *Gender & Society* 2: 58–81.

Reskin, Barbara F., and Patricia A. Roos. 1990. *Job Queues, Gender Queues: Explaining Women's Inroads into Male Occupations.* Philadelphia: Temple University Press.

West, Candace, and Don H. Zimmerman. 1987. "Doing Gender." *Gender & Society* 1: 125–51.

Williams, Christine L. 1989. *Gender Differences at Work: Women and Men in Nontraditional Occupations.* Berkeley: University of California Press.

——. 1995. *Still a Man's World: Men Who Do "Women's Work."* Berkeley: University of California Press.

Woods, James D., with Jay H. Lucas. 1993. *The Corporate Closet: The Professional Lives of Gay Men in America.* New York: The Free Press.

PROMETHEAN SOCIOLOGY

Harriet Friedmann

THE MODERN WORLD-SYSTEM: CAPITALIST AGRICULTURE AND THE ORIGINS OF THE EUROPEAN WORLD-ECONOMY IN THE SIXTEENTH-CENTURY, vol. 1, by Immanuel Wallerstein. New York: Academic Press, [1974] 1980.

Original review, CS 4:3 (May 1975), by Michael Hechter:

The Modern World System is a visionary work . . . more an aesthetic creation than a scientific one. . . . This may be one of the most important theoretical statements about development since the time of Max Weber.

Almost a decade after volume 1 of *The Modern World-System* (*TMWS*), Immanuel Wallerstein (1983, 75) wrote, "Historical capitalism has been, we know, Promethean in its aspirations." The same can be said for Immanuel Wallerstein. More than two decades ago he opened questions later blazed across headlines, and the subject of fast-breeding academic journals. If sociology has kept pace with "globalization" of the world economy, it is to the credit of the institutional and intellectual leadership initiated in 1974 by his remarkable study of the sixteenth century.

Wallerstein in 1974 forged a deeply influential perspective by merging American sociology with French social history. His importation of the *Annales* school into U.S. sociology compares with Parsons's early importation of Max Weber. He reconnected American sociology with a boldly original elaboration of themes from European scholarship. His accomplishment reflected a unique combination of synthesizing intellect, exhilarating theoretical ambition, and uncanny intuition of impending economic transformations and political shifts.

THE INTERCONNECTION OF EVERYTHING

Time and place, thanks to Wallerstein's work, became widened and deepened in sociological research. Historical sociology was beginning to open questions about the traditional-modern rupture conventionally thought to have arisen with industry and urban labor markets. Wallerstein's timely book imported the historian's chronology of the modern period into sociology, dating modernity two to three centuries earlier. Others, notably Charles Tilly (who as coeditor of the Cambridge series *Studies in Social Discontinuity* brought Wallerstein's book out in a prestigious edition), deserve at least as much credit for building interdisciplinary and international bridges between sociology and history. Yet *TMWS* struck a chord. It was no small matter to generate sociological excitement about the sixteenth century.

More audaciously, Wallerstein linked everything on earth over the subsequent 400 years. Wallerstein generalized the historical insight that wage labor in Western Europe grew via grain imports from its increasingly servile periphery. Studies by *Annales* historians linking Eastern and Western Europe in the sixteenth century had appeared in English translation a few years before publication of *TMWS* (e.g., Burke 1972) but were of interest mainly to specialists. Except for Tilly, even social theorists interested in classes, power, elites, and other classical questions were not visibly captivated by the insight that Western European capitalism fed its workers with imports of grain from Eastern European nobles who got the surplus by intensifying feudal obligations.

What historians called the "second serfdom" Wallerstein renamed "coerced cash-crop labor," emphasizing its connection to free labor in core areas. This he connected to the parallel identification by dependency theorists of contemporary center-periphery relations between rich and poor countries. Adding a controversial layer, which he called the semiperiphery, Wallerstein constructed a continuous and comprehensive system of core-periphery relations for the world.

THE THEORETICAL LEGACY

Wallerstein was justly criticized for refusing to locate his concepts in relation to sociological theory. In those days, much criticism compared Wallerstein's concepts to those of Marx. Yet Wallerstein did not explicitly address the connection. With characteristic rhetorical flair and linguistic imprecision, he referred to his interest in Weber and Marx on the first of a nine-page introduction. This was devoted not to theoretical or methodological discussion of his place in the field, but to explaining his arrival at the conception of a single social system, and his famous methodological analogy to astronomy. Readers were left to speculate on the influence of other theorists of world capitalism, such as Rosa Luxemburg, who also insisted on the importance of non-capitalist regions beyond the direct domination of capital.

One important legacy may be his implicit contribution to the rediscovery of Karl Polanyi. It is suggestive that Polanyi wrote *The Great Transformation* just before the great postwar expansion, and Wallerstein wrote volume 1 of *TMWS* just before the contraction became evident. Wallerstein and his collaborator, Terence Hopkins, were influenced by Polanyi at Columbia. Although there is only one footnote to Polanyi out of more than a thousand in *TMWS,* the approaches are close: the distinction between trade and markets (the latter organizing the division of labor); the complex relations among states, capitalist organizations, and social groups or communities; the fluidity and tensions characterizing territories, institutions, and ways of life when the market holds sway; the historical cycle between freeing markets and resisting or protecting against their destructive consequences. It is difficult to know how much of this approach, which is very rich, to attribute to Wallerstein, and how much to a revival of Polanyi.

WALLERSTEIN'S INTUITION

TMWS appeared at the peak of intellectual, political, and academic interest in international power and exploitation. With the defeat of U.S. power in the Vietnam War, and demands for a new international economic order, the time was ripe for a shift in perspective from East-West military confrontation to North-South economic confrontation. Détente began at the same time, encouraging a shift in attention from divided Europe to what was first called the "Third World" and then the "South."

Although center-periphery relations have figured in several long-standing approaches to social and economic organization, Wallerstein took up the one that was politically engaged and often polemical. Latin American dependency theory had already reached considerable complexity; a little of it had appeared in English, and parallel work had appeared in French (by, e.g., Samir Amin). But the most widely read texts in English were by André Gunder Frank, a close associate of Wallerstein. Wallerstein's three zones elaborated Frank's dyadic concept of development and underdevelopment, and (as Frank was to do as well) used it for historical analysis and a model that can account for literally everything.

In the ensuing years, it became clear that Wallerstein's vision had anticipated interest in the global economy. In retrospect it is generally agreed that a long economic downturn, with attendant social and political restructuring, began some time between 1968 and 1973. *TMWS* coincided with energy, money, and food crises of the early 1970s, and may be considered to have launched in sociology an outpouring of research on the world economy and state system. The influence extended to France in the early '80s: When the Socialist government blamed international finance for its abandonment of a national economic project, Wallerstein received public attention with a Franco-American theory to explain the limits on French policy imposed by the modern world-system.

IDEAS AND INSTITUTIONS

As Prometheus inspired humans to turn their thoughts to the gods, Wallerstein carved spaces for renewal of sociology on a classical scale. It is difficult to separate the influence of *TMWS* from new institutions formed in its wake. The ASA section name bears his trademark: Political Economy of the World-System. "World-system," with mandatory hyphen, is Wallerstein's neologism. While the name reflected a theory attached indelibly to Wallerstein's name, there was never a hint of doctrine. The section is practically a miniassociation encompassing historical, political, ethnographic, economic, gender, race, and area studies. It is macroscopic and microscopic in focus. It is exceptionally lively and iconoclastic and comprehensive, fostering integration of perspectives from other disciplines and cultures.

The same tension between Wallerstein's specific ideas and his critical vision prevails in related institutions: the journal *Review*, the Fernand Braudel Center, the workshops of international scholars, and the biannual thematic conferences. They have stimulated interdisciplinary, comparative, and global research, and provided a complex of fora for international scholarship and debate. Wallerstein never tried to impose his ideas, but acted as animator and patron, a role he could not have played without the visibility and influence of *TMWS*.

THE INTELLECTUAL IN ACADEME

TMWS is engaging and accessible, despite its impressive scholarly apparatus. It is written in the style of European intellectuals, playing with the implicit contemporary implications of historical analysis. Only this can account for the popularity and influence of a sociological study of the sixteenth century. It appealed to those of us who entered the field excited by what is retrospectively called classical sociology, which invented new ways to explore the big questions raised by a changing social world.

Wallerstein's brilliance and erudition were brought together by provocative argumentation. Perhaps nothing so grand could have been accomplished without the boldness to go beyond rigor. His remarkable synthesis was achieved by a combination of synthetic genius and intellectual sleight of hand, sometimes using rhetorical tricks and definitional fiat in place of careful conceptual analysis. His later work continues to push the boundaries of academic discourse into the messy real world of politics and ideas. I always find something thought provoking and maddening in his sweeping pronouncements: most recently, for example, on the similarity between Wilson (and Roosevelt) and Lenin in favoring technology over liberation (1995, 481). His faults as a rigorous thinker, in my view, are inseparable from his major contribution as a sociologist: to synthesize, provoke, excite, and inspire. He is reliably unorthodox and brilliant. *TMWS* began a sustained challenge to complacent common sense.

Wallerstein revived the Promethean project of classical sociology: holistic analysis in service of freedom. Like Prometheus, who stole fire from the gods and tricked them, capitalism has created civilization by stealing and tricking the forces of nature. As punishment Prometheus was chained to a mountain, his immortal liver eaten each day by an eagle, and each day growing back to be eaten again. Perhaps the metaphor applies to the cycles of capitalist society, and perhaps also to the fortunes of those who try to comprehend it whole.

REFERENCES

Burke, Peter, ed. 1972. *Economy & Society in Early Modern Europe: Essays From Annales*. New York: Harper Torchbooks.

Wallerstein, Immanuel. 1983. *Historical Capitalism*. London: Verso.

———. 1995. "The End of What Modernity?" *Theory and Society* 24 (4): 471–88.

5   RACE AND GENDER FORMATION

WHAT'S RACE GOT TO DO WITH IT?

Aldon Morris

THE DECLINING SIGNIFICANCE OF RACE: BLACKS AND CHANGING AMERICAN INSTITUTIONS, by William Julius Wilson. University of Chicago Press, [1978] 1980.

Original reviews, *CS* 9:1 (January 1980), by Thomas F. Pettigrew and Cora Bagley Marrett. From Cora Bagley Marrett's review:

> The position of [the black middle class] may be far more precarious than Wilson suggests. . . . [The Bakke] case and similar challenges to special minority programs indicate to many observers that affirmative action programs are not firmly entrenched. . . . The progress of the middle class may be shorter-lived and less sweeping than the Wilson presentation might imply.

In 1978 the University of Chicago Press published William J. Wilson's book, *The Declining Significance of Race* (hereafter referred to as *DSR*), whose provocative title conveyed its stunning new message. The book's popular and scholarly impact was immediate and widespread, and it has remained on the press's top 100 best-sellers list.

Thanks to its success, Wilson became famous, securing millions of research dollars and winning a MacArthur "genius" award. *DSR* was important to his election as only the second Black president of the century-old American Sociological Association. Wilson's stature has also made him a valued consultant to President Clinton.

Numerous colleagues provided critical feedback on this essay and I thank them all. I especially thank Christopher Jencks, Cheryl Johnson-Odim, Michael Schwartz, Walter Allen, Charles Willie, Donald Brown, and Terry Murphy. I thank Clarence Page for agreeing to be interviewed. My greatest debt is to William J. Wilson, who agreed to lengthy interviews and graciously provided relevant sources.

Why did *DSR* have such an impact? I argue here that this book had a huge impact because (1) it carried a message that was enormously appealing to many Americans; (2) its title skillfully alerted the public to its message; (3) Wilson's race and institutional affiliation legitimized the message; and (4) the message developed in the book allowed America's race problem to be conceptualized from a different angle of vision.

DSR is theoretically ambitious. It attempts by way of a macrohistorical argument to explain how racial stratification has worked in America, from slavery to the 1970s. For the modern period, Wilson argued that only some Blacks were at the bottom of the stratification system, and what kept them there was not their skin color or current racial discrimination. For Wilson, a brand new phenomenon had emerged in modern America that fundamentally changed racial stratification: Social class rather than race now determined the life chances of African Americans. From an economic standpoint, America had become a color-blind society.

One explanation for the phenomenal success of Wilson's message can be derived from an analysis of the social and political context of America during the 1970s. By 1978 most Americans — especially whites — wanted to believe that the nation's racial nightmare was finally over. Whites longed for release from both the guilt racism produced and pressures to initiate additional changes. They wanted to embrace the idea that a color-blind America had arrived.

During the 1960s and '70s changes had occurred that appeared consistent with the dawning of a color-blind society: In the 1970s Blacks were achieving visibility in areas previously closed to them, especially television, and large numbers of Blacks had, for the first time, entered professional and managerial positions. Wilson personified the trend. He became the University of Chicago sociology department's first Black professor in 1972, and by the time he published *DSR*, he had become its chairman. In the 1970s, scholars (Freeman 1973; Featherman and Hauser 1976) amassed significant evidence showing that during the 1960s and '70s young educated Blacks made significant progress in the labor market. Others (Schuman et al. 1985) found that during the same period whites were discarding their view of Blacks as inferior and had begun to embrace the principle of racial equality. Thus by the 1970s there was a new Black presence in the media and white-collar occupations. These changes were buttressed by a white populace who had developed a kinder, gentler view of African Americans.

Despite these gains, racial conflict persisted in the 1960s and '70s. At the height of this racial quagmire, *DSR* offered a way out. Its title alone made it clear that the book's message landed on the side of those who believed that significant racial progress had been achieved. Without its title, *DSR* would not have had the impact it did, nor would it have sold so many thousands of copies.

Wilson anchored his argument on the documented increase of college-educated Blacks in white-collar positions, arguing that Blacks from advantaged family backgrounds were the ones who obtained college degrees and the necessary skills to enter high-status positions. For these young, talented college graduates, the primary linkage between their skin color and their place in the stratification order had collapsed. For them, just as for whites, class position, not race, determined their life chances: Their futures were bright, for they were headed to the expanding white-collar sector of the economy.

But if the news was so good, why were inner cities teeming with poor Blacks who often appeared on the nightly news in handcuffs? For Wilson, current racial discrimination was not responsible for the presence of this huge Black underclass. He argued that, although the legacy of past discrimination created it, impersonal economic forces are responsible for the current predicament. A segmented labor market locked the Black poor into dead-end, low-paying jobs. For Wilson, these poorly trained and educationally limited Blacks were becoming members of a permanent underclass. Wilson's analysis of the Black underclass in *DSR* and *The Truly Disadvantaged* has shaped contemporary research in poverty and informed public policy on these matters.

Yet, even in the case of poor Blacks, current racial discrimination was not salient. In fact, Wilson ruled out current discrimination as an important factor in the labor market writ large. Thus, the gap between the earnings of older educated Black workers and their white counterparts was explained by Blacks' lack of experience and lower seniority. The modern labor market had been cleansed of racial discrimination.

The centrality of class divisions within the Black community was an important component of Wilson's message. For him, the segmented labor market created a prosperous middle class and a poor underclass that was deeply divided along class lines. Thus, an economic schism between the Black "haves" and "have-nots" was growing and crystallizing. As a result, there was no longer a uniform Black experience. Wilson saw these class divisions as rooted in the civil rights movement, which pursued middle-class goals. Despite available evidence to the contrary, Wilson claimed that the overthrow of Jim Crow practices was a limited goal of the Black middle class, and that lower-class Blacks were not involved in the civil rights movement. Through such assertions, Wilson portrayed internal Black class relations simplistically. He ignored research showing that Blacks possess high levels of Black race and class consciousness simultaneously (Legget 1968; Geschwender 1977). Thus, there were also racial realities that united Blacks across class lines.

But what of affirmative action and other antibias policies? Wilson argued that affirmative action benefited young, privileged, educated Blacks who already possessed the skills and credentials required for entry into well-paid, high-status positions. However, for the Black underclass affirmative action was irrelevant, for it could not address the impersonal economic barriers responsible for their poverty. For Wilson "the very attempts of the government to eliminate traditional racial barriers through such programs as affirmative action have had the unintentional effect of contributing to the growing economic class division within the Black community" (19). One reading of this is that affirmative action was not needed, given that racial discrimination in the labor market had been eliminated and that such policies caused Black class divisions.

Despite the book's title, Wilson's argument claimed only that race had *declined* in significance in the labor market. This approach enabled him to argue that racial conflicts would continue to occur, but in the sociopolitical order outside the labor market. These conflicts would be fought out in the inner city over housing, public schools, and local politics. Racial conflict in the future would be limited to fights between the Black and white have-nots. The hidden hand of the economy and the emergence of a state that promoted racial equality had finally lifted the white upper and middle classes, as well as the Black middle class, above the politics and economics of race. Future concerns should be focused on altering the economy in such a way that the Black underclass and poor whites could be incorporated into the labor market. If this vexing problem could be solved, the basis of racial conflict could be erased even for the have-nots.

The Wilsonian message was encouraging for white liberals because it exonerated them of blame and presented an analysis that seemed to explain the contemporary racial scene in radical terms. For white and Black conservatives it provided intellectual fuel for the rising movement intent on dismantling affirmative action and other policies they believed promoted reverse discrimination. For whites generally the message was embraceable, for it suggested that America had finally overcome its racist past. Clarence Page, a columnist for the *Chicago Tribune,* explained that the book attracted wide media coverage because "there was a strong wish at the time for Americans to put our racial sins behind us and achieve the dream. In the media there was a yearning for evidence of Black progress. Old news is no news" (1996). Similarly, the majority of the scholarly reviews of the book welcomed the good news of Black progress, as well as the claim that current racial discrimination had been superseded by class factors.

The fact that Wilson was Black and a professor at the University of Chicago played an important role in legitimating the book's message. *DSR* would not have made the same impact if the author had been white. In fact, in the early 1970s a number of white conservative scholars, including Moynihan (1972), Glazer (1975), and Wattenberg and Scammon (1973), had developed the building blocks of Wilson's argument. Moynihan, for example, in a 1972 article revealingly titled "The Schism in Black America," stated, "At a time when the nation was preoccupied with civil rights measures — measures having to do with the issues of race and caste — I said, in effect, that the real problem was going to be that of social class" (7). These writers, like Wilson, emphasized the gains of a Black middle class, and identified a rising class of poor Blacks trapped in the inner city. They emphasized Black class divisions, and, for the same reasons as Wilson, they were unenthusiastic about affirmative action. Thus Glazer wrote, "It seems clear that the main impact of preferential hiring is on the better qualified — the professional and technical, who are already the beneficiaries of an income bonus on the basis of their relative scarcity . . ." (73).

Wilson echoed many of these arguments and gave them a legitimacy unavailable to white authors. Wilson agrees that his race was central to the impact of the book: "I think that many of the white liberals who came to my defense would have been more reluctant to defend a white scholar who had written the same book" (1996). Also important was Wilson's prestigious position. Most of the reviews of *DSR* identified Wilson as a Black professor at the University of Chicago. Earlier,

Moynihan had complained that the good news about racial progress needed to be exposed because we "ought to know about it, and permit it to cheer us up" (19). Race and institutional position made Wilson an ideal carrier of the message.

A number of white scholars wrote important critiques of *DSR* (Pettigrew 1980; Margolis 1979). Yet, the race of the Black critics of *DSR* was also consequential to its reception. Many Black scholars were extremely concerned with what they believed to be the dangerous ideological implications of the book. In 1978 the Association of Black Sociologists issued a widely printed statement stating that "it is the position of this organization that the sudden national attention given to Professor Wilson's book obscures the problem of the persistent oppression of Blacks" (Willie 1979, 177).

Critiques by Black scholars tended to focus on a set of related issues. They worried that the book would give legitimacy to the rising conservative movement that opposed affirmative action. The Bakke and Weber cases were particularly relevant in this context. Black scholars were concerned with the accuracy of the argument that fundamental class differences divided the Black community; many white reviewers seemed to relish reporting such divisions. Wilson had shifted the debate from white/Black inequality to internal Black comparisons.

Black scholars were also concerned that Wilson misread precarious Black gains as permanent changes, forever backed by a supportive state. An analysis that separated struggles over access to schooling and decent housing from the labor market was, they felt, seriously flawed. These critics also questioned Wilson's unsubstantiated claims that Blacks now had access to power and privilege. They pointed out that Wilson ignored the literature on institutional racism, preferring to define racism as only overt acts of discrimination by whites.

Many of the Black critiques were closely reasoned and well argued (e.g., Marrett 1980; Payne 1979; Thomas 1979). Yet, Wilson's white liberal reviewers tended to dismiss Black critics as emotional and shrill. They were seen as overreacting due to their vested interest in the Black middle class.

On the other hand, Wilson was portrayed as a dispassionate, courageous scholar. White liberal academics argued that Wilson was the radical, for his work was, after all, a class analysis. They concluded that Wilson was under unfair attack and that race problems were less complex and more easily solved than fundamental class problems (e.g., Greeley 1978; Record 1980; Van den Berghe 1978). Wilson described the white scholars' reactions when he concluded that their view seemed to be:

Here is a Black scholar who has written what is really a book that represents left thinking. . . . He is under attack for many wrong reasons and the least I can do is support him. . . . Here is a guy who has really put his neck on the line. He has gone against the grain. He is running the risk of alienating himself from many people in his race and he has written a progressive book so I think I really want to support him. (1996)

As a result, the Black critiques were largely ignored.

In retrospect, many of the intellectual and political concerns of those Black scholars are paramount as the twenty-first century approaches. Racial conflict in the labor market persists as elements of the state wage a mighty campaign to end affirmative action. The brief era when Black college graduates earned as much as whites has passed, and fewer Blacks are attending college than in the 1960s. Whites appear less prejudiced attitudinally, but research shows that they are usually opposed to measures designed to implement racial equality. Moreover, research continues to show that Blacks exhibit greater racial bonds than class bonds in contrast to whites (Jackman and Jackman 1983, 48–50). Those Blacks who entered high-status jobs in the 1960s and 1970s were disproportionately channeled into positions concerned with managing the firm's race relations and affirmative action policies (Collins, 1997). As Sharon Collins argues, it is becoming clear that they do not even have power to influence the battle over affirmative action.

Important works deserve scrutiny. Thus, while I am critical of *DSR,* my overall view is that this book has made important contributions. It stirred a fruitful debate over race. *The Declining Significance of Race* reinforced the need to analyze race/class interactions, although it fell short of a relational class analysis that encompassed the ways in which the white middle and upper classes shape racial outcomes. The book directed attention to critical issues pertaining to poverty, including a focus on the systemic and enduring qualities of Black poverty. At the same time, I believe that the analytic flaws and political angle of *DSR* were as responsible for the book's success as were its virtues.

REFERENCES

Collins, Sharon. 1997. *Black Corporate Executives: The Making and Breaking of a Black Middle Class.* Philadelphia: Temple University Press.

Featherman, David, and Robert M. Hauser. 1976. "Changes in the Socioeconomic Stratification of the Races, 1962–1973." *American Journal of Sociology* 82 (November): 621–49.

Freeman, Richard B. 1973. "Changes in the Labor Market for Black Americans." Brookings Papers on Economic Activity. Washington, D.C.

———. 1978. "Black Economic Progress since 1964." *The Public Interest* 52 (Summer): 52–68.

Geschwender, James. 1977. *Class, Race and Worker Insurgency.* Cambridge: Cambridge University Press.

Glazer, Nathan. 1975. *Affirmative Discrimination: Ethnic Inequality and Public Policy.* New York: Basic Books.

Greeley, Andrew. 1978. "Racism Fading but Poverty Isn't." *Chicago Tribune,* March 21.

Jackman, Mary, and Robert Jackman. 1983. *Class Awareness in the United States.* Berkeley: University of California Press.

Leggett, John. 1968. *Class, Race, and Labor: Working-Class Consciousness in Detroit.* New York: Oxford University Press.

Margolis, Richard J. 1979. "If We Won, Why Aren't We Smiling?" *Change* (April): 54–55.

Marrett, Cora Bagley. 1980. "The Precariousness of Social Class in Black America." *Contemporary Sociology* 9 (1) (January): 16–19.

Moynihan, Daniel. 1972. "The Schism in Black America." *The Public Interest.* (Spring): 3–24.

Page, Clarence. 1996. Interview. January 19. Chicago.

Payne, Charles. 1979. "On the Declining and Increasing Significance of Race." In *Caste and Class Controversy,* ed. Charles V. Willie. Bayside, N.Y.: General Hall.

Pettigrew, Thomas F. 1980. "The Changing — Not Declining — Significance of Race." *Contemporary Sociology* 9:1 (January): 19–21.

Record, Wilson, 1980. Review of "The Declining Significance of Race." *American Journal of Sociology* 85:4 (January): 965–68.

Schuman, Howard, Charlotte Steeh, and Lawrence Bobo. 1985. *Racial Attitudes in America: Trends and Interpretations.* Cambridge: Harvard University Press.

Thomas, Charles B. 1979. Review of "The Declining Significance of Race." *Afro-Americans in New York Life and History.* (January).

Van den Berghe, Pierre L. 1978. Review of *The Declining Significance of Race*, by William Julius Wilson. *Sociology and Social Research* 63 (October).

Wattenberg, Ben J., and Richard M. Scammon. 1973. "Black Progress and Liberal Rhetoric." *Commentary* (April): 35–44.

Willie, Charles, ed. 1979. *The Caste and Class Controversy*. Bayside, N.Y.: General Hall.

Wilson, William J. 1996. Interview. January. Chicago.

EMPIRE AND KNOWLEDGE:
MORE TROUBLES, NEW OPPORTUNITIES FOR SOCIOLOGY

Steven Seidman

ORIENTALISM, by Edward Said. New York: Pantheon Books, 1978.

No previous *CS* review.

Sociology was the invention of the West. The breakthrough period occurred between the 1880s and World War I. Distinct national traditions of sociology materialized—in Germany (Weber, Simmel), in France (Tarde, Durkheim), in Italy (Pareto, Mosca), in England (Hobhouse, Spencer), and in the United States (Du Bois, Small). It is not coincidental, though rarely noted in its disciplinary histories, that this period was also the high point of Western imperialism.

The nations that produced sociology simultaneously forged imperial empires of unprecedented scope and power. In particular, the United States, England, Germany, and France exercised dominion over much of Asia and Africa. Indeed, by World War I, 85 percent of the earth's surface was under the dominance of the West. It is curious then that "empire," or the dynamics of colonialism and imperialism, were *untheorized* by classical sociologists. To be sure, Weber, Sumner, Spencer, and Durkheim were aware of imperialism and at times addressed this social fact in political and, even occasionally, in sociological writings. However, *the dynamics of empire were not incorporated into the basic categories, models of explanation, and narratives of social development of the classical sociologists.*

The failure of these sociologists to integrate the dynamics of empire into their core perspectives does not mean they went untheorized. Important efforts to explain empire and write it into the dramatic center

My thanks to Ali Mirsepassi for his helpful comments.

of the story of modernity were proposed by marxist contemporaries of the sociologists, such as Rosa Luxemburg, Rudolf Hilferding, and Lenin, and by "liberal" social thinkers such as John Hobson and Joseph Schumpeter (see Mommsen 1980).

The worldwide movements of decolonization in the post–World War II period prompted further efforts to conceptualize the relation of empire and society. However, in contrast to the previous generation of theorists (and many of their successors, such as Arendt, Aron, or Rostow) who were "Western" in origin and social and intellectual identification, alternative theories of empire were proposed by individuals whose perspectives were profoundly shaped by the experience of being a colonial subject. On the one hand, the existing rudimentary Marxist theories of imperialism were elaborated into complex models of uneven national development and into a world-systems perspective (e.g., Samir Amin, A. Emmanuel, André Frank, Harry Magdoff, and Immanuel Wallerstein). On the other hand, "post-colonial" intellectuals such as Frantz Fanon, Albert Memmi, C. L. R. James, and Aimé Cesaire emphasized the cultural and psychological aspects of colonial domination and resistance. Edward Said's *Orientalism* is very much in the latter tradition of theorizing empire.

Growing up in the British colonies of Egypt and Palestine and self-identified as an Arab and Palestinian, yet educated at Princeton and Harvard and assuming the post of professor of English and Comparative Literature at Columbia University since the 1960s, Said straddles the East and the West—the world of revolutionary politics and the genteel world of Western high culture. Said's hybrid social and intellectual positioning accounts for much of the brilliance and ambiguities of *Orientalism*. Born out of the politics of the Arab-Israeli wars between 1967 and 1973, and the theoretical "revolutions" in the West associated with poststructuralism, *Orientalism* is both an ambitious scholarly effort aimed at producing a genealogy of "Oriental" studies and a relentlessly political book intent on documenting the entanglement of the Western Enlightenment tradition in the domination of the non-Western world. It is a book that is deeply critical of liberal humanism for masking a history of Western colonial dominion in the mythic figures of human progress, truth, and freedom. And yet, Said defends the values of individualism, high culture, and tolerance by detailing the evils of dogmatism and stereotypical thinking.

Although Said is the author of many important books addressing literary theory and contemporary Middle Eastern politics, *Orientalism* has been his most influential. It has not only shaped the disciplines of English, comparative literature, "Oriental" studies, and cultural studies but also is arguably the key text in what is today called "colonial discourse studies" and "post-colonial theory" (see Williams and Chrisman 1994; Young 1995).

Drawing on Foucault's efforts to conceptualize knowledge and power as interrelated and as a potent social force, and Gramsci's focus on the cultural conditions sustaining domination in class-structured societies, Said intended *Orientalism* to expose the extent to which "Eurocentric" cultural meanings, from folk beliefs and popular travel writing to literary and scholarly knowledges, were pivotal in Western imperialism. Specifically, Said argued that while empire is surely about territorial dominion and material gain, it is just as much, and inseparably about, cultural meanings. Said's thesis pressed beyond the limited claim that ideas legitimate imperialism to the proposition that culture made empire possible by producing the desire for it and establishing a normative framework for imperial practices.

In *Orientalism,* Said argued that a condition of Western imperialism has been, and still is, the representational division between the "Occident" and the "Orient." Said highlighted several key features of this cultural trope. First, it is through the concept of the Orient that Westerners "know" the particular societies of the East. India, China, and Egypt are understood as instances of the Orient. Second, the Orient is meaningful only in contrast to the Occident. Both terms are defined in highly stylized, formulaic, and static ways. For example, the Oriental is figured as passive, sensuous, childlike, or irrational and despotic. Third, these very qualities position the Orient as morally inferior to, and in need of the authority and dominion of, the Occident, whose democratic and rational essence marks its superiority.

Although Orientalism, as folk belief, can be traced back to Ancient Greece, Said focuses on the production of this symbolic figure in modern Western knowledges, in particular in the discipline of "Oriental studies," which took shape in late-eighteenth-century Europe. Said approaches the accumulation of knowledge of the "Orient" not as indicating the progress of truth but as part of the making of the Orient as an object of knowledge and power. Western knowledges fashioned a concept of the Orient that reflected what Westerners wanted and imagined the East to be, rather than what it really was. This was a symbolic construction that presupposed and contributed to Western political-economic dominion.

Said's originality pivoted on the thesis that imperialism is as much about narration and cultural meanings as it is about political economy. Culture shapes colonial desires and offers symbolic incitements and justifications for territorial expansion. In particular, Said emphasized the role of scientific knowledge, not the "irrationalism" of religion or myth, in the making of empire. The crowds of philologists, historians, and social scientists that pushed their way onto the historic scene of Western modernity literally created the Orient as a cultural fantasy and projection of Western desire and power. Their knowledges accrued material force from the concrete practices of imperial policies and administration. Hence, *Orientalism* is not only a contribution to theories of imperialism, but also proposes "empire" as a core category for analyzing "the social" and social knowledge.

Said has had enormous influence across many disciplines and fields of knowledge. In particular, as an exemplary study of colonial discourse and its role in the making and unmaking of empire, *Orientalism* has helped to generate a rich field of literary, historical, and social scientific studies (e.g., Brantlinger 1988; Breckenridge and Veer 1993; Carrier 1995; Inden 1990; JanMohamed 1983; Mutman forthcoming). *Orientalism* has not, however, been without its critics. Said has been taken to task for neglecting material or social structural analysis and the politics of resistance, essentializing the West and Orientalism in his totalizing critique of Orientalist studies, leaving unaddressed the tensions between his poststructuralist approach and his avowed humanism, and waffling between a postmodern critique of representation and a lingering objectivism (see Ahmad 1992; Bhabha 1994; Clifford 1988; Mani and Frankenberg 1985; Lowe 1991).

Said has had, sad to say, little influence in sociology. While theories of dependence and world-system perspectives have made sociologists aware of the dynamics of empire, they remain peripheral to Western, especially American, sociology. Moreover, these perspectives evidence the economism of Marxism, rather than the semiotic and Foucauldian emphases of Said. I would conjecture that the almost complete neglect of *Orientalism* by American sociologists is, in part, connected to their resistance to Foucauldian and poststructural perspectives, a refusal that contrasts sharply with our brethren discipline, anthropology (e.g., Asad, Clifford, Fabian, Fischer, Marcus, Pratt).

How might sociologists profit from Said's work? First, Said urges us to consider empire, alongside class, gender, race, social differentiation, or nationalism, as a core macro-and-microsocial dynamic. This means rewriting the history and sociology of "modernity" and the discourses of modernity, including sociology, in relation to the dynamics of empire. Second, *Orientalism*, but also *Culture and Imperialism*, stands as a powerful exemplar of a type of cultural sociology that is both attentive to symbol as meaning and as power and attentive to the mutual interrelation of symbolic, narrative constructions and "material" structures of rulership and resistance. Moreover, Said makes the problem of difference or the social production of "Otherness" central to cultural social studies. Indeed, his work makes the question of "the Other" a key problem for social knowledge. He forces us to consider seriously how we should study social differences without essentializing and positioning them as inferior and subordinate. Third, Said compels us to approach knowledge itself as a social force, as a part of the making of the world, and not always, as in the case of Orientalist studies, in benevolent ways. Said documents how scholarly knowledges can become part of a system of social control through constructing and enforcing normalizing identities and social codes. If knowledge is intertwined with power, knowledge producers such as sociologists must assume responsibility for their practices. Said presses us to imagine human studies as an elaborated, multilevel type of social reason that incorporates into its practices a reflexivity about its socially "constitutive" role.

REFERENCES

Ahmad, Aijaz. 1992. *In Theory: Classes, Nations, Literatures.* New York: Verso.

Bhabha, Homi. 1994. *The Location of Culture.* New York: Routledge.

Brantlinger, Patrick. 1988. *Rule of Darkness: British Literature and Imperialism, 1830–1914.* Ithaca: Cornell University Press.

Breckenridge, Carol A., and Peter van der Veer, eds. 1993. *Orientalism and the Postcolonial Predicament.* Philadelphia: University of Pennsylvania Press.

Carrier, James, ed. 1995. *Occidentalism: Images of the West.* New York: Oxford University Press.

Clifford, James. 1988. *The Predicament of Culture: Twentieth-Century Ethnography, Literature, and Art.* Cambridge: Harvard University Press.

Inden, Ronald. 1990. *Imagining India*. Oxford: Blackwell.

JanMohamed, Abdul. 1983. *Manichean Aesthetics: The Politics of Literature in Colonial Africa*. Amherst: University of Massachusetts Press.

Lowe, Lisa. 1991. *Critical Terrains: French and British Orientalisms*. Ithaca: Cornell University Press.

Mani, Lata, and Ruth Frankenberg. 1985. "The Challenge of Orientalism." *Economy and Society* 14 (May): 174–92.

Mommsen, Wolfgang. 1980. *Theories of Imperialism*. New York: Random House.

Mutman, Meyda. Forthcoming. *Veiled Fantasies*. Cambridge: Cambridge University Press.

Williams, Patrick, and Laura Chrisman, eds. 1994. *Colonial Discourse and Post-Colonial Theory: A Reader*. New York: Columbia University Press.

Young, Robert. 1995. *Colonial Desire: Hybridity in Theory, Culture and Race*. London: Routledge.

THE GENDERING
OF SOCIAL THEORY:
SOCIOLOGY AND ITS DISCONTENTS

Barbara Laslett

THE REPRODUCTION OF MOTHERING: PSYCHOANALYSIS AND
THE SOCIOLOGY OF GENDER, by Nancy J. Chodorow. Berkeley:
University of California Press, 1978.

Original review, *CS* 8:4 (January 1979), by Rose Laub Coser:

This book will have consequences in sociological as well as in
psychoanalytic theorizing at the same time as it may provide
some of the underpinnings for a theory of feminism.

Nancy Chodorow and I have known each other for more than fifteen
years as colleagues and as friends. Part of that friendship has developed
out of our mutual intellectual interests in gender and family relations
and in social theory. In our many conversations that have engaged
those interests, there has been mutual critique as well as appreciation.
This essay continues in the spirit of those conversations.

*The Reproduction of Mothering: Psychoanalysis and the Sociology
of Gender* (hereafter, *Mothering*), published in 1978 by the University
of California Press, was a major intellectual event in the emerging field
of feminist scholarship and in social theory. Its original success reflected, in part, the desires of feminists to find a grand theory that could
address the normative questions with which they were so concerned —
women's subjectivity, sexuality, and constructions of self in the contexts of gender inequalities. It came at the height of feminist struggles
for intellectual space and legitimacy in the academy, and also argued
for the potential of psychoanalytic theory to be incorporated into sociological thinking. Attention was almost immediate.

The intellectual contributions of *Mothering* were at least twofold.
First, it presented an argument that problematized women's mother-

ing—nurturance, child care, and socialization, as well as pregnancy, childbirth, and lactation. Eschewing a biological explanation, Chodorow's central quest was, "Why do women mother?" Her answer drew on psychoanalytic theory, especially object-relations theory, and developed it using feminists' interest in and insights about the socially constructed nature of gender relations. Focusing on the pre-Oedipal period of development in which the primary relationship of infants is with their mothers, Chodorow argued that the development of gendered personalities in women and men is such that women have a deeply internalized psychological impetus to reproduce the intimacy of their relationship with their mothers, their primary and primordial caretakers, and are able to do so through becoming mothers themselves. In contrast, Chodorow contended that personality development for men fosters separation, not connectedness, the search for emotional distance, not emotional intimacy, and that this was especially the case in nuclear families built on a division of labor in which men are the primary breadwinners and women are the primary homemakers and nurturers (i.e., the Parsonian model of Western nostalgia, to paraphrase William J. Goode, 1963).[1] It is thus, Chodorow argued, that the reproduction of mothering in women occurs at a deep intrapsychic level, and cannot be adequately explained by the concept of "sex roles," by socialization theories, by coercion in male-dominated cultures or in male-dominated institutions, or by male economic privilege.

Second, Chodorow connected the development of gendered personalities in women and men not only to the reproduction of the desire to mother among women, but also to problematics in the relationships between women and men and to women's inequality. In so doing, she presented a powerful argument for the potential usefulness of psychoanalytic theory for sociologists in general, not feminists alone. In contrast to theories of social structure and/or the gendered division of labor in which women's mothering as socially, culturally, and biologically organized behavior was taken as a given, Chodorow raised a question to be answered, rather than one whose answer seemed self-evidently "natural." Gender relations, the gendered division of labor, and gender inequality—key concerns of feminists and feminist scholars—became, in Chodorow's hands, a theoretical problematic for so-

---

1. By providing such an abbreviated version of Chodorow's theory, I obviously cannot do justice to its nuances and complexities.

cial theorists in general, rather than a taken-for-granted dimension of social structure.

While *Mothering* was an event of moment for sociologists of the family and of gender as well as for feminist scholars across many disciplines, it became, almost immediately, the object of criticism among sociologists, including (perhaps especially) feminists. At the meeting of the American Sociological Association in Boston in 1979, I attended a panel session in which *Mothering* was discussed by prominent women sociologists then identified with the newly emerging field of feminist scholarship. I no longer have the program from those meetings but recall the participants to have been Alice Rossi, Judith Lorber, Rose Laub Coser, and Jessie Bernard. (Coser was the reviewer of *Reproduction* in *Contemporary Sociology.*) If my memory serves me, with the exception of Rose Coser, whose comments were both appreciative and critical, the commentaries were almost uniformly negative. Lorber argued that economic relations, not psychoanalysis, explained women's oppression and their decision to mother. Rossi was disturbed by Chodorow's rejection of biological explanations and evidence. Jessie Bernard commented on the need to just get on with it and test empirically if and how psychoanalytic theory might be useful to sociologists.[2] There was a way, however, in which *The Reproduction of Mothering* quickly became, despite (or, perhaps, because of) its widespread recognition and influence, a book that sociologists loved to hate. It has, nevertheless, continued to receive attention by scholars, both feminist and nonfeminist.[3]

The original and continued impact of Chodorow's theory needs to be understood within the intellectual context in which it developed — the Parsonian model of family life, with its taken-for-granted set of gender roles and relationships that were seen as "functional" for the society (if not necessarily always for women) and the concerns of contemporary feminist scholars to disrupt precisely what that model took for granted. But Chodorow's work posed a challenge to feminist schol-

2. The comments by Rossi, Lorber, and Coser were published in *Signs: Journal of Women in Culture and Society* in the Spring of 1981 (6:482–514) and it is to those I have referred in preparing this essay. Chodorow's published response in the *Signs* symposium merits reading today as it did then.

3. As editor of *Signs: Journal of Women in Culture and Society* between 1990 and 1995, I know that *Mothering* remains a major focus of debate among feminist scholars; recently, however, it is being considered in more positive, although not uncritical, lights. (See, for instance, Segura and Pierce 1993; Luttrell, 1997.)

arship as well. Making analytic use of Freudian-inspired psychoanalytic theory, she validated its usefulness to analyses of gender relations, rather than relegating the theory in toto to the dustbin of a patriarchal intellectual history, as some feminists were then doing. Chodorow was not alone either in her uses of psychoanalytic theory or in her questioning of the adequacy of functionalist theories of family life. Her rich articulation of a feminist critique, however, came at just the right moment to be taken up and noticed. Having identified "gender" as a theoretical category, *Mothering* became a classic work in feminist theory, and influential in many disciplines — for example, political theory and literary criticism. Ironically, although Chodorow is a sociologist, it has been more resisted than embraced in that field.

Should Chodorow's psychoanalytically focused theory of gender relations be of sociological interest now, in 1998, especially since she has revised some of her ideas since the publication of *Mothering?*[4] My answer — that Chodorow's theoretical work continues to have major contributions to make to sociology — reflects current theoretical debates that are not about personality or microlevel social relationships, but about macrohistorical processes of social change and social reproduction, that is, debates about social structures, human agency, and their intersections under concrete and historically specific conditions (see Abrams 1981). Quite simply, Chodorow's theory provides a way to theorize human action and the link between individual agents and larger social structures. She does so not by relying on a simplistic logic of market relations as unmediated by the subjective and interpretive capacities of social actors, but by directing attention to the power of emotions, to family relationships, to gendered cultures and experiences, and to the sociological relevance of sexuality and sexual identities as they are constructed by persons within patriarchal societies. Chodorow's attention to the ways in which personality develops and to the place of emotion in the construction of meaning contributes to our understanding of how and why people act as they do more richly than the theories either of "rationality" or of socialization that infuse many contemporary sociological models of action. She also gives, appropriately in my view, intellectual weight to gender relations, sexuality, and emotional

4. In *Feminism and Psychoanalytic Theory,* Chodorow discusses some of the ways in which her thinking has changed over time; she has, for instance, rejected her earlier implication "that women's mothering was *the* cause or prime mover of male dominance." (See Chodorow 1989, 1–19.)

life in ways that can inform the kinds of political, economic, cultural, and organizational questions with which sociologists have traditionally been concerned. Pierce's (1995) analysis of the gendered emotional dynamics in contemporary law firms, for instance, and my own work on the history of American sociology (Laslett 1990) use Chodorow's theory to understand organizational and historical dynamics.

Pierre Bourdieu (1977) argues that economics is everywhere, and that to differentiate the economic and symbolic, treating them as qualitatively different realms of social experience and activity, is to participate in a mystification of the links between them in all social formations. Chodorow's theory of "mothering" is a similarly radical and demystifying argument: "Gender" is present in all social relationships.[5] We carry and construct "gender" in our multiple realms of experience and activity through the emotions that energize our actions, through the symbols and meanings we construct to make sense of those actions, through our explanations — to ourselves and others — of how and why we become the social actors that we do.

For all their rich potential to engage with contemporary social theory, however, Chodorow's interests have remained focused on, indeed have become more firmly attached to, theorizing the person, not linkages to social structure. This is, in my view, a limitation of her work, although it does not by itself invalidate its sociological relevance, especially as it has developed over the last twenty-five years. Yet she has, perhaps not surprisingly, given her fascination with psychoanalysis "for its own sake" (1989, 6), become even more focused on persons as creative actors. In one of her recent publications, "Gender as a Personal and Cultural Construction" (Chodorow 1995), part of a book-length project on which she is currently working, Chodorow expands on themes that have been present in her work since the beginning, but that also reflect her recent psychoanalytic training and her current work as a clinician as well as an academician.

In this work, Chodorow is more exclusively concerned with how persons construct meanings, in this instance the meanings of gender, within the highly specific contexts of individual lives and clinical expe-

5. While gender relations are present in all social situations — indeed, gender is present even when women are not (see "Gender: A Useful Category of Historical Analysis" in Scott 1988) — it does not follow that gender is uniformly *salient* in all times and places; see "Seventies Questions for Thirties Women: Gender and Generation in a Study of Early Women Psychoanalysts" in Chodorow 1989.

riences. But she does not, unfortunately, explicitly link insights from her present location at the intersection of sociology and psychoanalysis either to sociological analysis or to social theory. Her current focus, however, whatever its limits, has important things to say to those of us interested in understanding human agency, in learning how people use the available social, cultural, and organizational resources and constraints to construct their own lives and become actors *on* as well as *in* societies. (See Chodorow 1994 for further elaboration of her argument in "Individuality and Difference . . ."; for another, related, theoretical statement see Mahoney and Yngvesson 1992; for empirical examples, see Lawrence-Lightfoot 1994.) Her case studies also illustrate how situations beyond the realm of personal life can become infused with meaning and the power of feeling. And her theory allows us to understand how jobs can become sites of struggle over masculinity and femininity (Pierce 1995), how sports and locker rooms can become sites of struggle over sexuality, and how both can become sites for struggles over control (Disch and Kane 1996).

Yet, some of the critique that Rose Coser articulated in the original *Contemporary Sociology* review of *Mothering*—that Chodorow does not pay enough attention to structure—remains. Although, from the outset, Chodorow has clearly recognized that meanings, actions, and relationships are constructed within particular social contexts, her fascination with persons has resulted in an inattention to how personal action and society connect. Drawing linkages between the questions that intrigue her and other approaches to social theory, however, is not necessarily Chodorow's responsibility alone, although not doing so may limit recognition of the relevance of her work to social theorists. Like us, she needs to be free to pursue her intellectual interests and sociological imagination where they take her. The challenge—to draw out the implications of Chodorow's contributions to social theory—is also ours. In 1998, it continues to serve our intellectual interests to take that challenge seriously, as did the publication of *Mothering* in 1978.

REFERENCES

Abrams, Philip. 1981. *Historical Sociology*. Ithaca: Cornell University Press.
Bourdieu, Pierre. 1977. *Outline of a Theory of Practice*. Cambridge: Cambridge University Press.

Chodorow, Nancy J. 1989. *Feminism and Psychoanalytic Theory*. New Haven: Yale University Press.

——. 1994. *Femininities, Masculinities, Sexualities: Freud and Beyond*. Lexington: University of Kentucky Press.

——. 1995. "Gender as a Personal and Cultural Construction." *Signs* 20: 516–44.

Disch, Lisa, and Mary Jo Kane. 1996. "When a Looker Is Really a Bitch: Lisa Olson, Sport, and the Heterosexual Matrix." *Signs* 21: 278–308.

Goode, William J. 1963. *World Revolution and Family Patterns*. New York: Free Press.

Laslett, Barbara. 1990. "Unfeeling Knowledge: Emotion and Objectivity in the History of Sociology." *Sociological Forum* 5: 413–33.

Lawrence-Lightfoot, Sara. 1994. *I've Known Rivers: Lives of Loss and Liberation*. New York: Penguin Books.

Luttrell, Wendy. 1997. *School-smart and Mother-wise: Working-Class Women's Identity and Schooling*. New York and London: Routledge.

Mahoney, Maureen, and Barbara Yngvesson. 1992. "The Construction of Subjectivity and the Paradox of Resistance: Reintegrating Feminist Anthropology and Psychology." *Signs* 18: 44–73.

Pierce, Jennifer. 1995. *Gender Trials: Emotional Lives in Contemporary Law Firms*. Berkeley: University of California Press.

Scott, Joan W. 1988. *Gender and the Politics of History*. New York: Columbia University Press.

Segura, Denise A., and Jennifer Pierce. 1993. "Chicana/o Family Structure and Gender Personality: Chodorow, Familism, and Psychoanalytic Sociology Revisited." *Signs* 19: 62–91.

FEMINIST SUBVERSIONS

Linda Gordon and Barrie Thorne

OUR BODIES, OURSELVES: A BOOK BY AND FOR WOMEN, by
The Boston Women's Health Book Collective. New York: Simon
& Schuster, [1973] 1992.

No previous *CS* review.

In its influence in the United States, *Our Bodies, Ourselves* may be in
the same category as the Bible and Rush Limbaugh. Since initial publication in 1971, its trajectory has been a rags-to-riches adventure,
encapsulating some of the dynamics of the women's movement in the
late twentieth century. Both book and social movement hold in tension
the rough edge of a critique of male (and class and race) power with
pressures to sand it down into a smooth message of self-help and informed consumerism. Moreover, because of its connection to a social
movement, the book moves freely between the popular and the academic; it cuts across disciplinary boundaries, drawing upon and influencing many bodies of knowledge. The coincidence of the shared
twenty-fifth anniversary of this journal and of feminism's best-selling
book affords an interesting opportunity for reflection on the ways in
which feminism has influenced sociology.

In 1969, at a conference of "Bread and Roses," a Boston socialist-
feminist organization, a group of women who came together at a workshop about frustrations with physicians decided to continue meeting. One-and-a-half years later they produced the first version of *Our
Bodies, Ourselves*—194 pages, printed on newsprint by a small New
Left press and priced at seventy-five cents. Advertised by word of
mouth and notices in women's and New Left publications, it had sold
250,000 copies by 1973, when the group signed with Simon & Schuster. The authors, a collective of eleven, insisted on provisions rare in
commercial publishing: All profits go to the women's health movement, and the publishers are required to make copies available at 40
percent of the cover price for nonprofit health groups. By 1995 the

book had sold 3½ million copies, not including sales of three sibling books, *Changing Bodies, Changing Lives* (for teenagers), *Ourselves and Our Children,* and *Ourselves Growing Older.*

The book is now famous for its positive and explicit discussion — and pictures — of sex and reproduction. The first edition began with an introduction on "Women, Medicine and Capitalism," and then turned immediately to the most burning topic for young feminists of the time — sexuality. This was followed by chapters on VD, birth control, abortion, pregnancy and childbirth, and a concluding essay on medical institutions. The 1992 edition, 750 magazine-size pages, priced at twenty dollars, begins with a subject possibly even more troubling for women — body image and food — then moves on to alcohol and other drugs, sports and exercise, alternative healing, psychotherapy, environmental and occupational health, and violence against women, before turning to sex and reproductive health. After childbirth, it continues with a long chapter on women's aging, and concludes with a lengthy section on the politics of medical care.

What makes *Our Bodies* so influential? To answer we need to recall how sexuality, the body, and gender were handled in scholarship, medicine, and popular discourse in 1971. There was virtually no open discussion of sex and reproduction in schools or the popular media, and physicians condescended to women and regularly withheld medical information from their female patients. Social science and humanities scholarship (outside the small, marginal, and suspect field of "sexology") included neither sex nor bodies; it treated the male experience and perspective as universal. Sociologists had no grasp of the concept "gender" except for the Parsonian conception of family-based "sex roles," and their work largely ignored women as social actors. Feminism appeared only as a relic of history.

The influence of *Our Bodies, Ourselves* is inseparable from the impact of the women's liberation movement, the largest social movement in the history of the United States, and one that still evokes intense resistance. The large gender gap in grasping the significance of this book was evident recently when CNN recognized the book's twenty-fifth anniversary by interviewing its two leading authors. The CNN producer reported that when she first proposed the interview to a large staff meeting, all the women in the room said, "Great idea!" and all the men said, "What is it?"

Our Bodies' appeal to women, like that of the women's movement as a whole, lies in the immediacy and, sometimes, the urgency of the information it contains. It can function as a manual in which to look up specific problems, from battering to breast-feeding, candida to cunnilingus. It does not defer to expertise; it will never tell you, as did Dr. Spock and his colleagues for so many years: "If in doubt, call your doctor." Its assumption that readers want this large quantity of information is unexceptionable today, but only because of its own extraordinary influence.

The book fits today's self-help fashion because it helped to construct that mode. *Our Bodies* could be analyzed to show that books can be what readers make of them — an example of the poststructuralist emphasis on the indeterminacy of meaning. Or, taking a social-constructionist approach, it can be understood as a cultural artifact whose significance changes over time. More precisely, it stands as evidence that the meanings of texts are powerfully shaped by social ethos and social movement. It could be read as demonstrating the trajectory of the second-wave women's liberation movement from radical to cultural feminism, from an insurgent challenge to institutionalized power to . . . eating healthy and learning to love our bodies. But this declension model misses the dynamics of social-movement influence, which include the trade-offs between breadth and radicalism; and it fails to appreciate the centrality of feminist emphasis on connecting structural forces with everyday life.

Our Bodies exemplifies feminism's subversive theoretical influence in its insistence that body and sexual norms are politically constructed. Today, some of the most theoretically sophisticated scholarship aims to integrate the body into poststructuralist and social-constructionist perspectives. *Our Bodies* blazed this trail and, moreover, assumed the task not only of making this anticommonsense argument but also of leading nonacademic readers through it, which in turn required a standard of proof much higher than is customary in academic discourse.

All of the book's editions rest on a critique of authoritatively legitimated expertise, presented in popular language but fundamentally identical with the similar critique presented by scholars. The authors repeatedly remind us of their lay status and of the historically destructive errors (and worse) of medical professionals and moral authorities. The book continues to devote substantial attention to a critique of the political economics of the health, pharmaceutical, food, and other, related industries. Take, for example, the chapters about body image and food. After a feminist cultural critique of fear of fatness and a crash course in nutritional awareness, the book discusses the influence the food industry exercises over the FDA and USDA; the advertising wars and constant introduction of new products by the few conglomerates that control food manufacturing; how the dollar spent on food is distributed among grower, packer, packager, transporter, and so on; how women workers are treated in the food industry. The authors also remind us repeatedly of the collective process of the book's production. In typically New Left fashion, the first edition told us how "sisters added their experiences, questions, fear, feelings, excitement. . . . We all learned together." The last edition adds a more theoretical take on the process — "We are increasingly proud of our dependence upon one another in a culture that so prizes independence" — but also repeats the personal — "We have seen one another through four divorces and three marriages, one case of hot flashes and some long dramatic affairs with men and women."

Just as some feminist and minority scholars have challenged dominant definitions of what counts as theory and as science, so *Our Bodies* integrates abstract, synthetic (masculine) knowledge with bodily, experiential (female) knowledge that produces immediate personal consequences. Nowhere is this integration more essential than in medicine, which faces the conundrum that the primary evidence of illness is pain, unknowable by the physician. Many professions have laid claim to their status on the basis of social-control agendas, but few have had a more directly tyrannical practice than medicine in its attempt to heal bodies while minimizing the authority of the body in question — the patient.

For at least 150 years one response to expertise — in particular to "regular" medical authority — has been self-help movements that shade into mysticism, from the water cure to Sylvester Graham to feminist moon therapies. The agenda of *Our Bodies* is different. Its goal is not to deny the benefits of expertise but to democratize access to it and insist that its more important validity test is not the opinion of professional peers but that of "patients." It emphasizes the diversity of bodily existence and experience, resisting the (social-)scientific and medical tendency to create norms and measure deviations from them. In this priority, the book is not uniquely feminist — i.e., for women — but constitutes a larger democratic and libertarian challenge to expertise. The book uses citations to medical and other scholarly journals sparingly, directing readers to studies they could actually read, and it provides carefully selected bibliographies for every chapter. The recent editions use humor to make points and to leaven political passion, as in a cartoon that shows a woman on a gurney saying to her surgeon, "I hope you can justify this hysterectomy to my women's health group."

Of course, *Our Bodies, Ourselves* was a prime mover in the construction and diffusion of feminism and particularly of a large women's health movement, perhaps the most vibrant contemporary expression of grassroots feminist activism. The National Women's Health Network emerged in 1975 out of the kind of activism the book stimulated, including women's outrage at the dangers of the oral contraceptives so cavalierly and prematurely mass-marketed in the 1960s. The impact of this movement has been so large that much of it has become invisible as women's health demands have been integrated into mainstream medicine. There are women's clinics in major hospitals and HMOs; childbirth practices have accommodated many feminist demands, such as birthing rooms, nurse midwives, labor coaches, family participation in birth, and new methods of labor and delivery; some medical schools now produce health newsletters for women; the inclusion of women in clinical trials is now required (for decades standard drug trials used only men); and there has been a (belated) upswing in research funds for women's diseases, such as breast cancer. The changes do not affect only women; the women's health movement has been the largest single pressure for a more democratic medicine for everyone.

Our Bodies, Ourselves exemplifies the transformative influence of feminism on both popular and academic knowledge. Over the last twenty-five years the impact of the women's movement on the academy has been in a transdisciplinary direction, and the most challenging edges of feminist theory and scholarship rub against the grain of disciplinary structures and practices. The feminist influence opened for scholars an array of new topics and challenges to traditional assumptions, such as the distinction between public and private. *Our Bodies* draws together and unfolds a broad swathe of the feminist insights, for example, into the political construction of bodies and the gendered dynamics of institutions, that have challenged and enriched the social sciences. Now sociologists notice and think about gender; indeed, by the 1990s the Sex and Gender Section, founded in 1973, had become the largest research section in the ASA. But the movement of feminist ideas into sociology has been uneven — widely transformative, but also co-opted (e.g., by the practice of using gender as a variable rather than using it as a theoretical category) and contained (ironically, by the institutionalization of feminist sociology as a subfield). In sociology, as in other disciplines, the majority of male scholars do not read feminist work, attend feminist sessions at conferences, or incorporate gender analyses into their teaching.

This symposium's emphasis on "influential books" skewed the evaluation of scholarly significance toward books by individual social theorists. Because feminist ideas are in constant interaction with a vibrant social movement, they develop quickly, and any one work is rapidly surpassed. Feminist ideas have evolved collectively, mixing genres, rather than through the vehicle of individual "theory stars." Social theory is a self-conscious genre whose canonized heroes — a symbolic source of legitimacy and coherence in the fragmented discipline of sociology — are all men. And in sociology there has been a persistent separation between works labeled "social theory" and works labeled "feminist theory."

Our Bodies, Ourselves reminds us that knowledge is produced not solely in the academy, and that some of the most productive new veins of research and analysis arise from radical movements.

6 THE MEANING OF THIS LIST

SOCIOLOGICAL POLITICS AND *CONTEMPORARY SOCIOLOGY'S* TEN MOST INFLUENTIAL BOOKS

Gerald Marwell

This comment was first drafted about a month after *Contemporary Sociology* (*CS*) published its reviews of the "ten most influential" (MI) books. Because the board of editors had anticipated considerable reaction, they had set ground rules for comments. As usual, I didn't want to play by the rules. Most important, I could not contain my analysis to 300 words. Although they therefore decided against printing my comment in *CS*, the editors graciously asked to include it in this book.

My original comments appear below mostly as drafted. I have done the kind of editing that might be expected in writing a third draft after receiving editorial suggestions. Until its last section, where I have added brief comments, this essay does *not* take into consideration *Required Reading*'s additions to the original *CS* list or any other new discussion of procedures or analysis. Of this new material, I have seen only the names of books added to the MI list.

JEALOUSY AND OTHER EMOTIONS

I admit to being jealous. While I served as editor of *ASR*, it never occurred to me to pick out the "ten most influential articles" of the past twenty-five years. I missed a great opportunity to reward my (intellectual) friends and to advise younger sociologists on what kind of articles they should write if they wanted to be "influential."

Jealousy aside (or not), I am uncomfortable with *CS*'s anointment of the ten MI books. The exercise seems much too political to have been done on the American Sociological Association's dime and with the Association's imprimatur. Especially since I do not think it was done well. What bothers me most is a vision of some Ph.D. student in the year 2050 writing "To understand changes in the discipline over the past half-century, compare the content of the most influential books of. . . ." Is this how we want to be remembered? As a discipline dominated by Geertz and Said and the Boston Women's Collective. Is this how we *should* be remembered?

WHO IS INFLUENCING WHOM?

Our discipline teaches methods for describing social process and social facts, and "influence," after all, is a social process. I wish the arbiters at *CS* had bothered with method in creating their list. A concern for method may reflect a "positivist bias," but a summary dismissal of method reflects a bias too. A virtue of method is that it forces you to be clear about what you are trying to do as well as how you are going to do it. Since *CS* paid little attention to clarifying method or objective I am not surprised that although I personally agree with some of its choices, I don't think the list as a whole is very good or, more important, very defensible.

The concept of influence is interactional, implying that someone or something is influencing someone or something. The most egregious problem with the editorial board's approach is that they never tell us who is being influenced in their conceptualization of this process. The closest I can come from the *CS* editor's description of the process implies that the "who" being influenced is the editor himself, and possibly some of his friends and associates. I, for one, don't find that a compelling basis for selection.

Some more logical candidates for the "influenced" might be (1) professional sociologists; (2) sociological scholarship; (3) American intellectuals (*CS* is an American journal); (4) all intellectuals; (5) scholarship in all areas; (6) public discourse; (7) public life; (8) everyone who reads work in sociology. Any of these definitions is reasonable. But each would certainly imply a different MI list, and make different methods of selection more appropriate. So many of the readers of sociology are students that their list would probably include some of the textbooks that frame the way they understand the discipline. Citation data might be useful to measure influence on sociological scholarship or on social science. The present list almost certainly does not contain the books most influential on Indian and Brazilian intellectuals. Actually, when I look at the eight possible audiences, I doubt that any of them would be satisfied by the MI list at hand.

The editors were no better in defining the population of candidates from which the most influential "books" could be selected. Obviously, the CS list does not represent the ten most influential books written by sociologists. Several of the authors would never describe themselves as sociologists. I, myself, don't find some of the MI books particularly sociological, but would not claim my reaction to be representative, and certainly not definitive.

Furthermore, calling these the most influential books published in the last twenty-five years hides a much less impressive reality: At best, the selections are the most influential books published between 1973 and 1980, a much shorter window of opportunity. I presume that books published after 1980 had not yet had the opportunity to be sufficiently "influential," even if they are much stronger contributions to the discipline. They never had a chance.

Interestingly, CS's editor and most of his chosen essayists received their Ph.D.'s between 1975 and 1980. I am tempted to conclude that CS's MI list represents the books most influential on a specific sociological cohort.

RUMMAGING

Given my reaction to the list, I thought it might be interesting to see how dangerous I could become with a little knowledge gathered by rummaging through the *Social Science Citation Index*. I am no expert on the *Index;* I have never used it for research purposes. Not surprisingly, I made some mistakes, which CS's editor kindly helped me to find.

The data I used were for 1995. Obviously, one year is not a measure of "influence" over the past twenty-five. Some influence is subtle, changing the way we think so thoroughly that we no longer "cite" any particular source as producing that change. And so on. But time was scarce, and why should the more influential books be cited less at any time, including 1995, than their less influential contemporaneous brethren?

To give some perspective on CS's MI list, I selected a number of books published within or very close to the same seven-year window of time that might have competed for inclusion. I didn't have time for a systematic sample, so these are basically suggestions from friends. Coleman is included as an example of a recent book that might be

Table 1
Citations in 1995

	Date	Total	"Core"
CS List			
Bourdieu	1972	140	1–4
Braverman	1976	86	3–7
Chodorow	1978	110	3–4
Foucault	1977	227	3–5
Geertz	1973	218	0–2
Said	1978	86	0–0
Skocpol	1979	47	5–7
Wallerstein	1980	49	3–4
Wilson	1980	40	7–11
Our Bodies	1971	0	0–0
Comparisons			
Duncan	1975	22	3–5
Featherman and Hauser	1978	29	8–15
Giddens	1984	148	4–9
Goffman	1974	61	1–11
Jencks	1972	33	4–8
Kanter	1977	105	8–11
Kohn	1977	30	3–9
Lieberson	1980	29	7–11
Tilly	1978	51	6–16
Coleman	1990	65	7–9

influential (titles of the books may be found in the References). I am sorry if I missed *your* book. It deserved inclusion.

In Table 1 the "Total" column reports the number of citations to a given book in the 1995 *Index*. The other column — "Core" — contains two numbers for each book. The first and smaller number in the "core" column reports citations in four journals that are commonly used as the "leading journals"; *ASR, AJS, Social Forces,* and *Sociological Methodology.* The second and higher of the two numbers is an estimate of the number of citations by scholars writing in specifically sociological journals produced in America (ethnocentric, but easier); to the four leaders I add other ASA journals, journals with some version of the word "sociology" in their titles, and *Social Problems.* Journals whose titles suggested they might attract a considerable number of articles by nonsociologists were omitted.

In general, citation patterns support the continued impact of many of CS's MI books on American (and European) scholars, particularly on scholars who do not publish in core sociology journals. If we forget *Our Bodies, Ourselves,* the selection of which *CS*'s editor himself describes as an idiosyncratic coup d'editeur, the nonsociologist authors on the list obviously have vast audiences in the social sciences. Braverman and Foucault are sometimes cited in the core sociology journals (the numbers are modest), but citation to the others in these journals is almost nonexistent. Which leaves me wondering whether they were really influential on sociologists, and if they were not why they would make a list of influential books in a sociology journal?

Not surprisingly, sociologists are more likely to cite books by self-identified sociologists, regardless of how often they are cited by other scholars. The sociologists on *CS*'s MI list fit this pattern, but are not more likely to be cited than the sociologists on the comparison list. In fact, some of the comparison books that are least cited in the Total column have the most citations in the Core column. The continued attention to Featherman and Hauser is an interesting case in point.

WHAT IS SOCIOLOGY?

There may be little difference between the *CS* MI and comparison books in their influence as measured by citations. Substantively, however, differences between the two lists strike me as reasonably clear — although this can only be a personal evaluation. The *CS* MI list is tilted toward politics, including identity politics, and toward culture. These are the long-term projects of those who have seen sociology as having a historical "core" aligned with debates important to European intellectuals. In this vision there may be room, but perhaps not appreciation, for all the social psychologists (Goffman, Kohn), organizational analysts (Kanter), demographers (Featherman and Hauser, Lieberson), methodologists (Duncan), and other professionally oriented scholars who actually constitute the bulk of the productive discipline. It is in that sense that *CS*'s MI list is fundamentally political.

Personally, I think it is bad politics for the discipline. The profession contains many trained and intelligent people trying their best to understand various aspects of social reality in their own ways and on their own terms. You or I may find any specific work incompetent, unbelievable, or immaterial. But it requires real hubris to dismiss the work of cadres of Ph.D.s with a wave of the hand. Each time we try to claim the high ground for our way of thinking and doing sociology we implicitly relegate others to the low, allowing us to look over their heads and directly into the sun. We would be better off keeping our eyes on what our colleagues are doing. We might learn something.

AN ADDENDUM IN RESPONSE TO THE NEW MI LIST

The extended list of seventeen MI books now contains three of the books I had chosen for my "comparison" list (Kanter, Tilly, Featherman and Hauser), one book by another card-carrying sociologist (Hochschild — a favorite book of mine), and three more books by non-sociologists (Becker, Murray, Nie). I must admit that I think that the development of *SPSS* (Nie) had more influence on sociology than any of the books cited — although by now most users of *SPSS* may have never read Nie.

Again without explanation, the editor has chosen to include Murray's book, which I expect to have almost no influence on the field in the twenty-first century, and Becker, who probably is more influential. Of course, by whatever criteria these decisions are being made, these might be wholly appropriate choices. I just wish I knew what those criteria were. I certainly don't think of the extended list as an "improvement" over the original.

Perhaps we should try for the one hundred "most influential books," or even two hundred? If the editor does not try to rank them in terms of their relative influence (thank goodness he didn't open that can of worms), fewer and fewer people will complain that their favorites were omitted.

ADDITIONAL REFERENCES (To the Books in CS's Top Seventeen)

Coleman, James. 1990. *The Foundations of Social Theory.* Cambridge: Harvard University Press, Belknap Press.

Duncan, Otis Dudley. 1975. *Introduction to Structural Equation Models.* New York: Academic Press.

Giddens, Anthony. 1984. *The Constitution of Society: Outline of the Theory of Structuration.* Cambridge: Polity Press.

Goffman, Erving. 1974. *Frame Analysis: An Essay on the Organization of Experience.* Boston: Northeastern University Press.

Jencks, Christopher, Marshall Smith, Henry Acland, Mary Jo Bane, David Cohn, Herbert Gintis, Barbara Heyns, and Steven Michelson. 1972. *In-*

equality: A Reassessment of Family and Schooling in America. New York: Basic Books.

Kohn, Melvin. 1977. *Class and Conformity: A Study in Values.* Chicago: University of Chicago Press.

Lieberson, Stanley. 1980. *A Piece of the Pie: Black and White Immigrants Since 1880.* Berkeley: University of California Press.

TAKING THE LIST AS IT STANDS:
WHAT DOES IT SAY ABOUT SOCIOLOGY TODAY?

Rachel A. Rosenfeld

As a child, I decided that I wanted to be a professor, and, early in college, I decided I wanted to be a *sociology* professor. I hadn't studied sociology in high school, but when I had the first course in college it seemed a discipline in which one could justify doing anything—from reading novels to studying math to thinking about what happened in one's own life, such as growing up in Faubus-era Little Rock. One didn't need to make any choices! I've never regretted being a sociology professor. Although I now specialize in the area of social stratification, I still enjoy the diversity of subjects and methods in our field. The "most influential" books in *Required Reading* illustrate this range of topics and approaches. Others in this book discuss the meaning of "influential" and whether these books are. But what does this list say about the current state of sociology, if one takes it at face value?

Recently, there have been a number of published discussions of "what's wrong with sociology" and with the American Sociological Association (ASA), as well as innumerable passing commiserations or debates over this in halls of departments and meeting hotels. Stephen Cole (1994a) summarizes the intellectual problems raised in the special issue of *Sociological Forum* on this topic as "the absence of theory that can be utilized in empirical research, the fact that theory development seems to follow fads rather than make progress as in the natural sciences, the lack of cognitive consensus in the discipline, the emphasis on methodology as opposed to findings, the interference of political ideology with cognitive development, and the failure of the products of the discipline to be relevant for solving social problems in society"

I thank Peter Blau and François Nielsen for helpful discussion and comments.

(129). Some of these tendencies are cited as behind sociology's organizational woes, such as university administrations', funding agencies', and the general public's lack of respect for sociology and the ASA's expanding attention to professional rather than disciplinary matters (Huber 1995; Simpson and Simpson 1994).

The list in *Required Reading* provides useful data for thinking about these issues. I'll focus on the emphasis on conceptual and methodological tools, the underrepresentation of cumulative efforts, and the role of timing and accessibility. Underlying my discussion is my belief that the goal and role of sociology are to help us understand how societies work.

A PLETHORA OF CONCEPTS AND APPROACHES?

I was struck by how many of the reviews emphasized the broadly methodological or conceptual importance of the book rather than its findings, as Clawson and Zussman also recognize. For example, Wellman urged *Required Reading*'s editor to include the *SPSS* manual precisely because it provided sociologists (and others within and outside the social sciences) with such a powerful tool for statistical analysis. Simon describes Foucault's *Discipline and Punish*'s influence as an exemplar of research strategy, rather than because of its findings or even its theory of power, and Calhoun rates Bourdieu's *Outline of a Theory of Practice* as more influential than Bourdieu's other work because those publications are scattered across a range of empirical subjects. Smith-Lovin suggests that Hochschild's *The Managed Heart* has had only "shallow" influence on sociology because it does *not* provide a research strategy. Further, many of the books on the "influential" list have had an impact because of particular concepts or premises, such as "emotional labor," "tokenism," "gender," or "world-system," even when, as Goodwin explains so well, sociologists don't have an accurate understanding of these terms.

Clawson and Zussman, in their justification of the list, suggest it is important to know about these approaches and concepts because they help sociologists understand each other. This certainly has organizational benefits. Many people in the ASA or the International Sociological Association (ISA) live within a particular section or research committee or a set of sections or research committees. These settings are loci in which influence occurs. At least part of Wallerstein's impact on the field, for example, has been through the ASA section on Political Economy of the World-System (Friedmann). Feminism and gender studies led to the Sex and Gender section's becoming the largest in the ASA (Gordon and Thorne). The study that Featherman and Hauser reported on in *Opportunity and Change* was part of a general, cross-national research program of the ISA's Research Committee 28 (Social Stratification). These subgroups of the larger organizations provide sociologists with valuable intellectual exchanges and collegiality, and leadership in these circles is one path to leadership in the ASA or ISA as a whole (Rosenfeld et al. 1997). However, if we remain split into sub-fields, we lose a collective identity.

Further, as Clawson and Zussman, as well as Marwell, point out, many of the books on the list are not by sociologists. The array of concepts and methods from a variety of disciplines and sociological subareas provided in *Required Reading* provides a lot of stimulation for the sociological imagination. As C. W. Mills (1959 [1961]) advised in describing his own research strategies:

The idea is to use a variety of viewpoints: you will, for instance, ask yourself how would a political scientist whom you have recently read approach this, and how would that experimental psychologist, or this historian. You try to think in terms of a variety of viewpoints and in this way let your mind become a moving prism catching light from as many angles as possible. (214)

If I remember properly, one of the aphorisms Jerry Marwell quoted to us when I was in graduate school in the early 1970s was "if you give a boy a hammer, everything needs hammering."[1] Having a range of tools may not only help us understand our colleagues and stimulate the sociological imagination, but also keep us from hammering away too much.

At the same time, there are problems with being too interdisciplinary. Intellectually, we may be tempted to swallow other disciplines whole, giving up some of what makes us sociologists. As England and Budig illustrate, this isn't necessary. Sociologists have something to offer and need to make that known. Disciplines coalesced over the late-nineteenth and early twentieth-centuries. Their boundaries have not so

1. Nowadays, he probably says, "If you give a child . . ."

much disappeared as increasingly blurred. But there still seems to be a much more "social" view of the world in sociology, compared with other disciplines. Organizationally, if everyone is part of something else, then it becomes difficult to sustain sociology and identify sociological work. Different affiliations and identities compete for members, resources, and recognition. My own department considers the inter- and multidisciplinary activities of many of our faculty to be one of its strengths. Yet, in a recent faculty meeting, our chair commended someone whose interdisciplinary research was getting a lot of press "for publicly identifying himself as a sociologist." If we want to reproduce sociologists—those who take a "social" perspective (whatever that is)—which I do, then we have to balance the benefits and risks of including many perspectives.[2]

EMPIRICAL FINDINGS AND PUTTING THE PIECES TOGETHER

Having all these tools is wonderful. But they are wasted if they are not used. And if they are used to produce separate little pieces that are impossible to fit together, then nothing is built.

In *Sociological Forum,* Davis (1994) argues that the problem with sociology is that it is "incoherent," that it doesn't hang together. One reason for this incoherence is that sociologists don't say "what we learned rather than how and why we learned it" (184). It is often easier to identify sociological leaders by their approaches than by what they have discovered. Findings are important, as a few of the reviewers note, even while also highlighting conceptual or methodological contributions. Grusky and Weeden, for example, suggest the most important influence of *Opportunity and Change* may be as an exemplar of "the Wisconsin style," which emphasizes interpretations supported by careful data analysis. Williams states that the main contribution of Kanter's *Men and Women of the Corporation* was that it showed that widespread, negative stereotypes about employed women were wrong. Murray was influential, Lowi and Mink argue, in large part because he was using data. England and Budig criticize Becker for failing to present empirical evidence to support his hypotheses. And Smith-Lovin

2. Notice that I'm not taking on the difficult task of specifying more precisely what sociology is or whether there is a core (as do Cole 1994b and Huber 1995).

points out that findings can have influence even when they haven't been established (just as concepts can have impact even when they aren't understood).

Mills (1961) says, "The purpose of empirical inquiry is to settle disagreements and doubts about facts, and thus to make arguments more fruitful by basing all sides more substantively. Facts discipline reason; but reason is the advance guard in any field of learning" (205). Kanter went out literally to look at what was happening within a particular organization, and her observations led to, and supported, her conceptualizations. Others had seen similar instances of women's lower achievement, but seen it differently. Both Williams and Laslett note that a contribution of gender studies is the emphasis on variation as compared with absolutes: Asking under what conditions there is greater or less gender dissimilarity and inequality takes one further than simply looking for whether there *is* a difference. Goodwin defends Skocpol against those who see *States and Social Revolutions* as an exercise in pure induction by stressing how she used the comparative case method to "develop, test, refine, and (not least) debunk a number of theoretical hypotheses about revolutionary process" (35). Murray took the data and surrounded them with syllogisms. The issue is not whether we should be inductive or deductive — one is rarely one or the other in actual research — but that empirical evidence is important as it interacts with general sociological logic, particular theories, and specific concepts.

Postmodern and feminist theories, among others, take this further by emphasizing that "facts" is not a straightforward concept, even (or especially) in a court of law (Scheppele 1994). Seidman argues that Said's *Orientalism should* be more influential in sociology, not only as an example of cultural sociology but even more generally as a way to study social differences. We do not, however, need to go into a paralyzing whirlpool where finer and finer division of social categories or acceptance of scholarship as a mere play on words prevents any generalizations about social reality.[3]

Davis (1994) also complains: "We neither refute nor confirm and expand ideas; we just become bored with them and move on to some

---

3. Similarly, we need not go so far into seeing everything as socially constructed that we deny that there *is* a physical reality.

'cutting edge' novelty" (181). Reviewers of these "influential" books are aware of this problem, too. Gould puzzles over Tilly's influence through *From Mobilization to Revolution,* given that researchers in the area of social protest did not follow up on its model of large, broad empirical tests of formal theory. Grusky and Weeden emphasize that replication that also extends a line of research is an indicator of influence. Burawoy argues that Braverman's *Labor and Monopoly Capital*'s influence was not so much because of its own depth, but because of the research it stimulated. *Labor and Monopoly Capital* was one of the books we were all reading at Wisconsin in the early 1970s at the time that Hauser, Featherman, and Sewell were continuing their research, research that—as Grusky and Weeden note—did include explicit consideration of institutional structures as sources of change. (Erik Wright hadn't arrived yet.) At the same time, Grusky and Weeden describe the tension between the need for cumulative research and the problem of declining intellectual and empirical returns when a path is worn too deep.

Required Reading, then, gives us hints about balancing concepts, different ways of knowing, empirical evidence, and theory building, although it leaves the solution to this problem as an exercise for the reader.

TIMING (AND ACCESSIBILITY) ARE EVERYTHING?

Many of the reviews point out that the book's ideas weren't entirely new, but that they emerged at a propitious time and in an understandable, convincing way. Clawson and Zussman mention some of these books that spoke to social concerns and social movements of the 1960s and 1970s. In addition, although Simon argues that *Discipline and Punish*'s influence now is not because of its specific substance, he describes how it resonated with prison unrest and reforms at the time it was published. Friedmann states that international crises and changes in the early 1970s made "the time ripe" for Wallerstein's *The Modern World System.* England and Budig, though, speculate that acceptance of Becker's *Treatise on the Family* among economists was because of the man—literally—in the period before feminist research had even a limited impact on this discipline, while both the combination of the times and the man made *The Declining Significance of Race* influential.

In addition, many of these same books are described as interesting and clearly written. Friedmann says, for example, "It was no small matter to generate sociological excitement about the sixteenth century" (150). *A Treatise on the Family* is "at least somewhat accessible to noneconomists" because it presents its ideas verbally as well as mathematically (102). Murray seduced readers with his seemingly straightforward logic. Hochschild is widely read because her work is readable, although this readability may be at the expense of methodological details. It is not surprising that there is overlap between the authors on the "most influential" list and those on Gans's list of best-sellers. As he suggests, best-sellers as he measures them are probably widely used as supplementary readings in undergraduate courses, which means they are written in such a way that someone relatively untrained in sociological methods, theory, and jargon can understand them. On the other hand, *Outline of a Theory of Practice,* Calhoun says, took longer than Bourdieu's other books to gain attention because it was more difficult to read, but because it was "sufficiently oblique in style" it appealed to theorists of very different camps (86).

It would be strange if sociologists did not respond to what was going on in the society around them, if indeed they want to understand this society. Such understanding is much of what sociology can offer those outside of the research community, while approaches to this understanding are our contribution to other disciplines. Funding agencies and state universities increasingly demand that the research they support have practical payoffs. COSSA and the ASA have made efforts to provide channels through which sociologists (and other social scientists) can be heard by government and other policymakers. Those who are able to communicate, all else equal, will be those to whom people listen.

This seems all to the good. Weber (1949), in his essays on methodology, advised that values enter research through choice of problems, although they should not enter thereafter. Given the malleability of "facts," it is difficult for one's predilections not to influence research design and interpretation of evidence. But there is the same general problem even when political and moral values are not involved, as when adherence to a particular theory skews the way one studies a given subject. High standards for research, appropriate to the given approach, are a responsibility of the discipline as a whole, as well of the individual researcher, through editorial policies, criteria for awards and other honors, published ethical statements, and public discussion of controversial findings. The ASA and its sections play an important role here (Simpson and Simpson 1994). At least some sociologists, like some biological and physical scientists, worry about how their research will be used. One doesn't always have control over this. The alternative is to go back to not stating one's findings or not having findings at all. Trying out our ideas publicly, rather than simply among those within the same subfield, can force us to think more clearly about what we are doing as well as stimulate further investigation, as has been true, for example, in the public/private schools and comparable worth debates, as well as those about the urban underclass.

Not everyone needs to do policy-relevant research. If all research were targeted at contemporary problems, we would lose the ability to find more general patterns and test and expand theories. One problem sociologists and other social scientists have is that we aim at moving targets. Morris, for example, suggests that Wilson's arguments about the declining significance of race relied too much on what was happening in a period when African Americans *had* approached parity with whites in college attendance (controlling for class) and wages of the college educated. Further, none of us (even economists) can predict all the social problems the future holds. By pursuing our varied theoretical and empirical interests, we may be more likely to have at hand resources for interpreting change and dislocation when they happen.

CONCLUSION

Required Reading may or may not include the "most influential" books of the last twenty-five years, but it does illustrate many of the trends at least some sociologists have viewed as problematic. Sociologists use diverse approaches and theories, may deemphasize empirical findings and cumulative research (or, alternatively, slip into ruts too easily), and be overly sensitive (or not sensitive enough) to contemporary social problems. Organizationally, these tendencies present challenges of maintaining disciplinary identity and membership, upholding research standards, and providing ways of letting others know what sociologists do. I'm optimistic that at worst we will continue stumbling along as we have and at best we will more consciously balance the benefits and costs of the way we are.

REFERENCES

Cole, Stephen. 1994a. "Introduction: What's Wrong with Sociology?" *Sociological Forum* 9: 129–31.

———. 1994b. "Why Sociology Doesn't Make Progress Like the Natural Sciences." *Sociological Forum* 9: 133–54.

Davis, James A. 1994. "What's Wrong with Sociology?" *Sociological Forum* 9: 179–97.

Huber, Joan. 1995. "Institutional Perspectives on Sociology." *American Journal of Sociology* 101: 194–216.

Mills, C. Wright. [1959] 1961. *The Sociological Imagination*. New York: Grove Press.

Rosenfeld, Rachel A., David Cunningham, and Kathryn Schmidt. 1997. "American Sociological Association Elections, 1975–1996: Exploring 'Feminization.'" *American Sociological Review* 62: 746–59.

Scheppele, Kim Lane. 1994. "Legal Theory and Social Theory." *Annual Review of Sociology* 20:383–406.

Simpson, Ida Harper, and Richard L. Simpson. 1994. "The Transformation of the American Sociological Association." *Sociological Forum* 9: 259–78.

Weber, Max. [1904, 1905, 1917] 1949. *Max Weber on the Methodology of the Social Sciences*. Trans. and ed. Edward A. Shils and Henry A. Finch. Glencoe: Free Press.

WHO'S IN? WHO'S OUT?

Charles Lemert

A story has been circulating for years now — one so disturbing that I would have wished it away had I not heard it so often from so many. In time the plausibility of the story dawned, if only because I came to realize that variants of it are played out just under the level of collective consciousness in departments with which I am all too well acquainted. The story, in its standard version, is this:

A department of sociology in a better than average university systematically purges its faculty roster of a junior member whose teaching and scholarship embrace authors and books considered theoretically heterodox by the department's seniors. The method of execution is relatively gentle. She is told she has no future there. She departs, leaving behind graduate students she is no longer able to help with their work. The expelled faculty member is neither white nor otherwise possessed of the social attributes favored by the now older order of academic sociologists. Still, most versions of the story account for the banishment by unregressed, monocausal reference to one of our field's more subtle excluding codes. Her seniors simply felt that her view of sociology was "too unsociological."

Like trade unions, political parties, and country clubs, sociology is a complex institution, which is to say that sociology also practices social selection. It, thereby, becomes what it becomes by investing its cash reserves so as to include those thought to be good while excluding those considered bad. Yet, unlike unions, parties, and clubs, sociology is an institution that reproduces itself more or less quietly. Elsewhere, the few hardy souls who are still looking for Jimmy Hoffa, the Elder, are innocent kin to those who were surprised a short while ago to learn that Spiro Agnew, on the occasion of his death, had actually been alive all those years. But, twenty years from now, sociologists may not ask, Whatever became of what's-her-name? — a junior colleague banished to the Dakotas or her brilliant student now practicing law in San Jose. We will not remember their names. We will not have known them. As Pierre Bourdieu and Erving Goffman, among others, have taught us, an interesting question to ask of banishing institutions like the Teamsters, the Republican party, and official sociology is always, Who's In? Who's Out? — and why?

Required Reading will annoy many people nearly as much as did its earlier version on the pages of *Contemporary Sociology*. This is good. Dan Clawson and his colleagues in the editorial work of American sociology's most widely read journal have done something audacious. By selecting a list of books from among their favorites, they have dared to suggest that in the last quarter century the field has not patrolled its borders carefully enough so as to prevent a detectable migration of its intellectual center. In their introduction to the book, Clawson and Zussman strain needlessly to make it seem that the rhyme and reason of their original list was more high-minded than it was. Gerald Marwell is right to say that theirs is a list of favorites, every bit as much as he is wrong to infer therefrom that the list, being of favorites he (and his) would not have chosen, is of pernicious consequence.

In the fuss over the original *CS* list precious little blame has been cast on those ultimately responsible for the list. It was, after all, agents of official sociology itself, acting in the name of the American Sociological Association, who handed over control of one of its most important journals to such a gang of editors. And what a gang it is — feminists, occasional Marxists, fellow travelers on the indefinite fringe of the cultural left, and other varieties of left leaners. Just a few years ago, most of these now officially endorsed editors would have been considered impossibly off-beat. One or two may still be. They are, with occasional exception, all of about the same professional age — an age that covers almost exactly the twenty-year period of their book list which, in not incidental turn, happens to be the period in which an older generation's scientific ideal of sociology gave way to a more honestly political one. When they were starting out, few of the current *CS* editors are likely to have supposed that they would one day crash the gates of one of the field's most efficient instruments of gatekeeping. What upsets some people about a book list like theirs is that such people as these are keeping one of the gates.

It may be, as Gerald Marwell says, that any book list of this kind, however it is composed, is "bad politics for the discipline." Even if his concern does not quite issue from the same political and intellectual interests that motivated objections to the list by Jerry Watts, one of the

CS editors, the caution is understandable. Still, Marwell, himself recently in a position to keep the gate to the field's most prestigious scholarly journal, makes an assumption that betrays the likelihood that, had he done as Clawson did, he would have kept his own gate according to different, if better disguised, political tastes. In respect to his widely shared concern about unsociological politicization, Marwell assumes what his data refute — that the *CS* list is somehow willy-nilly and that it thereby "claims the high ground," while relegating those on the *out* to a lower moral order. With uncommon empirical decency and admirable common sense, Marwell's comparison study demonstrates to his own surprise that, while some others might have been included (as in the book some now are), the *CS* list is entirely reasonable even by his more conservative, *ASR* standards.

What Marwell does not examine (and it would be difficult to know how one easily might) is the many hundreds of sociologists who would never — not for a minute — give his "core" journals more than a passing glance. This well-known but quietly kept secret tells of mysteries vastly more complicated than the difference between book and article cultures to which Clawson and Zussman refer. I have personally heard of sociologists who find the famous core journals not just quite beside the point but nearly as "unsociological" as the seniors of that unmentionable department found the work of the junior colleague they expelled.

Differences of scientific taste, no less than of political appetite, are what makes the world of professional sociology go round. If, therefore, as Marwell says, the field is legion, then the differences Marwell so graciously defends at the conclusion of his essay must arise on the prior, necessary condition that a great number of sociologists read, and are influenced by, such heterodoxic types as Foucault, Said, and the Boston Women's Collective. And (not to forget her just yet), it is a virtual certainty (though by definition of the situation unmeasurable) that the purged junior faculty member — and her students, and others at risk among her cohort — do. They do most certainly.

As a result, Marwell's evidence, no less than Herbert Gans's study of book sales, bear compelling witness, unimplicated by association with the once off-beat political tendencies of the members of the *CS* editorial board, that this list of required readings is far from frivolous. Which evidence leads, so far as I can tell, to the more daunting inevitability that, to use Marwell's phrase, "our way of thinking and doing sociology" is changing, or has changed — like it or not. Some who, in 1972 (the first year of the period in question), were *in* are now *out*. Some *out* then, are now *in*. So goes the world.

What is important for our field's collective self-understanding (if so ideal a state is attainable) is, first of all, that such a list could have been drawn up by such newly reputable types as the *CS* editors who had been authorized to run the book review show for a few years. Worse yet, some who were once pitifully *out* are today committing ever more ghastly atrocities than publishing lists of disputably required readings. They are relentlessly taking over the agencies and instrumentalities of official sociology. In which respect, the question that invites further attention is one that reaches well beyond the niceties (or indecencies) of one or another list of favorite books.

Why has the field changed as it has? In my view it has not so much changed as settled back into its proper place in the scheme of things academic. Those who take the evidence of the *CS* book list as a sign that the field has slipped from a once pure and comfortable degree of scientific discipline suffer a case of historical nearsightedness. They forget that the idea that sociology could be, and should be, a rigorously scientific field is a dogma of tender vintage.

For the duration of its century-long institutional history, sociology has mostly been the home of any number of incongruent activities, among which the scientific ideal has had to compete for public attention. In the earliest years, around the turn of the last century, not even the earnest labors of scientific sociology's institutional founders could dispel the magical hold of all those writers and journalists, social and religious workers, or public intellectuals and all-purpose social activists who worked the freshly plowed field of academic sociology. Even though the early Chicago school made all the right moves to establish sociology as an academic science, its faculty and students served the more worldly interests of institutions for which science was a resource but not an overriding purpose. Booker T. Washington's Tuskegee Institute and Jane Addams's Hull House are the most famous examples. In France, Durkheim, after declaiming his rules for sociological method, moved to Paris, where he became a sometimes notorious public intellectual. Even Weber, his insurmountable fears of public disorder and scientific corruption notwithstanding, could not keep himself out of prominent political romances. It was not until the generation that came to official sociological power after the Second World War that there was anything like a consensus that sociology ought to be, as it is said with tiresome regularity, a cumulative science meant to stand high above the world's political turmoil. That bright but brief moment of triumph lasted for twenty years at most—from the late 1940s to about (if I may mention the sacred year) 1968. Before this period, the field had not quite taken a definite institutional form. After, it reclined to its more characteristic state of scientific instability.

I am well aware that saying this as I have will do nothing to convince those who believe what they were taught about what sociology ought to be. It might help, however, to remark that the heterodox CS list, while it includes several who, like Foucault, may view "social science" as an oxymoron, mostly includes writers who are quite serious about their science. Skocpol, Tilly, Bourdieu, and Wallerstein have not, to be sure, practiced a scientific sociology that would neatly submit to the standards of the core journals. But they have, most evidently, changed the core and other distinctive features of the sociological landscape. This, no doubt, is why their names appear just as prominently on the Marwell or Gans lists as on the CS one.

But, even if they were on no one's list, it would be hard to imagine how any one could believe that the fact that we understand state politics, social movements, culture, and the world economic system differently today is not a direct effect of the writings of Skocpol, Tilly, Bourdieu, and Wallerstein, among others, who, in their separate but manifestly self-conscious ways, did their work on the shoulders of earlier, even classical, sociological giants. Though, in the four cases, the work led to reasonably obvious advances, the same can be said of work that faced controversy. William Julius Wilson's empirically thick studies have forced a rethinking not just of the relations of race to class but, even, of the most fundamental scientific *and* policy terms appropriate to the understanding of urban poverty. Nancy Chodorow, among students of gender and family structure, is as disturbing as Wilson is among experts in his fields. Yet, *Reproduction of Mothering* was the first theoretically sophisticated work to lead us out of the impossible confinements of the sex role theory taught by Parsons's generation. Much could be said of others on the list. In the end, all this boils down to the observation that sociology has indeed advanced (cumulated, if you must) in the past quarter century.

The problem for those who cling to the view that sociology ought to be a normal science is that much of its scientific work is done in and amid a great number of other concerns of sufficient seriousness that *no* one on the CS list (and few even on the Gans or Marwell lists) is simply a sociologist. Theda Skocpol, however she is regarded by sociologists, is generally considered one of the world's most influential political scientists, just as Tilly and Wallerstein are held in comparable esteem by historians — as is Bourdieu by anthropologists, Giddens by geographers, Wilson by policymakers, Chodorow by feminists, Kanter by the organizational behavior people.

What has changed in sociology is that, in becoming more like what it has always been over the long haul, it has very often reached out beyond the narrow confines of the discipline to a wide variety of resources and disciplines, thus to rethink itself and move ahead, thus, in many cases, to attract the attentions of a wider public, as Hochschild, Wilson, Bourdieu, Said, and Foucault have most notably done. This is why the most famous journals are the shrinking core of an increasingly smaller circle of sociological practices. This is why, against what they must know in their heart of hearts, some complain that a list like the CS one is heterodox when in fact it is verifiably orthodox. And, this is why everyone who cares about sociology must keep in mind the story of the young faculty member, and others like her, who are too often purged by an older generation of colleagues who are all too confident that they, and they especially, understand the difference between sociological and "unsociological" truth.

The future always belongs to the young, and those who kill their young in the name of doctrinal purity deserve to rot in the same hell of the forgotten to which they would consign those they fear. Whether they will or not, we shall see. But, worse yet, what we may not see is a blossoming of a fresh generation of scholars, some still in school, who are pressing hard through the ground laid out by the generation of the CS editors that, in its turn, has grown up into the nooks and crannies of sociological authority. Someone out there is buying and reading the more controversial books on this list. That modal someone is certainly younger, new to the field, and well taught by the example of friends and colleagues in other departments who laugh at the idea that official sociology possesses exclusive rights to the sociological imagination.

What is most surprising about the books reviewed in *Required Reading* is that some sociologists are surprised that such favorites as these are as influential as they are. What our field needs, now more than ever, is readers who read as voraciously and as widely as Weber, Du Bois, and Durkheim once did — and as so many of the younger in the field still do. The irony of this book's title is that for them the readings need not be required. That requirement falls to others, the very others who find themselves awkwardly *out* to what is increasingly *in*.

CONTRIBUTORS' NOTES

MICHELLE J. BUDIG is a Ph.D. candidate in sociology at the University of Arizona. Her research focuses on gender, race, and labor markets. She has presented research on organizational deviance, on the pay outcomes for male tokens in female occupations, and on the causal ordering of women's employment and fertility histories. She is currently using longitudinal data and event history analysis to examine race differences in the time ordering of women's employment and pregnancy states. She is also the coauthor of papers about the wage penalties of motherhood and about the effects of high prestige degrees on employment outcomes.

MICHAEL BURAWOY teaches sociology at the University of California, Berkeley, and has written ethnographies of the workplace in Zambia, the United States, Hungary, and Russia. His books include *The Colour of Class on the Copper Mines* (1972), *Manufacturing Consent* (1979), *The Politics of Production* (1985), *Ethnography Unbound* (1991), and *The Radiant Past* (1992).

CRAIG CALHOUN is chair of the sociology department at New York University. Among his recent books are *Nationalism* (1998), *Critical Social Theory* (1995), and *Neither Gods nor Emperors: Students and the Struggle for Democracy in China* (1995). He is also the editor with Moishe Postone and Edward LiPuma of *Bourdieu: Critical Perspectives* (1993). Calhoun's current work focuses on social solidarity, collective identity, and popular politics.

DAN CLAWSON edited *Contemporary Sociology* from 1995 to 1997, including the "most influential" books issue of May 1996. He prefers the book culture to the article culture, but participates in both. His books are *Bureaucracy and the Labor Process: The Transformation of American Industry 1860–1920* (1980), *Money Talks: Corporate PACs and Political Influence* (1992), and *Dollars and Votes: How Business Campaign Contributions Subvert Democracy* (1998); his articles have appeared in the *American Sociological Review, American Journal of Sociology, Social Science Quarterly, Sociological Forum, Sociological*

Quarterly, Social Science Research, and a number of other journals. The recent revival of the labor movement is, he believes, the most exciting political development in many years and will shape both his research and political activism for the next decade. He teaches sociology at the University of Massachusetts, Amherst.

PAULA ENGLAND is a professor of sociology at the University of Arizona, where she is also an affiliate in women's studies. Her research focuses on gender and labor markets and on integrating sociological, economic, and feminist perspectives. She is the author of two books, *Households, Employment, and Gender* with George Farkas (1986) and *Comparable Worth: Theories and Evidence* (1992), and editor of *Theory on Gender/Feminism on Theory* (1993). She has also written numerous articles on gender and labor markets. From 1994 to 1996 she served as the editor of the *American Sociological Review.* She has testified as an expert witness in a number of Title VII discrimination cases.

HARRIET FRIEDMANN is a professor of sociology at the University of Toronto. She is former chair of the American Sociological Association section on Political Economy of the World-System, and a longtime friendly critic of world-systems theory. Her research on the international political economy of food is one of the pioneering examples of a sectoral approach to a sociology of global production, accumulation, and power. Recent publications include "Warsaw Pact Socialism: Detente and the Decline of the Soviet Bloc," in *Rethinking the Cold War,* edited by Allen Hunter (1998) and "The Political Economy of Food," *New Left Review* 197 (1993), as well as the forthcoming chapter "The Political Ecology of Food," in *Food in Global History,* edited by Raymond Grew.

HERBERT J. GANS is the Robert S. Lynd Professor of Sociology at Columbia University. Trained as both a sociologist and a planner, he is the author of nine books, the first being *The Urban Villagers* ([1962], 1982) and the most recent, *The War against the Poor: The Underclass and Antipoverty Policy* ([1995], 1996). He is a past president of the Eastern Sociological Society and the American Sociological Association and a fellow of the American Academy of Arts and Sciences. This article is one of a series of studies and presentations on sociology and the public that began with his 1988 presidential address to the American Sociological Association, which was published as "Sociology in America: The Discipline and the Public," *American Sociological Review* 54 (1989): 1–16.

JEFF GOODWIN is an associate professor of sociology at New York University. He is the author of *State and Revolution, 1945–1991* (forthcoming) and has published articles in the *American Sociological Review, American Journal of Sociology, Social Science History, Theory and Society,* and *Politics and Society.* He is currently editing a volume entitled *Opportunistic Protest?* which examines whether and how a wide variety of social movements are the result of "expanding political opportunities." He was a student of Theda Skocpol's at Harvard University, and much of his work on revolutions reflects the influence of Skocpol's "state-centered" perspective. He has recently written a wide-ranging assessment of this perspective entitled "State-Centered Approaches to Social Revolutions: Strengths and Limitations of a Theoretical Tradition," in *Theorizing Revolutions,* edited by John Foran (1997).

LINDA GORDON is a professor of history at the University of Wisconsin, Madison. She has written several books on gender and the origins of social policy, including *Woman's Body, Woman's Right: A History of Birth Control in America* (rev. ed. 1990) and *Heroes of Their Own Lives* (1988), a history of family violence. Her most recent book is *Pitied but Not Entitled: Single Mothers and the History of Welfare* (1994).

ROGER V. GOULD is a member of the Department of Sociology at the University of Chicago. He has done research on the role of social networks in shaping elite and non-elite political behavior, in both historical and contemporary contexts. In a recent book, *Insurgent Identities: Class, Community, and Protest in Paris from 1848 to the Commune* (1995), he called attention to the importance of neighborhoods as a dimension of collective identity that coexisted and competed with class in the mobilization of urban protest. His current research focuses on feuding and revenge in honor societies.

DAVID B. GRUSKY is a professor of sociology at Stanford University, Honorary Fellow in the Department of Sociology at the University of Wisconsin, Madison, editor with Marta Tienda of the book series Studies in Social Inequality (Stanford University Press), and former National Science Foundation Presidential Young Investigator. He is currently studying the rise and fall of social classes under advanced industrialism, the structure of racial and cross-national variability in social mobility and sex segregation, the sources of modern attitudes toward gender inequality, and long-term trends in patterns of occupational and geographic mobility. He is editor of *Social Stratification: Class, Race, and Gender in Sociological Perspective* (1994) and editor with James Baron and Don Treiman of *Social Differentiation and Social Inequality* (1996).

BARBARA LASLETT is a professor of sociology at the University of Minnesota. She has written extensively on the historical sociology of gender, social reproduction, and the family and on the history of American sociology and feminist scholarship. Between 1990 and 1995 she edited, with Ruth-Ellen B. Joeres, *Signs: Journal of Women in Culture and Society.* Her most recent book, edited with Barrie Thorne, is *Feminist Sociology: Life Histories of a Movement* (1997). She is currently working on a collaborative study with M. J. Maynes and Jennifer Pierce investigating the uses of personal narratives in the social sciences.

CHARLES LEMERT teaches at Wesleyan University in Connecticut. His most recent books include *Sociology after the Crisis* (1995), *Postmodernism Is Not What You Think* (1997), *Social Things* (1997), *The Goffman Reader* (1997), edited with Ann Branaman, and *The Voice of Anna Julia Cooper* (1997), edited with Esme Bhan.

THEODORE J. LOWI is the John L. Senior Professor of American Institutions at Cornell University. He first looked at race and welfare in *The End of Liberalism* ([1969], 1979). He revisited welfare, race, and the conservative coalition in *The End of the Republican Era* (1995). He served as president of the American Political Science Association in 1991 and is currently (1997–2000) president of the International Political Science Association.

GERALD MARWELL is Richard T. Ely Professor of Sociology at the University of Wisconsin, Madison, and a past editor of the *American Sociological Review.* He has published four books and more than sixty articles, served on the board of the University of Wisconsin Press, and been an editorial adviser for various journals and presses. He regularly checks who has been citing his work, and notices who has not.

GWENDOLYN MINK is a professor of politics at the University of California, Santa Cruz. She is the author of *The Wages of Motherhood: Inequality in the Welfare State, 1917–1942* (1995), which won the Victoria Schuck Award of the American Political Science Association. Her most recent books are *Welfare's End* (1998) and *The Reader's Companion to U.S. Women's History* (1998), which she edited with Wilma Mankiller, Marysa Navarro, Barbara Smith, and Gloria Steinem. She cochairs the Women's Committee of One Hundred, a feminist mobilization against punitive welfare policy.

ALDON MORRIS is a professor of sociology at Northwestern University. His book, *The Origins of the Civil Rights Movement* (1984), won the American Sociological Association Distinguished Contribution to Scholarship Award, the Gustavus Myers Award, and the Annual Scholarly Achievement Award of the North Central Sociological Association, and it was selected by *Choice* as one of the outstanding academic books of 1984. He also edited, with Carol Mueller, *Frontiers of Social Movement Theory,* and has published articles in numerous books and journals, including the *American Sociological Review.* Currently he is working on Black protest movements in the northern United States and on culture and social movements. He is also an editor of a forthcoming encyclopedia on American social movements.

RACHEL A. ROSENFELD is Lara G. Hoggard Professor of Sociology and a fellow of the Carolina Population Center at the University of North Carolina, Chapel Hill. A participant in social movements of the 1960s and 1970s, she received a B.A. from Carleton College in 1970 and a Ph.D. from the University of Wisconsin, Madison, in 1976. Her research interests include work-family linkages in advanced industrialized societies, job shifting in the early life course, and the contemporary U.S. women's movement. She is author of *Farm Women: Work, Farm, and Family in the United States* (1985) and editor with Jean O'Barr and Elizabeth Minnich of *Reconstructing the Academy* (1988). She was the first recipient of the Katherine Jocher-Belle Boone Beard Award for distinguished scholarship on gender from the Southern Sociological Society and also earned the Sociologists for Women in Society Award for Outstanding Mentoring. Currently a deputy editor of *American Sociological Review,* she has served on many editorial boards and panels.

STEVEN SEIDMAN is the author of, among other books, *Liberalism and the Origins of European Social Theory* (1983), *Contested Knowledge: Social Theory in the Postmodern Era* (1994), and *Difference Troubles: Queering Social Theory and Sexual Politics* (1997). He teaches sociology at the State University of New York, Albany.

JONATHAN SIMON is a professor of law at the University of Miami. He has also taught at the University of Michigan, New York University, and Yale Law School. Simon's work focuses on the role of penality in contemporary society and its relationship to other strategies of social control, including insurance and civil litigation. His 1993 book, *Poor Discipline: Parole and the Social Control of the Underclass, 1890–1990,* won the 1994 book prize of the Sociology of Law section of the American Sociological Association. He is currently writing a book with Theodore Caplow on the incarceration mania of the last two decades.

LYNN SMITH-LOVIN is a professor of sociology at the University of Arizona. She is a former chair of the American Sociological Association section on the Sociology of Emotions and is currently coeditor of *Social*

Psychology Quarterly and president-elect of the Southern Sociological Society. Her research focuses on gender, identity, social interaction, and emotion. Recent publications explore the gendered impact of childrearing on social networks (in the August 1997 *American Sociological Review*) and the interaction of gender and task cues in producing influence within task-oriented groups (*Advances in Group Processes* 14 [1997]). She is currently completing a National Science Foundation–funded study of identity and conversational interaction.

ANN SWIDLER is a professor of sociology at the University of California, Berkeley. Her work includes *Organization without Authority: Dilemmas of Social Control in Free Schools* (1979); *Habits of the Heart* (1985) and *The Good Society* (1991), both written with Robert Bellah, Richard Madsen, William Sullivan, and Steven Tipton; and *Inequality by Design: Cracking the Bell Curve Myth* (1996), with Claude Fischer, Michael Hout, Martin Sanchez Jankowski, Samuel Lucas, and Kim Voss. Her new book is *Talk of Love: How Americans Use Their Culture* (forthcoming).

BARRIE THORNE is a professor of sociology and women's studies at the University of California, Berkeley. She received her Ph.D. in 1971, and her trajectory as a sociologist has converged with the trajectory of contemporary feminism. She is the author of *Gender Play: Girls and Boys in School* (1993), coeditor of *Rethinking the Family: Some Feminist Questions* ([1982], 1992), and she is now working on a comparative ethnographic study of childhoods in two communities in California.

KIM A. WEEDEN is a doctoral candidate in sociology at Stanford University with research interests in the area of social stratification. She recently completed two studies of sex segregation: one used log-linear techniques to model long-term trends in occupational segregation in the United States, and the other (with Jesper Sorensen) developed and applied models for studying segregation across multiple dimensions of the labor market. Her dissertation revisits the issue of how positions in the division of labor are matched to different reward packages and examines whether occupation-level collective action acts as an underlying source of inequality. Another current project (with David Grusky) explores recent trends in class, occupational, and socioeconomic structuration.

BARRY WELLMAN learned to write and to do qualitative analysis at the Bronx High School of Science and Lafayette College. He learned to do statistics and to play with computers at Harvard University. He has been doing all of these things ever since as a professor of sociology at the University of Toronto. Wellman founded the International Network for

Social Network Analysis in 1976 and is now its international coordinator. He was the American Sociological Association's first electronic adviser, chair of the ASA's Community and Urban Sociology section, and is the leader of SIGGROUP/ACM's "virtual community" focus area. His research focuses on personal networks of social support and how people work and play on-line. He recently edited *Networks in the Global Village* (1998).

CHRISTINE L. WILLIAMS is an associate professor of sociology at the University of Texas, Austin. She has written extensively on men and women in gender-atypical occupations, including *Gender Differences at Work* (1989) and *Still a Man's World* (1995). Her current research focuses on the social context of sexual harassment, examining how workers in different occupations distinguish between sexual behaviors that are enjoyable, tolerable, and harassing.

ROBERT ZUSSMAN teaches sociology at the University of Massachusetts. The author of *Mechanics of the Middle Class: Work and Politics among American Engineers* (1995) and *Intensive Care: Medical Ethics and the Medical Profession* (1992), he is currently working on a self-consciously modernist history of selfhood organized around a study of autobiographical occasions.